PRAISE FOR BREN... ...AND TRUE NORTH

'There is so much to admire and enjoy in this profoundly interesting biography. As a picture of Perth society in the first half of the twentieth century it is as good as anything I know. As a sympathetic portrait of the difficulty women as mothers had to be creative and absorbed in their work, it is profoundly moving. As a picture of a rare closeness between two sisters it is, if anything, enviable. Brenda Niall could not write a poor book. But this is, quite simply, one of her very best.' *Canberra Times*

'A sensitive and well researched exploration of the interaction between creative artists and their significant environment.'
Geoffrey Bolton

'Brenda Niall has produced a graceful and perceptive biography of two extraordinary creative women. She treads carefully through the minefield of controversies about their family's exploitation of Aboriginal labour, as well as their own interventions in Indigenous art and politics. Her brief portraits of other members of the family, especially the two brothers who dedicated their lives to improving the land up north and their Lear-like father, are an additional bonus to this absorbing book.' *Australian Book Review*

'A rich portrait of two complex and inter-connected lives... And throughout is the marvellous incisive Niall ability to distil, to capture the essence of a situation or problem, to ask the penetrating questions, to display sympathy and empathy but never to shirk criticism or to be afraid of exposing frailty. The individual portraits are beautifully drawn and very nicely contrasted with both the sisters emerging as their own person but yet with much that is shared... The book breaks important new ground. It is celebratory but far from uncritical and it confronts complexity on every page.' John Thompson

'A compelling Australian story that is just as relevant to today's social fabric as it was when it first began more than 130 years ago.'
Courier-Mail

Brenda Niall is one of Australia's foremost biographers. She is the author of eleven books including seven acclaimed biographies. Four have won multiple awards, among them her renowned accounts of the Boyd family. In 2004 Brenda was awarded the Order of Australia for 'services to Australian literature, as an academic, biographer and literary critic'. She lives in Melbourne and frequently reviews for the *Age, Sydney Morning Herald* and *Australian Book Review.*

True North

The Story of Mary and Elizabeth Durack

Brenda Niall

TEXT PUBLISHING MELBOURNE AUSTRALIA

Photographs courtesy of Patsy Millett and Perpetua Durack Clancy.

textpublishing.com.au

The Text Publishing Company
Swann House
22 William Street
Melbourne Victoria 3000
Australia

First published by The Text Publishing Company, 2012.
Reprinted 2012.

Cover and page design by W. H. Chong
Index by Nikki Davis
Typeset by J&M Typesetters
Printed and bound in Australia by Griffin Press

National Library of Australia Cataloguing-in-Publication entry
Author: Niall, Brenda, 1930-
Title: True north : the story of Mary and Elizabeth Durack / Brenda Niall.
ISBN: 9781921758928 (pbk.)
ISBN: 9781921921421 (ebook)
Subjects: Durack, Mary, 1913-1994.
Durack, Elizabeth, 1915-2000.
Sisters—Australia—Biography.
Women authors, Australian—20th century.
Women authors, Australian—20th century—Biography.
Women artists—Australia—20th century.
Women artists—Australia—20th century—Biography.
Dewey Number: A828.309

CONTENTS

PREFACE

Before I read their letters to one another I thought of Mary and Elizabeth Durack's early creative partnership as an enticing subject for a group study of some writers and artists who worked in tandem. Mary's words, Elizabeth's images—how did the collaboration work? And whose imagination gave the children's books that they published together—*The Way of the Whirlwind* or *The Magic Trumpet*—their edgy, unsettling quality? With those questions in mind, I read the unpublished letters that the sisters exchanged during the Second World War, when Mary was living in Perth and Elizabeth in Sydney. It's unusual to find both sides of a long correspondence surviving intact; unusual too to hear so clearly the distinctive voices of the writers as they express strong emotions and reveal their inner selves.

These wartime letters, which the sisters later planned to publish under the title *The Young Know*, gave insight into their literary-artistic partnership. But as I read more closely, I began to feel that there was a larger theme that asked to be explored. The sisters wrote longingly about the past, especially the time they had shared at Ivanhoe station in the Kimberley in the mid-1930s. But they also showed unease and concern for the future. Loving the land but well aware of wrongs done to the displaced indigenous people, they hoped that their own generation might bring about a new order.

The letters sparkle with the sisters' wit and comic sense, but they have depth too. Frank and forthright in style, they show two intelligent young women grappling with issues with which few Australians of their time were concerned. When I thought about the Duracks' creativity, I saw that it was inseparable from their love of the north. My subject became, almost overnight it seemed, a story about place, dispossession and imaginative possession.

True North owes a very large debt to John Thompson, biographer and historian, who first urged me to look at the remarkable Durack archive in the Battye Library, State Library of Western Australia. He said that I would be fascinated by Mary and Elizabeth; he was right. My historian sister Frances O'Neill, trawling through the Durack archive with me in Perth, said: 'You can't waste this material. Mary and Elizabeth must have a book of their own, not just a share in a group study.' She was right too. As the biography took shape, Frances read it in draft form, chapter by chapter, and I thank her for the stimulating exchange of ideas that followed and for her encouragement throughout.

The book could not have been written without the unstintingly generous cooperation of Mary Durack's daughter Patsy Millett and Elizabeth Durack's daughter Perpetua Durack Clancy. A trip to the Kimberley in their company was a delight as well as a source of insight. They contributed in uncountable ways to my understanding of my subject and saved me from many mistakes. Whatever mistakes remain are my own.

For interviews and conversations about the Duracks and the solving of research problems I thank Anne Durack Barker,

Geoffrey Bolton, Susan Bradley, Veronica Brady, Michael Clancy, Mary Ryllis Clark, Helen Elliott, Robert Hester, Francis and Sarah King, Helen Muir, Maria Myers, Hugh and Maggie Niall, Philippa O'Brien, Rosalie Okely, Clare O'Neill and Terry O'Neill.

I am indebted to the staff at the Battye Library, State Library of Western Australia, the staff of the Mitchell Library, State Library of New South Wales, Richard Overell, Rare Books Librarian at the Monash University Library and Robin Scott, the IBVM (Loreto) archivist.

I thank Jane Pearson for her skilful and perceptive editing and the team at Text for a smooth passage to publication. A grant from the Literature Board of the Australia Council, for travel and research expenses in Perth and the Kimberley, made this long-distance project viable and rewarding.

Brenda Niall, Melbourne, 2012

An Introduction

One moment in time is a turning point in two closely linked but very different lives. It is 17 October 1950. The scene is an office block in Howard Street, Perth. It's early evening and all the workers have gone home, but the lights are on in a second-floor office. For many years this has been the administrative centre of Connor, Doherty & Durack, a pastoral company ruled by Michael Patrick Durack, known as MPD. The company's land holdings in the Kimberley and the Northern Territory, estimated to be about the size of Belgium, have been sold, and MPD himself has died, suddenly, at the age of eighty-five. Now the company no longer exists; the office has to be cleared, and the task falls to MPD's widow Bess, her second son Kim and her two daughters, Mary and Elizabeth.

At sixty-seven Bess Durack has the classic beauty that does not fade with age. She has an air of ease and privilege to which a concierge at a first-class hotel would instantly respond. There's an impression of serenity and sweetness about her, but these words don't do her justice. It is true that she sets great store on the correct forms of social life (the importance of writing 'nice little notes' is one of them) but she is a strong woman who keeps her family together by thinking the best and ignoring the things she cannot control.

Kim, tall and fair-haired, with strikingly bright blue eyes, has a look of the open spaces about him, but he could equally well be taken for an academic, if not for his work-hardened hands. The daughters, too, are hard to place. Mary does not have her mother's beauty, nor is pretty the right word for her, but she is undeniably attractive. In a full-skirted cotton dress, with a cardigan against the chill of the October evening and a bright headscarf, she is neither the typical suburban housewife nor the casual bohemian writer, but something of both. There is nothing casual about Elizabeth. From her blonde hair, well-cut and discreetly tinted, to her varnished fingernails, Bet, as she is known in the family, appears as a charming product of her own art. And yet this elegant young woman is most at home in the remote Kimberley, on a dusty trek or painting in her grass studio beside the Ord River.

Up the marble staircase, poorly lit through the extravagant stained glass window, the Duracks enter their father's domain, feeling like trespassers. It is the first time they have opened the outer door for themselves; it feels strange, even intrusive, to use their father's set of keys. To open his safe seems like sacrilege. His big mahogany desk is just as he left it, with a few scribbled notes and unanswered letters tucked under the blotter. On the wall behind it, faded maps mark the trek across the continent, from Queensland to the Kimberley, made when MPD was young. They show four cattle stations: Newry and Auvergne, in wild Northern

Territory country beyond the West Australian border; Argyle Downs, the home station on the Behn River; and Ivanhoe, a mere eighty kilometres from Wyndham, the little port on the northern West Australian coast from which MPD came and went, taking a week or ten days to get home to his family in Perth.

His family is in shock; even at eighty-five MPD had seemed indestructible. They all know how it feels when a great, ancient gumtree crashes: the devastation of broken branches on the ground, the sudden emptiness on the skyline. It's like that now, less than two months since his death and six months since he sold the station properties that were his life's work, his inheritance from the earlier generation of Durack pastoralists. The heroic scale of the Duracks' pioneering achievement, overlanding with cattle from Queensland to the Kimberley, is undeniable, but MPD's sons and daughters have learned the high cost that achievement exacted from the indigenous people and from the land itself. They have all spent years in the Kimberley and they love it more than any other place. They all had ideas of doing things differently when their generation succeeded their father's rule. But under financial pressure, and with a touch of the King Lear about him, MPD dispossessed himself and his children. The tangible remnants of his kingdom are here, in this office. The bond with the land, intangible, remains in his sons and daughters.

Not that he disinherited them entirely. From the thousands of square kilometres sold to clear debts to the bank, pay out shareholders and provide for himself and Bess, he chopped off a segment of wild country in the Northern Territory where his eldest son Reg would need to be as much a pioneer as was MPD himself. There would be just enough money to keep Bess in frugal comfort in her old age. Mary, a writer and mother of five (later six) young children, has been given her first and much-needed car. For Bet, an artist, mother of two, who has never had a house of her own, MPD found a block of land and money to build one in Perth. For complex reasons he left Kim's future insecure.[1]

Now, as they stand awkwardly in the silent office, they have much to think about. The immediate need is simple. Empty the office and leave it for the next tenant. There is a haphazard collection of junk that no one wants: lumps of silver lead in bags with other mineral-bearing stones and the rolled skins of snakes and crocodiles.[2] But what to do with all the papers? Bess Durack has no doubts. She does not want those messy, dusty documents. Her house in King's Park is too small; its cupboards are already full. Her advice: 'Just put all the papers in the bins in the alley and then we can go home.'

Kim is neutral. He doesn't care about the papers. He cares deeply about the land that was sold. His ideas about reclaiming it and enriching the soil have been disregarded by his father, and his future now looks bleak. Bet cares about the land, but in a different way. She feels dispossessed and sad, though not defeated. Someone else will own the place where she used to paint, and her grass-hut studio beside the Ord River will be knocked down. But after fifteen precarious, nomadic years, she has the consolation of a house for herself and her children: a secure base from which to continue her career as a painter. Some years earlier she completed the illustrations for *They Reached a Land*, a family history written by Mary but not yet published. As far as she is concerned the family story has been told.

MPD's eldest son, Reg Durack, is up north, working long days to build a rough dwelling for his wife and children on the wild acres of his inheritance, Kildurk. The younger sons, Bill and

David, are far away too. Bill is in western Queensland, working on the land, not yet ready to return to the career in architecture that the war interrupted. David is with an engineering company in Honduras, after a stint in Borneo.

Only Mary is moved and excited by the family papers. She does not think much about the account books and other financial records; many of these are summarily dumped in the bins. But the letters and diaries—she wants at least another look at them. She disregards her mother's warning: 'If you keep the belongings of the dead, dear, you have no room for the living.' So, some of the papers are loaded into Mary's new Austin car and taken to her house; others will follow, and somehow be fitted in. Mary has always wanted a study but she is lucky, these days, to find a corner for her desk and typewriter. Her house had once seemed quite roomy, until five children and their possessions contested every space with her abundant writing projects. She has too many ideas already: novels and plays at the top of the list. Completing her Durack history, which draws on family memories more than documents, would have satisfied her. She has never thought of herself as a historian, but her father's papers are impossible to resist. Later, she writes a 'letter to the future', explaining what the letters and diaries mean to her, and what she hopes to make of them:

> As file after file, drawer after drawer was thrown open the past history of the company was gradually and haphazardly revealed. All the ghosts and whispers of past endeavours, the worries, hopes, heartbreaks, schemes, plans, enthusiasms of over sixty years were rustling and jostling one another within that small space.

...The old heavily bound carbon letter books with their thin paper were well preserved, the ink faded but the paper remarkably strong—and from the pages of these emerged the young men of the past generation—all taking themselves and their times so seriously, full of responsibility, tenacity and purpose—old scandals are revived, animosities revealed.

Should I never have the opportunity of getting down to it I am writing this to give some idea of what is to be found in the files and documents kept...so that the whole remarkable and in a sense tragic story might be translated into some meaning and significance to ourselves and our country.[3]

That night, Mary Durack, journalist, playwright, novelist and short story writer, changed her life. Five tin trunks, crammed with papers, provided the imaginative impulse for her most ambitious work, the pastoral family saga that would be published in 1959 as *Kings in Grass Castles*. The decision to undertake this work was significant too for her sister Elizabeth. They had been collaborating since childhood: words by Mary, images by Bet. Mary's decision to write a full-scale family history, based on documents, would leave no room for Bet's drawings; those already done, for *They Reached a Land*, would be scrapped along with Mary's text. How did Bet feel, that night in the office, and later, as Mary's plans emerged? She had already outgrown the role of illustrator; she had been exhibiting her paintings since 1946, and had an independent career as an artist to which she was passionately committed. Bet was never grudging about Mary's successes. All the same, she might have felt a pang of envy. Mary had always come first with their father, and in the act of taking home those five tin trunks, she had taken imaginative possession of the life and legend of Michael Patrick Durack.

Decades later, the sons and daughters of MPD would still be living in the shadow of a heroic legend. So much striving on the part of the earlier generations: what had it all been for? Triumph or tragedy? Discovery or invasion? How to count the cost to the indigenous Kimberley people whose lives were changed by these and other ventures? The three Durack siblings who stood in their father's office that night in 1950 were powerless to reverse that history. Their older brother Reg had made his decision to stay in the region, following his father but doing things differently. Kim had plans to redeem the land, diversify its use, repair the damage of the cattle industry and make the Kimberley fertile.

For Mary and Elizabeth, with their homes and children in Perth, the link with the north was intangible but equally strong. It was the source of their creativity. 'Our north', as they sometimes called the Kimberley, could not be possessed except perhaps in imagination.

CHAPTER 1

Beginnings

For Mary and Elizabeth Durack, every year began in November.
Like other children in suburban Perth, they put on their school
uniforms in February and followed the school calendar from one
hot Perth summer to the next. But they had their own calendar,
their own seasons. Their year was ruled by the weather in the
distant Kimberley region. In the wet season, work stopped on
their father's cattle stations, and during this gap of about twelve
weeks, Michael Patrick Durack came home to his wife Bess and
his growing family. It was the high point of the year for Mary
and Elizabeth when the little coastal vessel berthed at Fremantle:

> Dad's annual return! How thrilled we were when we
> all piled into Bloomer's car...and down to Fremantle to
> meet the boat. Dad standing on the deck, his right hand
> extended in characteristic gesture and there surrounding
> him that extraordinary collection of wildlife. The grey and

pink galahs, always for you [Mary], the sulphur-crested cockatoos, the painted finches. the bundles of reeking, salt-encrusted crocodile skins, the geological specimens in hessian bags tied at the top with strips of kangaroo or bullock hide…the ribbon stone and the potentially valuable like the silver, lead and bitumen—all to find its way into 263 Adelaide Terrace.[1]

One year he brought them a pony on the boat. Another time the surprise gift was two baby crocodiles. Bringing wallabies was a mistake; even the big block of land surrounding the Durack house on Adelaide Terrace could not contain them, and they eventually went to the South Perth Zoo.

Sometimes one or two Aboriginal stockmen came with MPD and slept in outdoor quarters in the Duracks' garden. When MPD took them for a stroll around the city, heads turned in astonishment, so rare then was the sight of an Aborigine in the streets of central Perth. These men stayed a few days to see the sights before being taken to Behn Ord, a sheep property in the south-west, owned by MPD's brother Patrick, where they worked for the rest of MPD's stay in Perth. 'We all lived with the north as a kind of legend and a kind of dream,' Mary said.[2] Reality was their big house on Adelaide Terrace in the centre of Perth, close to the river and the business district. Mary and Elizabeth went to the Loreto convent, a few doors away, and the boys had only to cross the road to the Christian Brothers' school.

Their house took in, unreconciled, the duality of north and south—the Kimberley and Perth. The smoke-room, their father's domain, had a suite of furniture specially designed for him and upholstered in the skins of crocodiles, all shot by MPD. He said the chairs would last forever, and because they were so uncomfortable to sit on he might have been right. Surprisingly, given her traditional femininity, Bess Durack became a deft hand with taxidermy; some at least of the trophies on display were her work. The hall below the staircase, the dining room and the breakfast room all had a museum quality carried by Aboriginal artefacts, spears and boomerangs, and photographs of India, where MPD and Bess had travelled on their honeymoon. Folding doors led to the drawing room, where north yielded to south. This was Bess Durack's domain: a quiet room of soft mauves and greys, with exquisitely arranged flowers from her garden and high windows looking out on the esplanade and the river. In this room, Bet said, 'Mother drew the line.'[3]

The north–south line had been drawn in 1915, when living in Perth became a practical and almost inevitable decision. Although he took Bess to live at Argyle Downs in the first few years of marriage MPD had always thought that life in the north was too hard for white women. Nevertheless, Bess was happy there. Her memoirs show the pleasures of her new life, in the 'exotic and wonderful scenery', the strange lizards and goannas and the bright birds. She and MPD took a horse and buggy from Wyndham, stopping overnight at Ivanhoe Station, and crossing the Ord River to arrive at Argyle. It was a challenge for a city girl but Bess enjoyed it:

> It felt like home from the first moment I stepped inside but looked more like it when I had been busy for a week or two…a happy group of Aboriginal women welcomed me like a member of their family and were only too eager to help set the place to rights. We had a lot of fun together and they brought their babies to me to admire.[4]

MPD, however, was always on the move, and unless Bess could travel with him she would be left for long periods with only the Aboriginal women for company. Besides, the management of Argyle was in the hands of his then unmarried cousin Ambrose Durack. When Ambrose married, Bess might have to move to Ivanhoe Station. Ivanhoe had a charm of its own, but it was not the head station and the house was in disrepair. Whatever Bess did at Argyle—bringing order to the house, making a garden—might be left behind.

MPD had promised Bess's parents that she would not give birth in the north. Late in 1910, when she was pregnant with their first child, he took her home to Adelaide. After she had stayed some time with her family, he installed her in a comfortable little private hospital where she spent the days before the birth while he went about his business. Inspecting meat works, conferring with representatives of the pastoral industry—there was always something for him to do. The arrival of his first son took him almost by surprise.

> I am met as usual by the smiling face of my dear wife. It is only after greeting her that I observe the baby lying on her arm. It took me a few seconds to realise the fact of the little mite's arrival...[5]

In naming this first child Reginald as a change from the confusingly multiplied Patricks and Michaels in the Durack family, MPD added the second name of Wyndham, thereby signalling the child's link with the north where he was conceived, and where he would spend his first years. Mary, born in Adelaide in February 1913, was also a child of the north, with early memories of Argyle and Ivanhoe stations.

MPD and Bess (or Bim as her husband called her[6]) had no more than four years together in the north. The decision to buy a house in Perth had many good reasons behind it. The string of cattle stations owned by Connor, Doherty & Durack, in which MPD was the biggest shareholder and the dominant personality, had none of the amenities of city or country town life. No schools or doctors within reach, rough roads—more like tracks—to the little port of Wyndham, no refrigeration, no electric lights, no reliable supplies of fresh fruit or vegetables and few comforts. Added to these drawbacks was the isolation of the wet season, when travel became almost impossible. When Reg and Mary were small, the Duracks spent summers in Manila, where MPD was establishing sales outlets for the company's cattle, and the rest of the year in the Kimberley. Mary had vague memories of a happy time when an Aboriginal nursemaid called Dinah lovingly carried her about. She could not remember her mother's presence in these early days but she had an image of Dinah at the edge of the billabong, catching little fishes with a bent pin.

In March 1915, with their third child on the way, the Duracks bought their first home in Perth. Elizabeth, born in July 1915, set great store on having been conceived in the Kimberley; she disliked the fact that her birth in Goldsmith Road, Claremont, had put an end to exciting days in the north. When Mary was born her father inscribed an exquisite book of Japanese legends to 'my dearest wife in memory of THE DAY—February 20th 1913'. There was no such fanfare for Elizabeth: 'Dad, away in the north at the time, didn't see me till I was three or four months old, and then I only cracked the barest mention in his diary: "Bim at the wharf to meet me with baby Betty—a nice little thing."'[7]

When Bet was born, Bess Durack was thirty-two. With her own

family a sea journey away in Adelaide, she was starting a new life in a city she hardly knew. The comfortable house in Claremont, staffed by a housekeeper, a cook and a nursemaid, spared her the hardships of the earlier generation of Durack women. Yet she must have been lonely at first, perhaps bored and depressed, without her husband to share the everyday pleasures and worries of their children, and knowing how much of his exciting life she was missing. That MPD loved her was not in doubt, but in his long absences, absorbed in the challenges of the northern properties, Bess was deprived. It is possible that her relationship with her second daughter was affected by the fact that Elizabeth's birth came at the begining of long separations from the handsome, vital MPD.

Bet felt that Mary had the larger share of parental love. In a revealing vignette of early childhood, she described the two of them, aged four and two, being posed for a studio photograph. Playing ladies, they sat facing one another at a little tea-table. Just as the camera clicked on the charming scene, Mary reached across and grabbed the tea things for her side of the table, leaving Bet with none.[8] The retrieval of this early memory shows the second daughter's perception of Mary and herself. She loved Mary and depended on Mary's undoubted love for her. No other relationship, it seems, was stronger than the sisterly bond. Yet, inevitably, there was rivalry between them and, on Bet's side, awareness of Mary's special status. 'I fell into the way of taking it for granted that Mary came first—seeing she was first—with Dad, less with Mother, who was enormously even-handed towards the lot of us...'[9]

MPD's second son, Kimberley Michael (Kim), born in 1917, was seven months old before his father saw this 'robust little chap'.[10] The sixth child, David, born in 1920, also had to wait till MPD's next Perth visit came round to meet his father. The fifth child, who had the luck to be born while MPD was at home in 1918, was named William Aiden. His father greeted him as 'Quintus Superbus'. Bill, or Quinty, as he was called for some years, was thought to be the favoured son.

Having married late—he was forty-six when Reg was born— MPD might not have wanted six children to complicate his life and separate him from his wife for most of the year. Yet he managed in those magical months of the wet season to give them love and attention while kindling in each of them an intense desire to be part of his life in the north.

It was MPD's decision—though one that any practising Catholic would make—to bring up their children in his family's faith and to send them to Catholic schools. The galaxy of bishops, priests and nuns that was part of Durack life was strange to Bess, who came from an Anglican family. She accepted this, as she accepted his other decisions, and made a success of her life in Perth. She had to put the north behind her as an adventure and make Perth her reality.

There is no record of her protesting, other than the wistfulness with which she spoke about the first few years of her marriage.[11] Yet it is hard to believe that the big well-staffed house would have compensated for the solitary maternal role to which Bess was reduced after only six years of marriage. Sometimes she spent a few months with her husband. This was made easier after 1920 when she had a competent deputy in Nurse Sarah Stevens, an Englishwoman who delivered the youngest Durack, David, at Adelaide Terrace in 1920 and stayed on for many years as nanny to the children and companion-housekeeper to Bess.

Bess Durack was so sweet-natured that her children found it impossible to rebel against her. Nurse Stevens was tougher.

She was also a great educator. Although they disliked being left with her while their mother went north, Mary and Elizabeth acknowledged their debt to Nurse Stevens as a brilliant reader of the English classic novelists. Hour after hour she read aloud, and when she fell asleep over Dickens or Scott in her epic journey through their complete works, the children would prod her awake to get on with the story. She also read them stories from *Chums* annual and passed on her love of Gilbert and Sullivan by taking them to every Perth performance.

Another strong influence on the Durack children was MPD's unmarried brother Jack Durack, who took them to concerts and operas, lent them books and answered questions about anything puzzling in their reading. The two girls and their four brothers, all close in age, were used to making their own entertainment, and they gave one another such stimulating companionship that they scarcely needed to go outside the family. Mary and Bet wrote plays, and dragooned their brothers into taking part. Together they made up 'a tightly locked, self-relating family group, a closed circuit within the general mechanism of the small isolated city.'[12]

With Nurse Stevens at home and the Loreto convent a few doors away on Adelaide Terrace, Mary and Bet had a first-class education. Both girls were clever. Reg, marked out by the Christian Brothers as a future scholar, worked harder than they did and set a high standard. Mathematics, a weakness in most girls' schools of the time, was Mary's only area of failure. Bet was caught using lesson time to draw caricatures of the nuns and the other girls. The subversive sketches amused her Latin teacher, Mother Dominica Baker, so much that she asked if she could have them to keep. 'The nuns were sweet,' Bet said in later years. Her talent for art was recognised and her lapses in discipline indulged.

Because the convent, housed in a mansion known as The Bracken, was so close to home, the Durack girls moved easily between the two. Like most schools for the daughters of the well-to-do of that time, Loreto had high standards of decorum, or 'ladylike behaviour'. These fitted nicely with Bess Durack's expectations. Bess, who once rebuked Bet for using the word 'pregnant' in front of her teenage brother David, was at least as concerned as the nuns to instil lessons of correctness in speech and manners as well as the feminine accomplishments of French, art and music. Music and musical appreciation were brilliantly taught by Mother John, who had been the first to discern the talent of pianist Eileen Joyce. Mother Gertrude, a scholarly enthusiast for ancient history, roused Mary's interest in early Egypt.

At twelve years old Mary was devout and orthodox. She was so shocked on finding a book by the anti-clerical Anatole France in her father's library that she thought it was her duty to burn it. Doubts came in her later school years. Because Bess Durack was not a Catholic and MPD was mostly absent, Mary and Bet grew up with a degree of flexibility in religious matters, and when in adult life they lapsed from the faith and practice of their upbringing they did so without apparent guilt, kept up close friendships with the nuns, felt free to send their daughters to Loreto schools, and in later years became observant Catholics again.

Their imaginative move towards the north began early. To Bet's 'What'll we do today?', during the mid-winter holidays in 1925, Mary announced, 'We'll write a book.' Bet laughed—she had heard that one before—but this time Mary had it all worked out. 'No, truly, we'll write a magazine every mail to send to Dad, and we'll call it *Kookaburra and Kangaroo*. You can be Kookaburra.' The Duracks modelled their work on their own reading. The illustrated books of Ida Rentoul Outhwaite and May Gibbs's adventures of the gumnut babies Snugglepot and Cuddlepie were favourites. Mary had a feeling for family history; a serial 'In the Heart of the Bush' was based on what she had heard about the Duracks in the early days. And Mary was in charge; she wrote the editorials ('really good for a kid of eleven,' Elizabeth wrote later[13]) and arranged with her mother to stitch their pages together and send them north on the boat to Wyndham for their father to read and admire.

Mary's other venture, at about the same time as *Kookaburra and Kangaroo*, was a series of poems, which her parents collected and published in 1923 as *Little Poems of Sunshine*. Sold in Perth bookshops or given away to friends, this little volume became an embarrassment to its author. Without MPD's pride in his creative daughter, the poems would have stayed within the family, evidence of a gift with words and an unusual persistence. But one hundred copies, bound in green cloth, were presented to Perth's foremost citizens, starting with Professor Walter Murdoch and the Mother Superior of the Loreto convent. Not only that: parental delusion and the Durack name brought the poems to a more general readership.

The collection was based on material already published. Between March and December 1923, twenty-three poems 'by Mary Durack aged 10 years' and a number of short stories appeared in the *Western Mail*. Spring, summer, autumn, winter were all celebrated in verse. There was a hymn and a prayer, a story headed 'Moral: Be Kind' and a poem addressed to 'Little Bunny Rabbit'. Although in later years any mention of her saccharine little poems would bring tears of rage to Mary's eyes, their publication gave her an identity as a future writer, someone with a career path to follow. Predictions of her fame roused Bet's competitive instinct. She did not want to be the stay-at-home daughter while Mary followed a career, but she knew that no one would want to publish Elizabeth Durack's 'Little Pictures of Frogs, Flowers and Faces'.[14]

Mary was a personality in Perth from the age of ten, when her parents published those embarrassing poems. She was sixteen when parental pride brought her forward again with a performance of her play about the French revolution, *The Avenger*. With tickets available from Mrs M. P. Durack, and proceeds to charities, it was advertised prominently in the *West Australian* and performed for one night only in the Hibernian Hall.[15] Wearing her gold silk evening dress to murder Marat in his bath, Mary played Charlotte Corday. Bet was Marat's serving maid, dressed in revolutionary red cap and full skirt. Two footloose English visitors—sophisticated young men, Bet thought them—played Robespierre and Marat. A reviewer in Perth's Catholic weekly paper said as kindly as possible that the play had nothing to do with historical fact.

Mary was seen as the clever one. She was also the good daughter, even-tempered and reliable. And although the girls, only two years apart in age, were close and affectionate companions, there was reason for Bet to feel aggrieved, especially with their father, because of Mary's special status. Her remedy, conscious or not, was to be the difficult one. Mary described her as 'volcanic'. Bet's patronising family nickname was Bumbles. When Mary was allowed to leave school at sixteen, without doing her matriculation year, and join her father in the north, fourteen-year-old Bet could not help feeling envious. Missing Mary's companionship and living for the long, tantalising letters from the north, she felt the pressure of being the only girl at home with three young brothers. An alliance with Kim, then twelve, became essential. It was a way to escape from her minor female role in a script too tightly directed by her mother and Nurse Stevens.

Although Bet learned to turn her gift for caricature against her father (as when she spoke of him as Old Poop-Deck and mimicked him wickedly), she wanted his approval and access to his Kimberley kingdom. Mary's admiration for her father shines through her account of his daily walk to his office. A handsome man, MPD was tall and straight, with dark eyes and a trim Vandyke beard, quite unlike the hairy bushman's style. He was known as 'Miguel' because of something Spanish in his appearance. Mary was proud to be seen with him on his regal promenade:

> There wouldn't have been anyone in public life that wasn't known to my father and occasionally he would get extra interest by walking down the street with an Aborigine. There was a big bloke called Masher whom he brought down on one occasion. He was an enormous Aborigine and he was staying with us for a while at Adelaide Terrace, but oh! he made a great impression. To see my father walking down the street with him and going into shops with him and things, oh, it was great fun!...
>
> It was more like a big country town [than today's Perth] and my father going down from the Terrace to his office in Howard Street (well, I'd sometimes go with him)...he'd be taking his hat off to practically every second person. Sometimes they'd stop and have a long talk, and I can always remember that he would take his hat off and bow very courteously to the statue of Sir Alexander Forrest on the way down.[16]

While Mary and Bet were growing up, the family was considered well off. Although the large leaseholdings of land in the north belonged to a private company, MPD was such a commanding figure that it was easy to think he owned it all. This was an illusion. And the wealth was always out of reach: 'when we find oil', 'when we find gold' kept the ever-receding, glittering promise ahead of them. The girls were brought up thriftily, without the party frocks that their school friends had and with school uniforms that were always a bit different from the required style, and therefore embarrassing. But their background in land, the big Perth house, their handsome father and beautiful, charming mother combined to make them socially acceptable. MPD's election in 1917 as Nationalist (later Country Party) member for Kimberley in the Legislative Assembly of State Parliament added to his status. But the Duracks were not 'old Perth' like the Bussells, the Drake-Brockmans and others; they were too recently arrived and as Irish-Catholics they would never quite fit in. As Elizabeth wrote:

> We were not Establishment Western Australian—that was much older, that was English and Church of England and Presbyterian and first-footing free settlers to the Swan River Colony...we were a mob of border-hopping parvenus making an unconventional entry to the precinct via the top end of Australia and we were Catholics to boot...[17]

Being Irish was an essential part of their story. As well as the alluring tales of the Kimberley, the Durack children were nourished by another, more distant, family legend. They had tangible proofs— photographs, artefacts, baby crocodiles—that the Kimberley region was real, even though it was out of reach. It was there, waiting till they were older. Their Irish past, in which their grandfather had the heroic role, was as remote as *Jack and the Beanstalk*, which in its fairytale style and moral tone it resembled.

The tale began with a peasant boy in County Clare, near the Galway border, with Patsy Durack, second of seven children, growing up in rural poverty with little education and no prospects beyond a lifetime of toil. The family had survived the Great Famine of 1848, but there was not much hope in the land. An uncle, Darby Durack, was doing well in Australia but Patsy's father, Michael Durack, did not have the passage money to take his family out of Ireland. One day, their luck turned. One of the wealthiest Anglo-Irish landowners, Lord Dunraven of Adare, was travelling to Limerick when his coach became so badly stuck in the mud that his manservant could not dislodge it. Seventeen-year-old Patsy, slight but strong, put his shoulder to the wheel and set the coach moving again. Many years later, Mary dramatised the scene from her memory of the story she heard in childhood:

> The great man had called [Patsy] back as he turned away and asked whether he was so rich that he had no need of a reward. Blushing with confusion Patsy had declared himself the eldest son of a large family hoping soon to emigrate to Australia and dig for gold. 'Then here's a piece to go on with,' said his Lordship, pressing a coin into the boy's hand.
>
> To one who had counted a few pence handsome payment for a day's toil this was riches indeed and it was not long before he had translated it into two hens, a sow and a holy picture for each member of his family. He told his children in later years how that sovereign had proved a magic coin for the hens laid well and the sow brought forth a fine litter so that in twelve months there was enough to bring them all to Australia.[18]

Patsy Durack arrived in New South Wales with his parents, brothers and sisters in May 1853. His father, Michael, and the older sons took work as farm labourers in the Goulburn district and the girls became domestic servants. An eighth child was born. Then, within two months of arrival, Michael was killed in an accident while at work felling timber. Patsy, at eighteen, became the man of the family.

Instead of staying in Goulburn, and making steady progress, as he might have done if his father had lived, Patsy took the risky course of going to the goldfields. He settled his mother Bridget and her younger children in lodgings in Goulburn, placed his sisters in jobs near the town, equipped himself on borrowed money and made his way to the Ovens diggings. His luck and enterprise paid off, and so did his good sense. Knowing when to stop in a time of gold fever, he took home one thousand pounds, and with it a wealth of worldly wisdom. In eighteen months on the goldfields he saw human nature in its extremes: greed and envy, high hopes and delusions, murder, suicide and despair. The boy from County Clare met Chinese and Afghans as well as Englishmen and Scots, Frenchmen and Germans among the diggers. He met drunkards sent into exile by wealthy English families, ex-convicts, educated men and illiterates, hardened criminals and visionary artists. He learned tolerance of those with religious beliefs different from his own Irish Catholic faith, and of those with none. At nineteen, he knew how the world worked. His own powers were in planning, organising, looking ahead and in persuading others to share his visions and join his ventures.

The story of Patsy Durack—'Grandfather Patsy' to Mary and Elizabeth—was one of always moving on. Farming in Goulburn was not enough. He saw better chances in Queensland, bigger tracts of land, cattle rather than sheep. His luck failed more than once. There were hard years in the 1860s, but prosperity in the 1870s, when the Durack property Thylungra, at Cooper's Creek, brought big profits. During this time of stable family life six children were born to Patsy and his wife Mary, née Costello: Michael Patrick (MPD), John, Pat, Mary, Bridget (Bird) and Jeremiah (Dermot).

Patsy's four sons became part of his grand design. Although he wanted them to have the education he had missed in his childhood in Ireland, it was hard not to put the land first. MPD and his brothers had some haphazard home schooling from a frail old Irish tutor who slept more hours than he taught. Aged fourteen, MPD was sent back to Goulburn with his brother John to board at St Patrick's College. Sixteen hundred kilometres away from their Queensland home, too far to go back for holidays, it was an ordeal at first for the homesick boys.

Because they were quick and clever they made up for the deficiencies of the earlier years, and were said to be promising scholars. But after three years, MPD was called home to manage the property while his uncle Michael and his father Patsy went with a group of family and friends looking for new land. The dream of a place secure from drought took them west to the Kimberley region, where in 1879 pastoralist Alexander Forrest had reported the discovery of at least forty thousand square kilometres of good pastoral land.[19] While Patsy was away, MPD was responsible for two properties, Thylungra and Galway, and for his mother, sisters, younger brothers and the homestead. It was a replay with variations on the experience of Patsy Durack, who used to say that because of the family migration and his father's early death he never had a childhood. Although MPD was sent back for one more year at St Patrick's, where he and his brother John matriculated in 1885, the land had already claimed him. He left school with a love of reading and a good grounding in the classics, but no serious thought of the professional career for which his teachers thought him well suited.

The stories of Grandfather Patsy, told to the young Duracks in Perth, were heroic tales of hope and survival. He was the organiser of the venturesome overland trek from Queensland to the Kimberley carried out under the leadership of his brother Michael (known in the family's descriptive style as Stumpy Michael). Starting in May 1883, the trek took two years and four months and followed a six-month trip to reconnoitre. It was not solely a Durack venture: costs were shared with Patsy's friend Solomon Emanuel, and other experienced bushmen were included, as well as Territory Aborigines Pannikin and Pintpot.[20] The expedition started with 7250 head of cattle and 200 horses, divided into separate mobs, independently led but camping together for the most part. As Patsy Millett summarised the story:

> By March of 1885 as the various groups made the Territory, half the cattle and many horses had become casualties to drought, disease, crocodiles or native spears...[In September 1885] they had reached the Ord at last and despite the heavy toll en route got through with at least the nucleus of a herd and enough men to start a chain of properties covering several million acres. The final cost of the journey was estimated at something like £70,000, a huge sum in those days, and their pioneering endeavour had just begun.[21]

In spite of the losses and hardships Patsy Durack was buoyed by the promise of more and better land for his sons. His quest was continued in 1886 when Stumpy Michael, Patsy's sons MPD and John, two cousins, Long Michael Durack and Jack Skeahan, and three friends, arrived by sea at the newly proclaimed port of Wyndham. Almost at once this Durack party was caught up in the discovery of gold at Hall's Creek, and the rush of prospectors created an instant market for their cattle. Like his father at the Ovens in the 1860s, MPD was too much a realist to succumb to gold fever. 'I never thought to encounter so great a collection of mixed humanity as have gathered here from the four corners of the earth,' he said, musing on the education he had gained as a spectator.[22] There were encounters with Aborigines, some benign, some hostile. When Patsy's cousin Big Johnnie Durack was speared to death in November 1886 a punitive expedition set out in search of those responsible. It failed to find them. Whether there was a later search is not known. A reprisal would have been brutal.

MPD's stories of the Aborigines in the Kimberley stressed their value as allies. Two men in particular, Pumpkin and Boxer, were intelligent and skilled. Pumpkin, who had come from Queensland with a Durack party, was given a large amount of authority by Patsy Durack. He exercised some degree of control over MPD when the younger man's judgment went astray. Boxer sometimes came to Perth with MPD during the wet season and was well known to the children.

Although the stories told to the young Duracks in Perth stressed the achievements of the pioneers, they also knew that Grandfather Patsy died a disappointed man in Fremantle in 1898, leaving MPD and his brothers a heritage of worries. As in the earlier generations, the eldest son took charge. MPD became manager of a company that merged the Durack assets in the properties Ivanhoe and Argyle with leases on Newry and Auvergne in the

Northern Territory, which were held by Irishmen Frank Connor and Dennis Doherty. In later years Mary Durack pondered her father's decisions:

> It might be said that they fretted their lives away in worry over this huge enigmatical heritage their father [Patsy] had signed into their hands while their relatives in the country he had left behind flourished on the backs of the Cooper sheep now sustained through good season and bad on the 'water underneath' of Aboriginal legend.[23]

As well as the stories of adventure in the north, the Durack children heard about the homestead life as their mother had known it. Bess Johnstone was in her twenties when MPD proposed. Her parents hesitated; they thought him too old for her, and an Irish Catholic was not a welcome son-in-law. But MPD was persuasive, Bess was in love and in 1909, the year of their marriage, the cattle empire was a brilliant success. MPD and Bess had a romantic honeymoon voyage to India. On their return in 1910, they travelled from Wyndham by buggy and four-in-hand to the homestead, Argyle Downs, that Patsy Durack had built in 1884. Argyle had special meaning for Reg and Mary, who spent their infancy on the property.

MPD always said that the Kimberley stations were a commercial proposition, not intended as a dynastic inheritance. He wanted Reg, Mary, Bet, Kim, Bill and David to make happy lives somewhere else. And yet by bringing them up on the enthralling legendary past of Grandfather Patsy and all the other pioneering Duracks, he made it almost inevitable that they would look north for fulfilment. Reg, at least as promising a scholar as MPD had been, went to the Kimberley 'just for a year' after leaving the Christian Brothers' school in Perth. Once there, the north 'got into his blood, worse than malaria'.[24] He left, returned, left again, and spent his youth disputing with himself as to where he belonged. He was at Argyle in 1931 when Mary, just out of school, spent a year on the stations. He was there again in 1933 when Mary and Bet came north together. He would have another chance to escape in 1950, before MPD died, but the north, inexorably, would claim him. And so, in a different and ultimately sadder way, it would claim his younger brother, Kim, who came north after agricultural college with high hopes of redeeming the land after the damage caused by the cattle industry.

The north was as powerful a magnet for Mary and Bet as it was for their brothers. For these two attractive, intelligent young women, the most likely destiny would have been early marriage and a life like that of their mother, but without the Kimberley complication of an absent husband. Their religion was a drawback: a 'nice Catholic boy' would be hard to find within the upper class Perth circle to which the Duracks belonged. But, unusually for a man of his time, MPD wanted his daughters to do something interesting, to find some way out of the usual domestic role. Hence, perhaps, his allowing Mary to go north in May 1931 to escape some of the social round in Perth and develop her gifts as a writer. At twenty, Mary impressed Perth newspaper editors. 'Life in the North: Miss Mary Durack's Impressions' filled three columns in the *Western Mail* with a thoughtful account of her experiences.[25] Even then, she had the art of balancing narrative and anecdote; reporters found her 'good copy' from the start.

Mary must have used the long evenings in the north to study and to draw on her father's knowledge of the region. An emerging historian can be seen in her early article on the history of the north-west. Ambitious for a nineteen-year-old with no training, it ends with an imaginative vignette, drawn from her father's diary, of 'dear, drear wretched old Wyndham', awaiting a call from its long sleep after the gold rush frenzy ended. Shaping the narrative of exploration through the achievements of individual explorers, Mary places the Duracks among the pioneer heroes of the region.[26]

The city in which the Duracks grew up was smaller and more decorous than its counterparts in the eastern states. You could see everyone you knew just by strolling down St George's Terrace, but the meetings might not be very exciting. Only in the Perth Repertory Club, the Western Australian Historical Society and the university was there a chance for young men to meet women informally, and even in these circles young women were very few. Elsewhere, the gender divide was maintained. Paul Hasluck, then a young journalist (later a writer, political leader and Governor-General) described the polite and limited world of the 1920s into which Mary emerged:

> Our world at this time was very much a man's world... We were polite and rather shyly well behaved in [girls'] company and always raised our hats very respectfully if they recognised us when we passed them on the street. It was part of good manners in Perth in those days not to greet a woman in the street unless she first recognised the man, and if she chose to ignore the man it would have been rude to salute her. We opened doors for them, and offered to carry parcels for them, and asked their permission to walk with them, being most careful of course to walk on the side nearest the traffic. Girls did not enter much into the planning of our amusement and recreation and we seldom saw them except in a social setting...Football

clubs never had girls hanging around them in those days, and girls did not intrude on our smoke socials, dinners or club functions.[27]

By 1929, when Mary was sixteen and Bet fourteen, the family was feeling the effect of the worldwide economic depression. The big house on Adelaide Terrace was sold and replaced by a more modest one in Goderich Street, a short distance away. Although MPD would not have liked to admit it, it looked as if his daughters might have to earn a living for themselves in one of the few occupations open to young ladies. He could give them a small allowance and hope for a good marriage; otherwise it would have to be teaching or nursing, unless—and this might have been his secret hope—Mary's promise as a writer somehow paid off. One daughter at home, helping her mother, was acceptable, but not two. The obvious choice for both girls was to begin with an arts degree at the University of Western Australia, where family friend Walter Murdoch was Professor of English. But the pull of the north was too strong. Mary left school without qualifying for university entrance; she wanted so much to be with her father and live in his enticing world.

She didn't really work in that first year. She was 'Dad's driver' as he toured the string of station properties that made up the Connor, Doherty & Durack pastoral company. As a child she had been entranced by MPD's stories of the pioneering past. Later, as she drove the hundreds of kilometres between the stations, she heard more and understood the human cost as well as the triumphs of the early days:

Into focus through the blur of years ride these hard, lean,

bearded men, quick-moving in their days of slow travel, pitting human will and energy against a strange land's hostility, dotting its great grey empty plains with their stock, their homesteads, their fences and yards; and beside them their women, wind-burned, sun-browned, wrinkled before their time, coping, normalising, dedicating to the will of God [their] griefs and anxieties...[28]

Although Mary could see how hard it had been, and still was, for the women of the north, her imagination was caught by the heroic model of the past. Responding to the natural beauty of the region and to its people—Aborigines as well as white settlers—she began to write about it. Compared with the Kimberley, Perth never had a chance of holding Mary's heart. Being one of Perth's favourite daughters was not enough for her.

In the 1920s and 1930s Perth was so small that whatever the Duracks did was sure to make a newspaper paragraph. MPD was interviewed after his first experience of flight.[29] The loss of Miss Mary Durack's pet crocodile, Monday, was a news item; a short paragraph a few days later announced its safe return to its two companions in a pond in the garden at Goderich Street.[30] What Mary wore to balls and charity dances was noticed, and, because she was only sixteen when she began her year as a debutante, her appearances on the social pages as a single woman went on too long in this period of early marriages. There she was in black chantilly lace at the King's Park Tennis Club dance in 1933, and in a Marina blue suit and black beret at the West Australian Turf Club's Easter race meeting four years later. 'Miss Betty Durack' appeared with her sister now and then ('black wool de chine, lacquered satin front'[31]), but having left Perth soon after the end of her schooldays, Bet was less well known than her sister.

Parallel with her social round, Mary had a semi-professional life in journalism, with six articles published in Perth newspapers in 1931, ten in 1932, ten in 1933 and twelve in 1934. The *Western Mail* and the *West Australian* were useful outlets for her first adult stories and documentaries that drew on her Kimberley experiences. She sometimes gave lectures to women's groups on life in the north. Friendly, sociable and charming, Mary was welcome everywhere. But it was not a life to satisfy her. Whether she knew it or not, the material that would shape her creativity was elsewhere—in the north and in all the events, dreams, hopes and tragedies of her family's pioneering past.

Bet was also restless in Perth. In 1933, she was not as pretty as Mary—'robust' was the kindly word for her plump schoolgirl figure. Nor was she as tolerant of the inevitable dullness of a limited social circle. Going north saved both girls from a social round in which marriage was the only happy ending. So it was that in April 1933 the Perth social columns reported that Mrs M. P. Durack and the Misses Mary and Betty Durack left on the *Koolinda* for a stay of some months on the family property Argyle Downs.

CHAPTER 2

Ivanhoe and Argyle

The north claimed Bet Durack in 1933, as it had claimed Mary. The next eight months at Argyle Downs gave her a place in the daily life of the station. She learned its rituals, took part in its daily work, listened to stockmen's stories, watched corroborees whenever invited to the station camp and, above all, imprinted on her memory the colours of the Kimberley. Back in Perth during the wet season, she felt that the meaning of home had changed. The months passed slowly until she and Mary set out again for the stations in April 1934. Her letters home show her exhilaration at the return, and a comic sense which makes the most of the journey and its mishaps. Travelling from Wyndham to Argyle Downs, after the week on the *Koolinda*, they stopped first at Ivanhoe Station. Only eighty kilometres from the port, Ivanhoe was the most accessible of the properties, but in Bet's exuberant account of their journey, every kilometre was an adventure:

Well I don't think there was any stop between Goose Hill
and Saltwater Creek but we stopped properly when we
got there and Reg held forth long and lustily on the utter
irresponsibility of taking car through water thigh deep.
Eventually he decided to take Dad's car first. This meant
unpacking it. Mary and I set to work with our usual ardour
and dragged out the swags, suitcases, apples, oranges etc
etc. Meanwhile Jack [Kilfoyle] was testing the bottom
again. 'Oh dear, dear, dear Reg. It'll be a good car that
gets us through this Reg. Oh dear, dear, dear, almost up
to a man's waist, eh Reg?' Reg places the car gingerly at
the water's edge. 'I think it best to rush it, son,' says Dad.
Reg of course thinks the opposite and of course says 'yes'.
However in low gear with all hands pushing we deposited it
safely on the opposite bank. Then started a long procession
of crossings and recrossings with the swags and suitcases
and apples and oranges etc. Reg carefully bandaged the
carburettor of his car and with a look of infinite misery
on his face turned its nose to the water. 'Mind you, I don't
think she'll do it.' Anyway with an extra push, she did. We
all patted ourselves on the back and wrung ourselves out
and rubbed our sweaty faces.[1]

The little comedy of the river crossing shows the clash of
personalities between father and son. They differ about the best
way to get across, but 'of course' Reg gives in. MPD was used
to having his own way and he found it almost impossible to
trust any of his sons to make decisions. He had perfected the art
of not listening to anyone who disagreed with him. Watching
Reg's struggle for independence Mary and Elizabeth were amused

and sympathetic; they could see how hard it was to deal with a kindly autocrat. As a schoolboy in Perth, Reg had seemed aloof. Now, in the isolation of the Kimberley, the sisters and brother became close.

As the eldest of the four Durack boys, it was inevitable that multi-talented Reg would try out life in the Kimberley. He became as much at home in the cattle yards as in a library, and he understood machines as well as horses. There was no electricity at Argyle until Reg installed a generator—after which he had to be last to bed at night because no one else knew how to switch it off. His wide reading in the 1930s was taking him towards socialism and Marxism and this made him confront the social injustice of the use of Aboriginal labour. At twenty-three, Reg was full of ideas and unfocused energy. From early 1934 he filled a gap at Argyle, when the death of MPD's cousin Patsy Durack left the station without a manager. MPD was nearly seventy, strong-willed as ever, but looking at times so disarmingly old and frail that his sons felt guilty when they challenged him—and angry when they lost, as they usually did.

And so, while his sisters were happy in the north, saving money for travel to Europe, Reg was already trying to extricate himself from his father's realm. He was still at Argyle in April 1934, when Mary and Bet joined him. They were paid union wages for helping in the kitchen, where they learned to make bread for the homestead and for the twenty or more Aborigines on the station. In their spare time they turned their attention to the children. As Bet wrote in a letter home:

We are making dresses for the little pics. Mary cut their hair yesterday and washed them with phenyl and lifebuoy.

You've no idea how pretty they looked. All the gins circled round to watch and they wanted their hair cut and washed too, with the result that we now have a staff with beautiful clean hair. We are making dresses for the little kids. Charlotte and Topsy are quite big enough to be useful. We are making them frocks with big bows at the back and teaching them to wait on table. The dresses are to be worn only at mealtimes; we are going to keep them in a box in the cook's room and they can play around in something less auspicious. They look awfully sweet like dear little schoolkids with their bobs and bows.[2]

Argyle had never been a grand dwelling, and in 1934 it was in decline. Once, when cattle prices were high, there had been a full-time gardener. Now, the flower beds Bess Durack had tended were overgrown. Spear grass was pushing the fences into crooked angles and the porch was sagging under the weight of the bougainvillea that covered it. A boab tree in the centre of what might have been a lawn and a twisting path made of flagstones from the river were reminders of the optimism of the 1890s when the first Durack women had made a home there. The house was made of stone, with mud, ant-bed and cement, and it had an iron roof which dazzled when it caught the sun. It was famous for the cockroaches that made their homes in the cracks of the stone walls. They would come out in the quiet darkness, 'scuttle about the verandahs and rustle in the kitchen like a shower of rain'. Cockroach hunts were useless: even if hundreds were killed in a night, still more would come in from the bush and breed in those hospitable cracks in the walls.[3]

Before Mary and Bet arrived at Argyle a series of Afghan and

Chinese men had done the cooking, bringing their own equipment with them and taking it away when they moved on. Mary wrote home asking if the firm could run to another basin and an eggbeater. Everything had to come from Perth; it took weeks for the boat to take her requests home and make the return trip to Wyndham with the small items needed to make the kitchen work easier. After a few months at Argyle, Mary and Bet saw a chance to prolong their stay in the north and make more money by moving to Ivanhoe Station where a permanent cook was needed. It meant taking responsibility without family support. The manager, Bill Jones, was old and frail; due for retirement but not ready to give up, he was huffy at the girls' being given any authority. He resigned, changed his mind, returned and finally had to give up after a car accident. Though Mary and Bet anticipated 'much dearie-me-ing' from their father they were confident that 'we will be quite alright'.[4]

Ivanhoe homestead lacked the dignity of Argyle. Its charm was in its setting, near the Ord River, and in the lookout, reached by an outside stairway, from which the girls could survey the landscape and see if any visitors were approaching. It had a 'dog of a kitchen', under-equipped and inconveniently shaped. Bet cut up a tablecloth for serviettes and adapted an area under the house for making butter. She and Mary changed the pictures on the dining room walls and made new curtains. Making things pretty, while also working hard in bread-making and dealing with the oversupply of meat every time a 'killer' was brought in kept them busy. For recreation they went swimming with the Aboriginal women and children in the afternoon, and after their early dinner they filled in the long evenings writing letters or working on their first book about life in the north. Bet's habit of going on long walks with the Aborigines dates from this time.

It was so lovely to go walking with them and to learn about the bush, and the way they'd tell you about the bush. And classify plants for you, and show you the different methods of the way they might have done it before the white man came because there'd always be casual food collected along the way. You know, we'd always kill a few lizards. And they'd have dogs, and we'd probably hunt, they'd hunt a kangaroo and that sort of thing. And then there were lovely walks from Ivanhoe to the Carr Boyd Ranges that were just near there, about eight or nine miles away, which made a nice walk...and then quietly get back to the station by dark.[5]

It was just as well that the Durack girls liked to walk. The horses on the homestead were needed for serious work, so the chances of riding were limited. But when MPD visited Ivanhoe he took his daughters on long treks to see rock paintings. Bet was overwhelmed by the experience of coming in from bright sunlight to see ancient totemic creatures—the Rainbow Serpent, the Lightning Brothers— on the huge rock surface.[6] These caves were on Auvergne, the Connor, Doherty & Durack property on the Baines River, over the Northern Territory border.[7] As the first major works of art that Bet saw, the cave paintings had a profound influence in kindling her later fascination with prehistoric art and human origins.

Back at Ivanhoe, Bet sketched the Aborigines: men, women and children. Her father and others among the white men on the properties were also included in her informal gallery. At the same time she did the illustrations to go with Mary's chronicle of life at Argyle, *All-About*. Today the pictures seem overly cute, as do parts of the text, but at the time they passed for realism and they had the merit of suggesting individual characters, not types. Published by the *Bulletin* in 1935, *All-About* sold well. A pompous foreword by Sir James Mitchell, Lieutenant-Governor of Western Australia, included the statement: 'All interested in natives as human beings should read this book.' It seems that many did. It delighted MPD, who took to haunting bookshops in the hope of seeing copies of his daughters' work, checking sales figures and keeping reviews in his pocket to show his friends. Writing to Mary and Bet, he enclosed the *Sydney Morning Herald* review: 'So there you are my dear girls you have risen to fame with a mighty rush and such that nearly brings tears to your old Dad's eyes. God bless and cherish you both.'[8]

At a time when the abuses of Aboriginal labour were coming under public scrutiny, *All-About* would have pleased their father for its mainly cheerful portrait of life on his stations. Its publication followed the Moseley Royal Commission of 1934, to which MPD and his men gave testimony. As far as can be seen from their letters of this time, Mary and Bet were not then worried about the family record coming under scrutiny. When the commission members came to Argyle in June 1934, it was more of a social event than an inquisition, in their eyes at least. Bet was annoyed when MPD forgot to introduce the visitors to his daughters, and when this was rectified she thought that one of them, a Mr Brackenridge, had 'fallen for Mary'. They both liked that 'nice young man', Paul Hasluck, then a Perth journalist seconded to the commission.

Moseley reported that the 'station blacks' of the Kimberley were better off than most Aborigines of the time: 'natives on pastoral properties experience conditions which as nearly as possible approach their natural life.' In the main, Moseley said, 'their wants are met.' He also stressed the advantages for the pastoralist in having a source of labour which, considering the number of dependents maintained along with those who worked, was not cheap, and for 'the old and infirm and children, where they exist [who] are kept by the station'. His words 'where they exist' suggest that he did not see many children and was not much troubled about the future. The Aborigines' needs, he said, fitted with those of the pastoralists:

> It would be difficult, if not impossible, to obtain white labour when such labour is required only during a portion of the year. As it is, in the 'wet' season, when little work is being done, the natives go on their 'walkabout' and are back again on the station when needed—indeed sometimes long before. It is a life of freedom, in that the native is under no obligation to remain on the station if he desires to go elsewhere. He has no such desire; he is in the country to which he belongs...[9]

Failing to ask what happens when a pastoralist abuses his power, the report bypassed the question which increasingly troubled the young Duracks. But they would have agreed with Mosely on the importance of the Aborigines' being in their own country and on the misery of those who lived in the towns, belonging nowhere, doing nothing, having nothing.

Here and there in Mary's generally upbeat account of the lives of the Aborigines on Argyle come signs of uneasiness. Mary was a good listener. She was becoming attuned to the pain of the women whose children of white fathers were forcibly removed by government officials. Telling the story of Polly and her daughter Daffodil, with irony and subdued anger, Mary was careful to note that 'the Missus' (whether a Durack wife or the wife of a manager is not stated) had been on holidays when the child was taken away.

> [Polly] hid her in the pandanus down by the creek, and at night put her under a rug in the humpy and kept guard at the door. The 'Government' brought torches to seek her out, and old Polly fought for her young like a tigress at bay, with all the primitive mother-instinct of creatures wild or civilised. But the white men had right on their side and were fired with a spirit of purpose. Daffodil must learn to read and write and sew fine seams with her slim brown fingers and learn the godlessness of her mother's people. Later, if she wished, she could go back again, provided she kept away from the blacks' camp and as much as possible from the old black mother who had fought so hard for her ignorance and wailed curses on the white man's head by all the devils of her heathen tribe.[10]

During their time at Ivanhoe, Mary and Bet allowed, even encouraged, 'transgressions' by the station Aborigines.[11] Ivanhoe was a separate sphere, and occasional police raids threatened to disrupt it. When police came looking for offenders, the sisters claimed to know nothing. Mary recalled their policy of collusion with the Aborigines against the police:

> When the police came round ostensibly on the lawful mission of keeping the camp dogs down (and incidentally serving the dual purpose of reimbursing their own salaries to the tune of one pound a head, by passing them off as dingo scalps) old Paddy would come up to me with an

expression on his shrewd face of 'we're in this together' and say: 'P'liceman comin'missis. Me and all-about dog go that way longa river. You tell'm we gone walkabout longtime.'[12]

Once, out walking with Bet in bright moonlight, Mary said, 'I had no idea there were so many charred stumps on this plain,' and as she pointed the 'stumps' came to life and darted off into the long grass. She and Bet walked on, a little unnerved. A few days later they heard that the police were hunting for an alleged murderer and his band who were thought to be hiding out in the ranges close to Ivanhoe. They never said a word to anyone about their moonlight walk.

In 1934, a young anthropologist, Phyllis Kaberry, introduced to MPD by anthropologist A. P. Elkin, came to stay at Ivanhoe and became a close friend of the young Duracks. Bet liked Phyllis but was sceptical about her application of scientific enquiry to the lives of the Aborigines. Kaberry's conclusions about the lives of tribal women sounded idealised.[13] Bet knew the risks of interviews: the women would say what they thought their questioner wanted to hear.

In later years Paul Hasluck recalled the general complacency of the 1920s and 1930s as far as the Aborigines were concerned. Few whites thought there was any problem. Aborigines were seldom seen in settled areas. Those who knew a little about them usually thought their race was dying. 'Smoothing the pillow' was all that need be done. But travelling with the Royal Commission convinced Hasluck that there was a future to plan for.

As a newcomer, Hasluck felt the remoteness that the Duracks had scarcely noticed. It took him four days by light plane to get from Perth to Wyndham, with overnight stops at Carnarvon,

Port Hedland and Broome. Wyndham was a small and desolate town of one street and about ten or fifteen buildings. In the gold rush of the 1880s, it had seven pubs; now there were two. The meatworks was the main structure. For entertainment, apart from the usual pub, there was a cricket pitch 'on hard brown earth, its boundaries marked by beer bottles thrust downwards into the ground'.[14] Contrasting with these ugly man-made structures was the beauty of the land and its remoteness. Hasluck wrote:

> Travelling northwards from Perth over the hazy red land and along the sharp edge of a painted sea, the sense of time faded and consciousness of place became blurred. One came down in the late afternoon of the fourth day to a shimmering mirage on the dry marsh at the head of Cambridge Gulf and it seemed another land where the time-scale, the landscape and the few and lonely structures made by man had nothing to do with the places left far behind.[15]

Hasluck estimated that there were only about two thousand white persons in the Kimberley and about fifteen thousand Aborigines. Of the latter, two thousand were employed, and nearly all, including workers, were 'fully tribal'. Most of the whites lived in the towns of Broome, Derby and Wyndham, and no more than two hundred lived inland. The only inland town was Hall's Creek, which had a white population of fourteen, and the biggest empty-bottle dump in the world. Fitzroy Crossing had a permanent white working population of six men—publican, policeman, postmaster and staff. About a dozen white women were living on the eight-hundred-kilometre stretch between Wyndham and Derby.[16]

One idle afternoon Hasluck and a colleague from the Commission went out climbing with Mary and Bet. Mary stood on a rock and declaimed a Rupert Brooke poem that evoked gentle hills and green grass. It was nothing like their own landscape of spinifex and sharp rocks with no soft surfaces. The men from Perth sat on 'carefully selected boulders' and listened to the sisters' stories of the grim past of Mount Misery, where members of a surveying expedition, besieged by Aborigines, had built a stockade for protection.[17] The charred stumps of the stockade remained. And that night, MPD entertained them with his own tales of pioneering days. For Hasluck it felt like a foreign country, it was so unlike Perth and the other coastal places that he knew.

Mary and Bet had the diversions of visitors from other stations. It would be flattering Ivanhoe to say it was on the main road, but its rough track was the most travelled route to a number of other stations. Bush hospitality ruled. If anyone called, you assumed they would stay the night, sleeping on green-hide strips on the wooden-based beds on the verandah. The girls saw their father on his regular circuit, and their brothers Reg and Kim came and went from Argyle. But for most of their eighteen months at Ivanhoe they depended on one another and on the Aboriginal women and children. Although officially Mary and Bet were in charge of the Aborigines, they were given motherly protection by the older women. Mary recounted an episode that showed their intuitive sympathy:

> Oh the drama of that place that strange old house where the ghosts walked…Once you [Bet] went up to Argyle with Reg and Tom. I was not nervous, but at night, all alone there, the sound of a roof contracting after the heat

of the day, like furtive footsteps, the keening of a dingo out on the plain, the dismal notes of the mopoke. There were THINGs abroad…footsteps, soft padded footsteps coming up the rickety old stairs. I was too terrified to move, but I called, 'Who's there?' not expecting an answer because ghosts don't talk, but a voice came back, 'Me! Gypsie!' 'What do you want?' 'Well, old Tommy reckon poor little missus too much meself. You go camp longa house.' It was alright when she was there though she was only a sleeping dark mass on the other side of the verandah.[18]

At Ivanhoe the departing manager, Bill Jones, had shown paternalism at its best. Mary wrote of his gentleness with the Aboriginal children. 'He had looked after them through their illnesses, taught them to ride and to swear almost as soon as they could walk.'[19] The women brought their babies to him to have their names approved in little ceremonies of his devising. As well as the babies born on the station, Mary noted, 'quite a lot' were coming in from the bush and the station Aborigines seemed happy to adopt them. This didn't fit in with the 'dying race' theory.

> We now have a Bruce, a Dougal and a Wallace whom they all call 'Wireless'. Personally I prefer their Aboriginal names. What's wrong with Barloe, Gurrungung, Rainyerru and Maroolong? But the people themselves insist on white man names, even the silly ones a lot of them were given in the past like Pumpkin, Slippery, Dodger, Mellonhead [sic] and the rest of them.[20]

Although Mary and Bet established an easy relationship with the

Aborigines—played with the babies, swam in the lagoon with the young women and children—they were becoming aware that the system was open to abuse. Their doubts scarcely surfaced in *All-About*, where text and illustrations gently combine to show laughter and good humour prevailing over frustration at the blacks' refusal to adopt white ways.

There were no clashes at Ivanhoe. Unlike the wives of most station managers, who had families of their own, Mary and Bet did not mind chaos. There was no clock: 'we just guess the time.'[21] It was a time of innocence—or ignorance—as Mary later acknowledged:

> When I left school in 1929 I came back to the North like a homing pigeon and did not then see the tragedy of the drought-stricken eroding plains, the dwindling herds, the shortage of stock horses, the lack of traffic on the roads. To me it was all simply 'life on a cattle station' and talk of hard times and poor seasons the habitual outback topic.
>
> Even the hungry 'bag-men' carrying their swags from station to station in search of work, the thin blue smoke of their fires across the creek I accepted as a changeless part of the outback scene. But the sight of their hunched, retreating figures disturbed me as did the station aborigines—the shadow people in their humpies on the river banks, humbly serving, unknowing, unquestioning.[22]

When Mary spoke to her father about the Aborigines, he was vaguely troubled, but saw no way of changing a way of life that had gone on so long. Having seen what he perceived to be 'an unaccountably sterile generation', he believed that the race was doomed.[23] Yet the children coming to Ivanhoe in 1934 showed

Mary and Bet that there might be renewal after all. But renewal for what? Mary wrote of the distress of one Aboriginal mother who asked her 'with tears in her eyes, whether her Jimmy might not be taught to read and write because she wanted something better for him than the ordinary life of a station black'.[24] That was the dilemma: leaving the station community to be educated in a mission school meant breaking the ties of land and people. And how many pastoralists would take responsibility for establishing a school for the uncertain, shifting numbers of children who came into the station?

The Duracks' experience shows the complexity of power relations on the cattle stations of the early twentieth century. In the debates of the 1980s some historians spoke of 'forced labour' and drew comparisons with slavery in the United States. Others emphasised 'creative adaptation' and the 'cultural leverage' granted to Aboriginal workers to stay on their land and maintain kinship ties.[25] The Duracks were close enough to see both sides of the issue. But they could not foresee the technological changes which would make the station Aborigines redundant. When helicopters and motorbikes replaced horses for mustering, their 'cultural leverage' would vanish, and with it the fragile accommodations of 1930s Ivanhoe.

For all the sisters' doubts, nothing would ever match the enchantment of their eighteen months at Ivanhoe. It affirmed the already-strong bond between them; it gave them the habit of working together—Mary's words, Bet's pictures—and strengthened their ambitions. But if they were sisters, friends and allies, they were also rivals. At Ivanhoe, Mary became aware that the plump schoolgirl Bet, or Bumbles, had become a strikingly attractive young woman. More than Mary, who had her share of admirers,

Bet could catch the attention of any man who happened to interest her. Mary watched, astonished, at Bet's new-found power of 'teasing enticement'.[26] In a green-and-white dress, with the sunlight turning her hair to gold, she easily eclipsed her older sister. But Bet was vulnerable as well as seductive, and when she fell in love it was passionate, long-lasting and disastrous.

The affair was inevitable from their first meeting. Tom Naughton—son of a well-known Riverina pastoralist whose Kimberley properties included Lissadell Station, near Argyle— 'turned up suddenly from the other end of Australia with a blaze of headlights on the verandah'.[27] The first impression of Tom in an impeccable white suit was dazzling. He must have seemed perfect for Bet, except that she was too young. Even his religion was the right one: he came from a big Catholic family, like the Duracks but very rich, and he had been educated by the Jesuits at Melbourne's Xavier College. He established a brotherly relationship with Reg and Mary and went out riding with them or alone with Bet. But soon a pattern of self-destructive drinking, followed by pathetic childlike bouts of remorse, showed itself. The young man who talked knowledgeably to MPD about stock and windmills, or the buoyant Huckleberry Finn with a fishing line and a panama hat, returned to Argyle after an absence, a dishevelled, despairing figure in torn and muddy clothing.

Bet turned down Tom's proposal of marriage. 'She says I drink too much,' he told Mary, adding, 'I suppose you wouldn't marry me, old girl, just for the hell of it?'[28] Understanding him better than the others did, Bet felt powerless to change the self-destructive course Tom was taking. But she couldn't forget him. She was not usually reticent, but she did not let Mary or anyone else know the pain and loss she felt as she watched Tom's plane become a speck in the sky over Argyle, 'a great grey emptiness of sky'. She didn't allow herself to cry:

> Only people who don't feel things much cry. But God! Thank God for the night and the darkness and the longing so much greater but easier, easier now alone in the dark on my own…Tears can come in the dark and run down into the pillow…face leaning down into mine in the grey dawning light, grey blur of the dawn, morning that picks up the colour again. A laugh and we are back again into another day. Fried eggs for breakfast and pouring coffee. He is talking to Reg about a fine new fence a thousand miles away from me, while an hour ago so close.[29]

In spite of Bet's refusal to marry Tom, the affair was not over. The sisters' time at Ivanhoe ended in May 1936 with their departure for Europe on an extended holiday. Just after they sailed from Wyndham, Tom made a romantic but misguided attempt to farewell Bet once more. He flew down Cambridge Gulf on his private plane and swooped down above their ship so as to drop a letter on the deck. Too late, too far: the sea took it away. Bet never knew what he had written. On the voyage she danced and flirted and seemed to enjoy herself. Mary, from whom Bet had concealed her sexual relationship with Tom, misread her sister, believing that there was a good deal of self-dramatisation on both sides, and no lasting feeling.

Although the Durack fortunes never recovered from the depression years, MPD was happy for his daughters to spend all their money on travel. The royalties from *All-About*, added to the savings from their time as station cooks, and the maturing of insurance policies, which had been taken out by MPD, all helped to pay for a year in Europe in 1936–37. This first trip abroad was an upper-class young woman's rite of passage; it should have been the Duracks' great experience. It was assumed that seeing Europe prepared the way for marriage—at the least it filled in the time of waiting for the suitable young man and gave a cultural advantage over the less privileged.

But Mary and Bet set off with none of the glamour of the great ocean liner. MPD had booked them on one of the meat boats that sailed from Wyndham. They had an impressive itinerary, first in England, where they did the usual sightseeing, and in Ireland, where they visited their father's brother, Dermot, and teased a pompous cousin with a pretence of colonial naiveté and bad manners. They went to Italy, including Sicily—the only place that really excited them—and, more adventurously, to North Africa.

In fact their time in the Kimberley was far more important for the sisters than the overseas travel that followed. Their letters home from Europe had lively and amusing moments, but little of the freshness of observation of those written from Ivanhoe and Argyle. Some of Bet's letters, so Mary said, showed 'barely concealed boredom'. The sisters argued and quarrelled. Everything Mary wanted to do was dull, so Bet said, while Bet's ideas, Mary thought, were silly and dangerous.[30] Bet wanted to spend all their money on a week at the Dorchester or the Savoy and then see what it would be like to be penniless in London. Mary vetoed that, and she vetoed an invitation to go dancing with an Arab Sudanese guide in a disreputable quarter of Tripoli. She was uneasy about Bet's plan that they should pose as journalists and interview Mussolini;

it was a relief to her when the attempt failed. Mary was always putting on the brakes. They had never quarrelled like this at Ivanhoe, where they had been equals, where there had been no clocks and no rules.

Although they were unsupervised during their travels, they were not really free. Letters from Reg, who was still locked into his ongoing disagreements with his father, were a reminder of the emotional and financial problems to which they would return. There was no luxury, little comfort and no future at Ivanhoe or Argyle. And yet when Mary and Bet felt homesick, their thoughts turned to these dilapidated homesteads, rather than to the well-ordered Durack house in Perth. They did all the usual tourist things in England and Europe, met 'lovely people' (as Mary was inclined to see nearly everyone), stayed in country houses and had a distant glimpse of royalty during the abdication crisis. But the green fields of England meant nothing when compared with the lagoon at Ivanhoe in afternoon light. It was home, Bet said:

> I felt a bit guilty when I stepped on the boat at Fremantle for that wildly exciting voyage up the coast when other passengers would say: 'It must be nice to be going home again.' But it was like home and always will be, I think— that wild, wonderful country with its great open vistas, its sweeping yellow savannahs, and its blue hills, dreaming and secret...You [Mary] and I standing on the verandah at Ivanhoe—there together for the first time—the close-folding purple ranges, the far sweep of the plain, and the distant river, and the gins carrying the dishes from the kitchen to the house in that quaint little procession and young Chunuma laughing up at us from the woodheap.[31]

In London, Mary and Bet rented a flat and pursued their careers in writing and art in a desultory way. Bet enrolled at the Chelsea Polytechnic, but was bored by the routine of sitting on a stool for three hours at a time, drawing a figure in one position. The experience was a let-down after drawing Aboriginal sitters at Ivanhoe. Soon she did not bother to attend the classes. Without telling Mary, she played truant, filling in the mornings by going to films, visiting the London Zoo to sketch the reptiles, and wandering round London, aimlessly, neither happy nor unhappy.

Mary worked on a novel for adults, set in the Kimberley but quite different from *All-About*. She was introduced to the critic, Edward Garnett, well known to have an interest in Australian writing. Garnett invited Mary and Bet to tea, and agreed to read Mary's work. Disappointingly, he found much of the novel (an early version of *Keep Him My Country*) too 'strange and new' to appeal to English readers: there was too much about station life and landscape and not enough on the romance between the hero and the 'half-caste' girl.

Mary accepted the verdict; she was tired of the novel anyway. Bet was angry with Garnett and what she saw as the tyranny of English publishing. Why couldn't the British public cope with the unfamiliar? '…damn it all, we read *And Quiet Flows the Don* [and] all of Dickens with his slums and his Fagins and his bleak houses…'

> Actually I don't think Mr Garnett's criticism of your book is good at all. What a suggestion…that you turn the whole thing into a cheap novelette…as it stands it is one of the best things that has been done about that country…the ghostly description of the cattle stampeding and the phantom rider

turning their head; and the bloodcurdling part about old
Pluto burying the body in the quicksand.'[32]

Mary had already tried to find an Australian publisher for the
novel. Angus & Robertson, who turned it down, had also rejected
Katharine Susannah Prichard's *Coonardoo*, saying that 'A & R have
done more than their share in presenting to the world pictures
of the hardships and sordidity [sic] of Australian life and another
publisher must father it.'[33] Like *Coonardoo,* Mary's novel tackled
the almost unmentionable theme of sexual relations between white
men and Aboriginal women.

Mary described her novel as an 'unladylike' book, which ought
to be published under a male pseudonym. Her first choice was
'George Johnstone', which made an invisible link by its use of
her mother's family name. When the Australian author George
Johnston began to publish, Mary switched to 'George Hurley'. The
viewpoint of the novel was intended to be that of a middle-aged
stockman, accustomed to brutalities from which women were
usually sheltered. But even with a male pseudonym it would not
have done well in the 1930s. The times were against it, as they were
against Henry Handel Richardson's *Ultima Thule*, turned down in
1930 as too gloomy to sell in years of economic depression. When
escapist writing was popular, and race relations sentimentalised
as they were in *Gone with the Wind,* the harsh realism of Mary's
novel would not find favour. It had to wait, and undergo many
revisions, before publication in 1955.

Some Australian writers and artists found a fresh vision in
Europe; the Duracks did not. Perhaps Mary and Bet had used
up their capacity for wonder before seeing Europe. At the time
when the banks were becoming the real owners of the Kimberley

properties, the region and its people had imaginative possession of the Durack sisters. So too in different ways the north caught their brothers Reg and Kim. When the land itself was eventually lost to the family, this third generation of Duracks would remain part of it, willingly entangled, emotionally bound.

CHAPTER 3

Love and Marriage

The sisters returned to Perth in February 1937, their futures unresolved. Mary thought of doing an arts degree, but Bet was appalled at the idea of living in her mother's house again. Although they agreed that Bess Durack was 'sweet and unselfish', life as an unmarried daughter at Goderich Street (God's Street, as Bet called it) was restrictive and dull. There was nothing to do, and Bet could not endure the combined pressure of her mother and Nurse Stevens. It would have been unseemly to rent a flat in Perth, nor could she afford it. Their father gave Mary and Bet £1 a week each for clothes and entertainment—not nearly enough for independent living.

Bet insisted on going back to the north. Unspoken, probably, was the hope of seeing Tom Naughton again. It might come right, after all. MPD and Bess refused to allow Bet to go alone. Perhaps because Mary shared, though less intensely, the wish for independence, the sisters took the boat once more from Fremantle to Wyndham and joined Reg at Argyle Downs.

Returning to the Kimberley took the sisters into the whole troubled question of station life. Reg had new ideas but his father did not allow him to act on them. After resigning early in 1936 Reg had lived in Sydney, where he enrolled in medical school, read widely in socialist and Marxist theory and mixed in semi-bohemian circles. In August 1936, he was pressured to come back and manage Argyle. Following the death of Uncle Jack Durack, manager of the firm's headquarters in Perth, MPD planned to take Jack's place and spend less time in the north. This turned out to be an illusion: MPD did not change his routine, and Reg was not given any authority.

In August 1937, a few months after the arrival of Mary and Bet at Argyle, Reg resigned again and went back to Sydney, leaving his sisters to find their own solutions. A brief note to his father was written in desperation. MPD, so Reg believed, would never stop and listen to his ideas for the future of the company and the problems of station management. More important, perhaps, was Reg's need to be independent. His father was angry, hurt and reproachful, and, as he looked at his older children, his King Lear qualities emerged. MPD wanted love as well as obedience, and it seemed to him that Reg was failing in both. MPD spoke of his old age, his need. Considering that in his seventies he was as vigorous and decisive as ever, this was emotional blackmail. The plaintive 'all I have given you' theme was especially hurtful. Reg replied in writing. He could not make MPD listen but perhaps he might make him read and understand:

> You gave me life and strength and health Dad, and the educational equipment to face up to life. For these I will be

forever grateful…You will never understand the strange resentment I have often felt for privileges—and they have been many—which have come to me beyond these things…I was upset at the hint in your letter that I have been somehow unfeeling in the whole affair. Why, my dear Dad, do you bring up the matter of your age? Granted you have many years to be with us yet—to say that life has lost its point of late!…Surely it has not narrowed down to the point of futility simply because it cannot be prolonged indefinitely and vicariously in one of us boys.[1]

MPD's way of dealing with dissent was to put it aside. His children loved him; he knew it and they knew it. A five-page letter, full of news, addressed to Reg at the Advance Bookshop in Sydney, affirmed the bond between them and probably helped to draw Reg back. No reproaches: an affirmation that his son is 'always in [his] thoughts'.[2]

Reg's struggles for independence from his father and his love for the Kimberley coincided with Bet's restlessness. Going north was not a solution after all. She had heard from Tom Naughton. He hadn't been on the wharf at Fremantle to welcome her back from Europe but he hadn't forgotten her; there were two letters waiting for her at Argyle. Although she refused to face it at the time, there were disturbing signs in the way he wrote. A deeply alarming letter from a friend explained Tom's precarious state. It was not just alcohol. Rich enough to get any drug he chose, Tom was taking opium. Bet kept all this from Mary, who would have been shocked, but she pleaded with Reg to lend her the fare to Melbourne so that she could see for herself whether Tom was truly lost. As she admitted to Mary years later: 'I never felt any better and all the time too I never abandoned hope that some day...'[3] Reg refused; he would have helped her in any other affair of the heart but not that one. In despair, she catapulted herself into a nursing career at Darwin.

The other family members were sceptical as to how she would put up with the routine of this new life. Nurses had to be neat and obedient and orderly: these were not Bet's strengths. And, as she admitted, it was not so much that she wanted to do nursing but that she wanted the label of 'I am a nurse'. Otherwise, what was she? She could not rely on the literary partnership with Mary. Although they both wanted to keep working together, they could not see their way to independence through the small returns of the publishing industry in Australia. So, without having told Mary her plans in advance, she departed for the Darwin Hospital where she had been accepted as a probationer. Her strongest motive was the hope that Tom Naughton might follow her there. Mary was annoyed: she had come north mainly to keep Bet company. Now she was left with MPD's undivided attention:

> Daddy is like a cat that has lost all of his kittens but one— and that one he is determined not to take his eye off for a moment if possible. Poor old darling he is so sweet and pathetic—simply goes to my heart and worries and irritates me at the same time.[4]

More susceptible than Reg or Bet to her father's emotional blackmail, Mary knew that she too had to get away. She dreaded being back under close scrutiny of the family: not just her mother, but the aunts and cousins of the extended Durack family. Yet her best chance of finding a job was in Perth, where she was known.

With her role as Bet's chaperone ended, she was free to go south and start earning a living.

Soon Mary was working as 'Virgilia' on the *Western Mail*. She was nearly twenty-five, with three published books (with Bet) to her credit, as well as many articles and an ambitious, unpublished novel. Editing the women's section as Virgilia and being Aunt Mary on the children's page was not exciting, but Mary made the best of it. The job was easy in some ways, but it took almost inexhaustible good will and sociability. Besieged by garrulous readers, Mary learned to hide in someone else's office or to pre-arrange phone calls summoning her to fictitious meetings. Perth was then such a small city that even on a weekend she could not go anywhere without being captured as Virgilia by a posse of devoted readers.

'The job protects me from my friends and relations,' Mary said. There were always family rows about the firm, and after the death of the tactful peacemaker Uncle Jack they had become worse. Whatever the issue—whether or not to sell some part of the Connor, Doherty & Durack holdings or the choice of a new manager for one of the properties—Mary was caught between opposing sides. Living at Goderich Street with her mother and younger brothers Bill and David, hearing complaints about her father from aunts and cousins and from the Doherty sisters, Vergne and Bylly, she was glad to escape 'the whole bloody family', and take refuge in her office. The Virgilia role made its own claims. She was expected to give up her weekends to good causes by attending charity picnics and busy bees. The Lady Lawley Cottage for Crippled Children committee—'a bunch of squabbling old fogies'—was another unwelcome entanglement.[5]

As long as she lived at home Mary could not separate herself from family problems, or feel detached from the station properties.

The unqualified joy of that innocent first year at Ivanhoe was gone; she knew more now about the realities of the Aborigines' lives. A troubled letter to her parents, written after her return from Europe, shows her concern about the wife of the manager at Auvergne: 'a very cruel woman'. 'Some of the goings on there would if reported reflect very badly on us for not putting a stop to them.' The manager was a 'good old fellow', but his wife, angry at a new political climate in which white authority was being questioned, was systematically abusive.[6]

Mary based a short story on the plight of a young Aborigine, Daisy, whom 'Old Woman'—the manager's wife—exploited and terrorised. Daisy is caught between the two worlds. Claimed by her tribal husband, she is taken away from the station and held in another kind of servitude until she begins to think that 'Old Woman' was not so bad. But when she returns with her baby, she is met by a tirade of anger about the worthlessness of all Aborigines and subjected to a harsher regime than before. Published in the *Bulletin* in 1939, this grim story provoked an action for libel (later withdrawn) on the grounds that the combination of the Durack name and the local detail made identification of 'Old Woman' inevitable.[7]

Ivanhoe remained for the sisters the most beautiful place in the world, where they first felt strong, independent and free of the ties of family. Yet they could not forget the Aboriginal children, nor absolve themselves of sentimentality in *All-About* and other early writings and drawings. The feeling in Mary's 'Old Woman' was matched by a passionate letter from Bet, written from Argyle, deploring the 'surface-scratching' of *All-About*:

Can we ever draw the line between the romanticised

pretty-pretty version of dear chubby little piccaninnies doing delightful things all the sunny day through and the little starvelings that are constantly abandoned by their parents and left at Auvergne, arms and legs like sticks, little shrunken chests, tummies round and distended. It's a question of either opening one's eyes to the situation and grappling with it with whatever instruments lie within one's reach or shutting one's eyes to the whole business and getting the hell out of it.[8]

Their younger brother Kim, having his first experience of the north, was seeing firsthand the prevalence of leprosy among the Aborigines. Those found to be suffering from the disease were removed to an island off the coast near Wyndham. Kim was appalled at the enforced exile:

> Today I watched another poor old gin taken down to Wyndham never to return. Not a very happy sight. In her last letter dear Mother showed her usual concern for our safety but that is not the point. Leprosy is very difficult to contract under ordinary hygienic conditions. We're alright, but what about the poor bloody blacks, living in conditions that can only go on encouraging the spread of disease...Don't make your book on black children of the North too picturesque.[9]

The book on the children of the north was probably *The Way of the Whirlwind* (1941), another collaboration between Mary and Elizabeth. Unlike the semi-documentary *All-About*, *The Way of the Whirlwind* is a fantasy, written for children. It has a simple plot: the search by a brother and sister, Nungaree and Jungaree, for their little brother, who has been stolen by Here-and-There, the Whirlwind. Along the way, they ask the animals and birds of the bush for help. Although Mary's descriptive skill and the eerie, sometimes grotesque, quality of the illustrations save the *The Way of the Whirlwind* from sentimentality, none of the painful issues skirted over in *All-About* are explored in this book. Its intended readership of white children is invited into an imaginative identification with Nungaree and Jungaree and given a sense of the strange beauty of the unknown north. A later work, *The Magic Trumpet* (1946), is a weird fantasy of an Aboriginal Peter Pan: a little boy who never grows up, never succumbs to the constraints of adult life. The same wistful note appears in *Piccaninnies* (1940) in which the bush is an enchanted place, drawing white children in. The first line, 'Come away little brother…', spoken by an Aboriginal child, sets the mood of this long poem.

Although the Durack fantasies have something of the narrative charm and visual appeal of Ida Rentoul Outhwaite's collaborations with her husband Grenbry Outhwaite, in *The Enchanted Forest* and other sumptuous books for children, there is something unsettling in the Duracks' works: they are not simply nostalgic. This may reflect the tension in their creators' love of the Kimberley and their concerns about the Aboriginal children. Writing fantasy for white children allowed them to compromise: they did not have to tell the whole truth. But they were not satisfied with 'surface-scratching' and pretty pictures. Mary's unpublished Kimberley novel was designed to tell the truth and shock its readers. 'The Abyss', a short story written in 1939 and thought too gloomy for publication, is quietly savage about white people who expect gratitude in return for even a small measure of justice.[10] Bet's portraits of Aborigines, begun at Ivanhoe and continued at Argyle, captured their individual qualities. Her landscapes are not gentle; the skies often threaten.

Mary's work as Virgilia was busy and frustrating; there was not much time for serious writing. Bet's attempt to find a role for herself as a nurse in Darwin began well. Patients liked her and, although she found her duties grim as well as exhausting, her sense of fun often lightened the spirits of those around her. She was shrewd enough to work the system, keeping on good terms with the matron, the laundress, the cook and the odd-job man. But for much of the time she was lonely and bored. On a little sketch pad she kept in her pocket, she drew scenes of hospital life, but these were just for exercise. She wanted another project with Mary. 'I'm sunk without you Mary, your words, my pictures...'[11] Inevitably, in the frontier town that was pre-war Darwin, she had admirers, but the hope of Tom Naughton's return kept her from taking any of them seriously.

There were parties, lots of them; Bet spent her salary and had to ask her father and Mary for money.[12] Then, in November 1937, four months into her training and with no one to share her shock and grief, she heard that Tom had died suddenly in Melbourne. If it was not quite suicide, it was not quite accidental either. Tom had opened the door of a moving car and fallen or jumped from it. He died about a week later from head injuries. It was assumed that he was drunk; no one really knew. Nor was anyone sure of Bet's feelings. There was a frenetic quality about her in the following months that signalled danger. Only with Mary and Reg, who had been Tom's friends, did she express some of her anger and grief: '...as long as you and I and Reg are alive Tom is alive too. But he played a dirty trick on us, didn't he? It's a hell of a long way before I can catch up to him and short cuts, though tempting, are pretty pointless for a heathen like me.'[13]

Within a few weeks of Tom's death, Bet was looking for a way out of her hospital training course. 'Of all the stupid things I don't want to be is a disciplined orderly obedient diligent docile unimaginative trained nurse.'[14] Accompanied by another young woman Bet took a ten-day voyage on a pearling lugger whose owner was besotted with her. Forty-three years old 'with not a bean in the world', Eric Foxton was one of a number of men—some marriageable, some not—with whom Bet passed the time unhappily in Darwin.

'What next for Bet?' Mary speculated. 'Will she marry some steady chappie for the security of a decent home or throw security to the winds and go off with some ratbag like the fellow with the lugger?'[15] Bet's public self was a 'bright young thing' who made sure she was noticed. Appearing at a party in a white evening dress with a red belt, she carried a white mouse with red eyes as an accessory. Writing to Mary and Reg she kept up a brittle self-dramatising mockery about the adventures of 'our little heroine'. The reality was different, as her later words show:

> By Christmas I was up to my eyes in it. Two timing, three timing, four timing. A Dutch destroyer, an English cruiser, balls, dinners, parties, beaches, a tiger's head on his chest that opened and shut its mouth when he breathed, storms and men and heat and rain and Mrs Abbott and heat and storms and men and rain and heat, boring when they wanted to get married and told their mothers and my face in the mirror talking to me: 'Fool! He's not coming, do you hear, and you're not a nurse's bootlace. Darling [Tom] why, why,

why did you do it? Can't you see that I could have stood anything, anything, only for you not to be. I cannot stand it, Oh God make it stop! Get out of this hospital.[16]

Bet left the hospital and worked for a few months as a librarian while living in a Darwin hotel. 'No place for a Loreto girl,' said a shocked Mrs Abbott, wife of the Administrator of the Northern Territory. Young ladies did not stay alone in hotels and Mrs Abbott would have been happy to have Bet at Government House.

Still in emotional chaos, Bet left Darwin in May 1938. She resisted going home to Perth, where she knew her mother's protectiveness would irritate and oppress her. Looking for family comfort, she took refuge with Reg in Sydney. It was a brief respite, though an important one; it was there that she met her future husband, Frank Clancy.

Within weeks of Bet's arrival, Reg left Sydney. Homesick for the north he took casual labouring work, calling himself 'Jimmy Gale'. He kept in touch with his sisters, whose letters, addressed to Mr James Gale, were sent to post offices around the country. Inevitably, in the small world of cattlemen, the disguise failed; someone told MPD that his son was fencing at Anthony's Lagoon, which was not far from the Durack properties. Choosing to forget the rebellion of the previous year, MPD made Reg manager of Auvergne, the wildest and most remote of the Durack stations. After an interval in Perth, where she did some journalism, Bet followed Reg to his new home in the north.

With Reg and Bet in Durack country at Auvergne, MPD must have felt that he was in control again. True, his second son Kim had come back from agricultural college with new ideas about soil erosion and a questioning attitude towards the cattle industry, but this he could put down to youthful enthusiasm. Nothing had prepared him for a new rebellion. It came from Mary, calm, rational Mary, his perfect daughter. Her choice of husband seemed utterly perverse. Airline owner-manager and pilot Horrie Miller, aged forty-five and soon-to-be divorced with a young daughter, had no obvious charm or good looks, and his source of income seemed insecure. Mary had met him on the Wyndham boat in 1934 and, with an invitation from Reg, he had visited Ivanhoe, dropping down from the skies one day in his little plane, just to see Mary. They had exchanged letters while Mary was in Europe, and a friendly relationship developed after her return. Writing to Reg, Mary did not give the impression of a romance:

> I see Horrie Miller for lunch now and again—find him waiting outside the office as I sally forth…Horrie is a funny old soul—hard to understand at times but he will do an unexpected lot for people he likes, or is sorry for.[17]

Horrie was mentioned again in a later letter, on his way to Sydney to finalise his divorce. Mary did not think he was much interested in his daughter, who by all accounts was 'a sweet little thing'.

In 1938, while Mary was working as Virgilia and arbitrating in family rows, Horrie was working in his office across the street from the *Western Mail*, not especially ardent, but very persistent. His courtship was more casual than gallant. Without preamble, during an absence from Perth, he sent Mary a ring, a square-cut diamond, wrapped in paper and enclosed in a letter. Mary meant to send it back by the next mail but, until then, she thought that it would do no harm just to wear it for a little while. Later in the year, he sent a cabled plea: 'If you still love me at all will you meet

me in Sydney or Melbourne and we will be married if possible
the day you arrive or the day after.'

Mary agreed. It must have been hard to break the news to her
father; she was so used to pleasing him. She wrote to her parents.
MPD's diary recorded the shock: 'Bess shows me a letter from
Mary but I cannot bear to read it.' Distressed and bewildered,
MPD wrote to Reg for support:

> If she married Horrie Miller that would appear the finish
> of her career & to a certain degree social ostracism. Not that
> Miller may not be a decent man in himself. I have nothing
> against him personally but I abhor the idea of her marrying
> a divorced man, a second hand article, cast out as it were…
> As you know Reg dear boy I am not a dogmatic Catholic
> but I feel that [we] have to live up to a certain tradition
> that the name bears—certain principles as it were and if
> Mary married a divorced man I would sort of feel that she
> had sullied my name…
>
> I always endeavour to look at both sides but there are
> no two sides in this; if Mary marries Horrie Miller she gives
> up her career and throws herself away. Mother is very sorry
> about it & regrets the unfortunate situation but probably
> does not feel it as keenly or as sadly as I do. Perhaps if I
> had loved the girl less I would not have felt it so deeply…[18]

For different reasons, neither Reg nor Bet shared their father's
indignation. The Durack name was a burden to Reg, as his 'Jimmy
Gale' masquerade had shown. The appeal to religion meant nothing
to either of them. And, having so often disappointed their father,
they might unconsciously have felt relieved to have Mary slip from

favour. Whether they really liked her future husband is hard to say but Bet at least managed to put a romantic spin on the affair by stressing Horrie's unwavering attraction towards Mary, and the glamour of this 'great shaggy-winged eagle' who had flown to Ivanhoe to see her.[19] As founder and manager of MacRobertson Miller Airlines, Horrie was an authentic pioneer of the skies. Mary saw him in the same heroic light as her own father and grandfather, conquerors of space in their cross-continental trek. As a sixteen-year-old schoolgirl in 1929 she had watched the last stage of the East-West Centenary Air Race and seen Horrie, the winner, emerge from his plane to take his gleaming trophy and the prize of one thousand pounds. That memory, and the newspaper headlines that celebrated the win, fixed Horrie's image in Mary's mind:

> I was standing by the wire fence around the Maylands aerodrome. I was in my school uniform. There were hundreds of cars, a great crowd, a hush of excitement and expectancy, and then a thin rod of sound upon the air, a speck in the sky and all eyes turned Eastward. It is hard to recapture it these days when planes are zooming overhead all day long. It was landing, taxiing through the grass, turning with a great spurt of sound, propeller spinning furiously. It had stopped. The crowd pressed forward. He was stepping from the cockpit, pushing the goggles back on to the helmet. He was shaking hands; lost in the cheering throng.
>
> Hitherto heroes had ridden like brave Sir Lancelot or Young Lochinvar…now they came on wings from the sky and dressed in brown leather, but just as far removed

from the others as the reality of a gawky kid in a shapeless school uniform.[20]

Horrie Miller was attractive enough to appeal to a young woman who wanted to fall in love. He was tall and lean and fair, with deep-set blue eyes and the authentic look of an aviator from central casting. His age was not against him; she had her parents' example of a similar disparity. Bess Johnstone's family had not welcomed the forty-five-year-old Irish Catholic MPD. Horrie's being divorced would have troubled Mary if she had been more devout. She had already lapsed in the belief and practice of her religion so there was only her family's attitude to consider.

For Mary, Horrie's deprived childhood and his lack of family ties would have been an added attraction. She liked to give, to help, to make things better for others. Her brother Kim thought that she had inherited from MPD the 'desire to fix people up'.[21] When Horrie's ex-wife died, Mary proposed adopting his daughter instead of leaving her with her maternal grandparents: an unrealistic idea that came to nothing. Horrie's upbringing had left him without much aptitude for fathering or for being part of a family group. He was not prepared for the Duracks' close, loving, critical and analytical relationships with one another. He never became one of them.

Although MPD could not see any merit in Mary's choice, Horrie's career was impressive. His grandiose given names—Horatio Clive—suggest ambitious parents. As much as peasant-born Patsy Durack, Horrie Miller was self-made, independent and venturesome. Born in Ballarat, Victoria, in 1893, he was left motherless in infancy, and he and his sister had only intermittent care from their father, a clerk of small means, who placed them

in a series of foster homes. Horrie left school young and moved
to Melbourne where he took whatever jobs he could find: as a
baker's errand boy, a cleaner and an odd-job boy in a car firm.[22]
An apprenticeship at the Sunshine Harvester works developed his
mechanical talents. He went to England in 1911 and worked for
an aviation company, learned to fly and came back to Australia in
1914 with a good knowledge of aerodynamics and enough practical
experience to build his own plane, which he did while waiting to
join the newly established Australian Flying Corps. He was trained
as a fighter pilot and saw action in France in 1917, but was sent
back to Australia in 1918 to serve as a test pilot. Aged twenty-five
when the war ended, he was unusually well placed to make his
mark in Australian aviation, which was then just emerging. In
1928, in partnership with the confectionary magnate Macpherson
Robertson, who supplied the funds, he founded MacRobertson
Miller Airlines, in which he was chief pilot and chief engineer
as well as managing director. When he met Mary Durack,
Horrie Miller was establishing air services in Western Australia.
In later years his company would support the Royal Flying Doctor
Service.

Mary's uncompromising words to her father—'I am sorry to go
against you Dad but I *will* marry Horrie'—sound calm.[23] They may,
however, express an urgent need to free herself from her father's
possessiveness and idealisation. Being the perfect daughter came
at a high price. But there are more prosaic reasons: she was nearly
twenty-six, most of her contemporaries were already married; and
the constraints of home were driving this even-tempered young
woman past all patience with 'the bloody family'. And although Bet
seemed bent on disaster in personal relationships, her power over
men was acknowledged between them. Horrie was an exception

in always preferring Mary and scarcely noticing Bet.

Mary was married in a Melbourne registry office on 2 December 1938, with no family members present. A proper marriage for a Durack daughter in Perth's Catholic Cathedral, with an archbishop presiding, was ruled out. According to Catholic teaching, Horrie was a married man, the civil ceremony was irrelevant and Mary was in effect placing herself outside the church by living with him. The couple made their home in Perth, where Horrie had a chilly formal acknowledgment from Mary's aunts, a gentle acceptance from her mother and an unrelenting silence from her father who could not bear to shake hands with his new son-in-law.

Meanwhile Bet spent the wet season of 1938 with Reg in the old homestead of Auvergne, the most dramatic of the Connor, Doherty & Durack properties. Set high above the Baines River, Auvergne combined spectacular views with indoor gloom and squalor. The homestead had mud floors, donkey-hide mats, and revolving tables made from cartwheels set on broad tree-trunk bases. During Bet's stay, a hurricane took the roof off, and the walls, already eaten away by white ants, collapsed. Reg was uneasy about Bet's evident unhappiness. He wrote to Mary:

> What with one thing and another and the roof blown off I would much rather she were not here. She is a worry to me and often I am frightened for her with her 'ups' so up and her 'downs' so down. I keep thinking that at any moment she will react to it all and start smashing things. Of course no one comes here in the wet, the heat has been particularly trying, and that and the perpetual dirt and dust of the place have not contributed any to the soothing of frayed nerves. Even a wireless would have been something…Bet has just

read this over my shoulder. She said I might have given her a break and told you something about her drawings—the mural designs, the lizards, goanna, crocodiles, etc. Yes. They are good. She's our dear sister and I love her a lot, and that's just why she worries me...[24]

Bet, who sent Mary her own version of life at Auvergne, said it was Reg who was likely to do the smashing. She described him roaming the riverbank at night with a rifle or inside the house shooting the invasive feral cats that were too wild to catch. He was sombre and absent-minded, 'bursting with strange new knowledge, strange ideas'. 'It was the time of the Spanish business [the Civil War] and I'm sure he was imagining each cat as a little four-legged Franco.'[25] It might have been better for Bet to join Kim at the more orderly and less lonely Argyle Station but the long ride in the extreme heat was thought too much for her. Besides, Reg needed company, and it helped her to feel needed. So she and Reg stayed on through the wet at Auvergne with a brief visit from Kim to break their isolation and bring them up to date with his plans for reforming the stations. His monologues on soil erosion matched Reg's anti-fascist tirades. 'Of course we are mad,' Bet wrote to Mary, 'but we are living in a mad place.'

We haven't seen a soul or had a drink since Lord knows when, and then the night before last the whole world went mad with a terrible storm. We will stay here for Xmas despite 'do comes' from Newry [Station] etc. Cook drunk and left the bread in the oven all night...Country breathtakingly lovely and the life so abnormal and we so incapable of doing anything about it. Kim and I walked along the riverbank last night—paperbarks ghostly in the moonlight—you know it all so terribly well—I just said to Kim, 'If you mention erosion to me I shall leap into the river,' so we talked of other things and of you. Don't gather that I am upset about anything. This is infinitely preferable to Goderich Street and I have always my beloved lizards and other beautiful creatures to comfort me.[26]

The mood at Auvergne lightened when Bet was courted by the writer and journalist Frank Clancy, whom she had met in Sydney. Frank wrote often, sent her books and delighted Auvergne's distantly scattered neighbours with eloquently worded telegrams. Frank did not realise that these would be read aloud on the pedal radio. One neighbour wrote it all down every day; such wonderful words were too good to waste.

Was Bet in love? She thought she was—and with Mary married, it was time for her to follow. Frank was an intellectual whom Reg respected; Bet was flattered that he took her seriously. He was witty and charming and his love helped her to forget Tom. Frank's letters showed her a mind 'matured and vital to a point of humorous cynicism'.[27] She liked the idea of living in Sydney among bohemian writers and artists. Frank would open up new worlds. He was serious-minded as well as funny, and he had been touched by tragedy. He was on board the Sydney ferry from which one of his journalist friends, Joe Lynch, fell one night in 1927. Weighed down by beer bottles he was carrying, Lynch's body was never found. The accident inspired Kenneth Slessor's meditative poem about time and mortality, 'Five Bells' (1939), and later John Olsen's celebrated painting of the same name.

When Bet's engagement to Frank became certain, Reg was

non-committal about it, with a touch of gloom; it was June 1939 and the chances of 'peace in our time' seemed to him remote:

> Poor Bet has such a wonderful capacity for life and living, but somehow it never seems to be dealt out to her very lavishly. She seems always to be making the most of what is offered her. I do not know much about Frank but liked what I saw of him. He is a rather talented chap, I think, and not without that Irish appeal which seems to be a characteristic of the Clancy family. Not too much money, though—as far as I can gather—which rather surprises me about Bet. I suppose they have as much chance of being happy as any other young couple of today.[28]

Bet's marriage was as contradictory as her personality. To marry a penniless writer with radical opinions satisfied her longing for an adventurous life, free of conventional forms. But to marry in St Mary's Cathedral, Sydney, from Admiralty House, Kirribilli, where she was staying with the Governor-General, Lord Gowrie, was surely the height of convention and privilege. The grand wedding came about because Lord and Lady Gowrie, touring the north in July 1939, had stayed at Argyle. Bet, who took her mother's place beside MPD, the host to the vice-regal party, easily charmed the Gowries and they invited her to stay with them at Kirribilli so that she could see her fiancé. Wedding plans, based on a Catholic ceremony in Perth, were discussed. Frank might not be the perfect match as far as MPD and Bess Durack were concerned, but he was an improvement on Horrie Miller; at least he was single and from a Catholic family. Persuaded by Bet to write to her parents asking their approval, Frank presented himself as responsible and serious, with a Jane Austen touch of respectful formality. Mary thought it was a cynical exercise, but it went down reasonably well at Goderich Street.

Back in Sydney, Frank became irritable and embarrassed at the vice-regal style in which Bet was living. As a radical republican he felt out of place. He and Bet had little privacy. She too was on edge, not sure if she wanted the big family wedding with all the aunts and cousins scrutinising her choice. It might be almost as bad as Mary's ordeal in taking Horrie back to Perth. MPD's sisters, Aunt Bird and Aunt Marie, had insisted on meeting Horrie while making their disapproval clear. How would Frank Clancy fare?

Frank allowed Bet to do all the irresponsible things Mary had discouraged on their travels in Europe. With civilisation cracking apart and a second world war inevitable, he saw no point in being staid and sensible. Together they climbed out on the cantilever of a city hotel in Sydney and waved to the people in the street below. Bet nearly had Frank arrested by pointing to him in a crowd and saying, 'This man accosted me.' And whenever they went onto a dance floor the members of the band would notice them and play *Liebestraum*. But although he was compliant with Bet's whims, Frank resented the formalities of the vice-regal household. He could not see or even telephone her without being identified and approved. When he called to take Bet out, he was scrutinised by equerries with English voices and exquisitely creased trousers.

A revealing letter to Mary, written several years after marrying Frank, shows Bet's fragility after the emotional turmoil of Tom Naughton's death, the sexual wasteland of Darwin and the retreat to weird, timeless Auvergne. No wonder the Government House people were baffled; they did not know that Frank showed her the way out of a prison of self:

I must say they had reason to think him most Unusual.
How could they know that a person could give things
that could not be measured in terms of money or houses
or servants? How could they know that a person could
remould something shattered within one? How a person
could give one confidence and fixity of purpose out of
doubt and vacillation?[29]

Like Mary and Horrie, Bet and Frank were married without
any family present. In place of the Melbourne registry office, they
had the grandeur of the Catholic cathedral, St Mary's, where the
handful of guests must have looked lost. Lord and Lady Gowrie
played the parental roles as hosts, and Gowrie's aide-de-camp gave
the bride away. The *Sydney Morning Herald* reported the occasion,
with details of Bet's wedding outfit and the diamond brooch lent
by Lady Gowrie.[30] The date was 19 August 1939.

When war was declared, just two weeks later, Mary and
Elizabeth Durack were separated by the breadth of the Australian
continent, as they would be for several years. From Perth to Sydney
and back, their long and intimate letters crossed and recrossed.
Their shared confidences and joint literary and artistic projects kept
them close—perhaps closer than ever—as they tried to balance the
claims of husbands and babies with the need to write and paint.

CHAPTER 4

Wartime

Scattered around the continent during the war years, the Durack sisters and brothers depended more than ever on letters. Nothing stopped the flow of words: the exchange of news, the expressions of self-doubt, the calls for support, the gossip, the need to know that the others were listening. Reg, still a solitary bachelor at Auvergne, wrote by the light of a kerosene lantern under a hurricane-damaged roof. Kim was at Argyle, also alone, planning and dreaming of a new order for Kimberley land. Elizabeth was in Sydney, where she had few friends. She signed her letters to the family as Bet or Bumbles, but she was becoming Elizabeth— a name for a serious artist and the name that Frank always used.

And even though Mary was back in Perth, with a home of her own, she too was lonely. She could not go back to work on the *West Australian*: like the state schools and the public service, it did not employ married women. More than ever in the war years the Duracks needed one another. Reg could not talk freely to his father;

Elizabeth was not at ease with her mother. Exasperation did not extinguish love but it strained their relationships. Mary became their centre, always responsive to their emotional needs. As the family mediator, she urged them to be fair to their parents. Her protest on behalf of their mother drew this reply from Elizabeth:

> Yes—I guess I am a bit heartless and don't 'understand' about Mother. The fact is that most, in fact, every human being needs to have someone they can be themselves with. The usually laid out course of affairs is that the daughter confides in the mother but in this case I have you and Reg who understand me dispassionately enough to say anything at all without feeling self-conscious. A mother's love to me was always too defensively protective—it frightened me into complete silence.[1]

Closeness to their brothers—Kim as well as Reg—probably worked against intimacy within the marriages of Mary and Elizabeth. Indeed, Mary seems scarcely to have expected it from Horrie. On one of his many absences from home she remarked that she was missing him 'despite the fact that we have so little in common'.[2] Their marriage, as Elizabeth remarked acidly, was 'doomed to last',[3] but its success came to depend on their having separate spheres.

Soon after their marriage in 1938, Mary and Horrie built a house on a corner block in Bellevue Avenue in the Perth suburb of Nedlands. Some family wit called it Mildew, from the combined Miller-Durack names. Nothing could have been less appropriate for a place of constant movement and sociability: 'cosy bedlam' as their daughter Patsy later described it. Designed by Mary's brother Bill, who had then just graduated in architecture, it must have seemed roomy in 1938, but its four bedrooms would be stretched to accommodate six Miller children and their parents.

Mary wanted children. Whether she wanted them to come so quickly, and so many of them, her natural response was to accept and somehow find ways to manage. Her first baby Patsy, born in August 1939, was 'adorable', clever, responsive, funny. Mary played with her for hours.[4] Horrie was not enthusiastic about Patsy: she was dark, not like him; Mary thought he was suspicious because the birth came early. Within little more than a year, in September 1940, a second child, Robin, was born. This blonde daughter was more to Horrie's liking; she became his favourite, shamelessly indulged. Perhaps to compensate, Mary was at first cool about Robin, who was 'plainish' at birth and not as immediately responsive as Patsy to the comedy of life. Julie was born in July 1942, Andy in August 1944 and Marie Rose in October 1949. The birth of a sixth child, Johnnie, in June 1955, completed a family which stretched Mary's capacities, emotional and physical. The strain of motherhood, evident in her letters to Elizabeth, is not reflected in Mary's published writings.

Motherhood was a full-time job, especially in the war years, when household help was scarce to non-existent. Horrie, too old for this domestic abundance and unsuited to fatherhood, did not give emotional support. He was by nature a loner, and his work often took him away. There was no place for Mary to write. A table in her bedroom, on which her papers mingled with children's unmended socks, was the best she could do.

Like Elizabeth in Sydney and Reg and Kim in the north, Mary was often alone. Horrie's way of life as a pilot did not change with marriage and for much of the time she was in effect a sole parent. Unlike her mother, Mary had no Nurse Stevens to help look after them and manage the household. Her only sure time for writing was at night, while the children slept, and from these late hours came the letters that held all the Duracks together, as well as articles, stories and poems. Mary had no large projects during the war years, but her output was formidable.

When she married, Mary said that a career would never have been enough for her, but that did not mean she was giving up her ambitions as a writer. If her children were happy and well fed, she was willing to leave some household tasks undone. And yet she felt the pressure of disapproval or envy. 'A few people I know feel a sense of real resentment if they "pop" in on me and find me at the typewriter. They say, "It's nice to keep up your writing but of course something has to go," and I feel their eyes are racing around the room to pick out something that has been horribly neglected.'[5] Her mother would never criticise, but Mary knew that she noticed lapses in standards: silver that was never cleaned, a tablecloth hastily ironed. The children learned independence early. Patsy, aged four, went to school alone on the bus, taking her fare of one penny.

Mary's sociable nature worked against her. The visitors who 'just popped in' were warmly welcomed. And as her reputation as a writer grew, she was easy prey to anyone with an idea for a story and a need for professional help. 'If you could just cast an eye over this,' they would say, and Mary would add another ill-prepared and probably hopeless piece of writing to the pile on her desk.

In the first years of her marriage, her writing was unfocused, her energies too scattered for any solid achievement. As with her father, so with her home city: Mary paid a price for being a favoured daughter of Perth. It was too easy to get recognition of a limited kind in Perth newspapers and radio programs, and not to look for a national readership for her writings about the north. Not that it would have come readily: for most Australians in the eastern states, the problems of the north were too remote to be interesting.

Mary's writings for children, *Chunuma* (1936) and *Son of Djaro* (1938), written in collaboration with Elizabeth before either of them was married, did well in the small Australian market. *The Way of the Whirlwind* (1941), rejected by Angus & Robertson as lacking in individuality, sold out its first printing by Consolidated Press within months and was reprinted in 1943. Much later, in a time of increasing literary nationalism, it was taken over by Angus & Robertson and, in a smaller format, it was reprinted four times between 1956 and 1959. These books did not have large overseas sales. The Aboriginal child characters were not immediately appealing in wartime Britain, and without these sales (which in the 1930s and early 1940s had been richly rewarding a London publisher for Mary Grant Bruce's Anglophile Billabong books) the sisters could not build a career. Elizabeth was annoyed at the production quality of *The Way of the Whirlwind*. With high expectations she had asked to have the first page of each chapter on black paper and to have the text in her own elegant handwriting. Because this was not done she dismissed the cover design of a quite lavish production as 'a mess'.[6] The publisher countered by telling her that the book was already too expensive; she could not expect them to invest any more in elaborate design.

Throughout the war years and beyond, Mary's maternal role stretched beyond her own children to her brothers and sisters. Elizabeth's storms were hers too, as were Reg's indecisions and Kim's hopeful and despairing moments. Elizabeth's most of all. Nearly all Mary's early writing projects were devised with the aim of helping her sister as well as herself. Their wartime collaboration on a comic strip for Sydney's *Daily Telegraph* worked well for both of them. Sometimes Mary's storyline gave Elizabeth her inspiration, and sometimes Elizabeth took the lead. A letter to Mary shows her impulse to get rid of a character: if Mary did not specially want to keep him, she would like to have him eaten by a crocodile.

The children's books and the comic strip did not stretch Mary's abilities. For more than a decade she had been making a place for herself as an authority on the north and as a voice of conscience on the treatment of Aborigines. In a 1944 article for the *West Australian*, she pointed out the fact that the exploration of the west would never have been accomplished without the labour of the Aborigines. West Australians should remember the obligation that the white settlers had assumed in 1897 with a solemn undertaking to set aside not less than one per cent of the gross revenue for Aboriginal advancement and their ultimate attainment of equal citizenship. This had not been honoured; the expenditure was pitifully small, and the general attitude was one of apathy and neglect. The Aborigines should be the first charge on the State, Mary wrote, because 'only by these people being deprived of their land was there any State to tax'. She believed while missions and government institutions must still exist, they should at least work on a constructive education policy to help Aborigines find their own place in society as individuals.[7]

Mary's time in the north gave her a rare degree of experience. Few white women knew the lives of the Aborigines as she did; fewer still combined intellectual authority with a passion for justice. While Australia's war with Japan was preoccupying most of its citizens, Mary affirmed her belief that racism was a greater threat to humanity than war.

Her main focus was on education and health. It was not enough to train the girls to be good domestics and the boys to be useful farm and station hands. 'Who wants a serf-race in Australia? They must be given the same educational advantages as children of our own race.'[8] She had seen the Ivanhoe children, so lively and promising in 1934, become listless adolescents. Angrily tracing their decline, she named them Lucy, Chunuma, Dot:

> I would have [white Australian people] see young Dot as she was when we were at Ivanhoe—quick and willing and eager for life, the pride she took in her hair and the few poor frocks we gave her. And I would like them to have seen her again as she was when I was at Ivanhoe last, for since her eye has gone she goes about like an old hag, face averted, a long piece of hair hanging down to hide the sunken socket, her whole life warped and ruined because in the conditions in which the natives live it would not be possible to restore her self-respect with an artificial eye.[9]

Writing late at night, while her own children slept safely in her Nedlands house, Mary was haunted by the Aboriginal children whose eagerness for life, she now believed, was all but extinguished. Most of all she grieved over Chunuma, the little boy who had been 'the personification of life and joy, of fun and impish gaiety'.[10] Now a lanky adolescent, he showed a 'heaviness, a dullness' in his eyes and face. Living in cattle camps, he was learning the worst that the white and the Aboriginal worlds could teach him. He had no future.

Mary never lost touch with the women and children she had known at Ivanhoe. She made many trips north, even when her own children were young. As her family increased in number this became a major exercise in strategic planning. 'One can do a whole lot of things only by not doing a whole lot of other things.'[11] Early in 1945, as a way to celebrate her father's eightieth birthday, she set off with him for a three-month tour, revisiting the Queensland places he had left, aged twenty-one, for the great trek west. It was hard to place her children for such a long absence. Patsy was six, Robin five, Julie three and Andy eight months old. Bess Durack was always willing to help, but her limit was two children. The Loreto nuns could be persuaded to take very small children in cases of need, but it would be another year before Patsy and Robin would be judged old enough for the convent boarding school where they were safe but unhappy. Mary engaged a housekeeper, a deaf Scottish woman called Mrs Bow, to look after the three younger children, while Patsy went to Mary's friends the Korwills. Horrie's work, as usual, ruled him out of these domestic arrangements. So, with a degree of ruthlessness that seems to contradict her maternal qualities, Mary set off with her father on a journey of memory for him and discovery for her.

There may have been a stronger reason for Mary's wish to take time away from her family. In 1944, not long before the birth of Andy, she discovered some letters from another woman which proved that Horrie had been unfaithful to her. Although she was deeply wounded, she seems not to have sought comfort from anyone. It would have been hard to do so, given her father's opposition to her marriage and the disapproval of other family members. At some stage Mary confided in Bet, but her eventual decision not to end her marriage was hers alone. Horrie waited for her forgiveness, which must have come at the price of a certain detachment from Mary and a lowering of her expectations.

Mary and MPD travelled to Melbourne where Elizabeth was then living with her two children. Frank's wartime job was coming to an end. He was unable to find a house for his family and the marriage was in trouble. MPD did not then face the fact that Elizabeth would have to fend for herself, but Mary was deeply worried about her sister. From Melbourne, MPD and Mary went to Sydney and Brisbane, and to Cooper's Creek, where Thylungra, the dwelling of MPD's boyhood with its thatched roof and mudbrick walls, had been replaced by a modern homestead. The Queensland journey opened up new perspectives on the family's past. Mary established close friendships with a number of her Queensland cousins, the descendants of Patsy Durack's sisters Mary Skeahan and Sarah Tully. Only one of the Aborigines MPD remembered was still living, but talking to him triggered memories that Mary stored up for the family history she was planning. She and MPD went by train to Charleville, took a flight to Katherine, a truck to Wyndham, and another flight to Perth.

Mary told an interviewer that her family history was near completion.[12] So it might have been, if there had not been so many claims on her time. In revisiting the western Queensland of her father's youth, Mary meditated on the meaning of place for his generation and her own. MPD had never seen the Kimberley as anything but a place for profit. In his mind the stations were always for sale. He could not understand the emotional power it had over his sons and daughters. But for Mary and Elizabeth, Reg and Kim, it was home. As Mary later wrote in her family saga *Kings in Grass Castles*:

> Surely never was the power of a country more clearly
> demonstrated than in the extraordinary hold that Kimberley

exercised over this third [Durack] generation, which, although educated away from it, never encouraged to belong to it, returned to it as naturally as the Aboriginal to his 'dreaming'—his spirit home.[13]

The Queensland travels added to Mary's knowledge of the Kimberley region and gave her the material for a major work: a family chronicle to be called *They Reached a Land*. Like her other books it was to be illustrated by Elizabeth. Probably because of the pressure of home and family, it moved slowly. It had been preceded by another collaborative idea for Elizabeth and herself which grew out of their wartime correspondence. This was a joint autobiography, the story of family life with their own impressions and ideas. Their letters to one another, in which they matched memories and filled in gaps in their knowledge of their times apart, became the basis of a book-length collection which they called 'The Young Know'. Elizabeth chose the title from a Chinese proverb of her own fertile invention: 'The Young Know, the Middle-Aged Regret, the Old have Forgotten'.

The perspectives and personalities of the Durack brothers emerged indirectly in 'The Young Know'. It was not likely, Mary and Elizabeth agreed, that Reg and Kim, Bill and David could be persuaded to join in as co-authors, but in passages quoted from their letters, which Mary, a natural hoarder of papers, had retrieved, the brothers' personalities were evoked. As the project developed, the letters lost some of their spontaneity. Candid and funny in the narrative of the ups and downs of domestic life, the correspondence could not carry the freight of the sisters' ideas about war and peace, religion and politics. Intellectual and personal histories contended with one another: there was no strong narrative thread to give the letters unity.

Mary was optimistic about finding a publisher for 'The Young Know'; she edited the letters and sent them off to Angus & Robertson. Not surprisingly, they were rejected. Wartime paper shortages would have been one reason; another was the fact that the sisters were not yet 'names'.

Seen in the perspective of their lifetime, the letters of 'The Young Know' are remarkable; they show the closeness of the sisters, the contrasts in personality, their questioning minds, the demands of marriage and motherhood, ambitions, successes and frustrations.

Mary and Elizabeth were in agreement about the folly and waste of war. Elizabeth thought that Australia should have stayed out of it. Mary took a less extreme position: it was not possible, she argued, to stand aside. Both admired the convinced pacifism of their brother Bill. They debated their own religious beliefs or lack of them; both would then have been called 'lapsed Catholics'. Mary was the more sceptical. Elizabeth agreed with her in rejecting much Church teaching, but she thought that the Catholic insistence on the importance of the individual outweighed much folly, and formed a bulwark against racism:

> Mary, for all you say I still think that only a broad return
> to the fundamentals of Catholic doctrine can ever make it
> nice again—of course I don't mean G. K. Chesterton, nor
> do I mean all the hocus pocus though a pity to deny so many
> of the comfort and fun afforded them by their candles and
> sodalities and holy water and what-not. I mean the Church's
> teaching concerning the importance of each individual
> being—from the moment of conception...Accepting

the importance of the individual so many things fall into order—the jigsaw puzzle takes shape—automatically all barriers of race and colour vanish as factors of any importance. It just remains as something interesting and delightful that certain sections of the human race have developed, during the ages, distinct physical and mental characteristics.[14]

Politics, religion and art: the letters ask questions about all these. Both sisters were still in the early stages of their creative lives. Mary was the more diffident about her powers. She saw her sister's talent as more important than her own. Elizabeth's early drawings, sent from Sydney, were a revelation:

I spread them all over the floor—those great black sheets of paper that had suddenly come alive with colour and movement, with life and exuberance and energy. I knew that this was what all the restlessness, what everything we had to put up with at your hands had been about…You will go much further in your line than I in mine because you have felt more and suffered more. I was going to say you have had the courage to live emotionally but I doubt really whether you had much option, whether you could have lived any other way.[15]

Elizabeth depended on Mary's weekly letters. As well as helping her to believe in her art, they were a link with home, which for her was the feeling of being loved. Her sense of home was indivisibly linked to Mary, Reg and Kim. They cherished her, complained to one another about her waywardness, enjoyed her sense of fun and high spirits, and worried about her emotional fragility. In urging Elizabeth to collaborate on 'The Young Know', Mary may have seen this project, like their other joint ventures, as a way of holding Elizabeth together and giving her something to do. At the least, when a phone call from Sydney to Perth was an expensive three minutes, letters were a substitute for talking to one another. It was possible that a book might come from them and, as long as Mary had no other projects in mind, 'The Young Know' was worth doing.

Neither of them faced the fact that 'The Young Know' needed a framing biographical narrative and a sense of an ending. The sisters' reflections often sparkled with individuality and intense feeling, but they had their flat and predictable moments too. More than once, as the correspondence progressed, Mary pressed her sister to decide whether or not she would be willing to publish her life story so far. Elizabeth declared that she would not hesitate; she did not care what anyone might think of her. But as the exchange proceeded through 1942 until early 1943 there were signs that indiscreet Elizabeth had some areas of discretion. Both her marriage and her career were as volcanic as her nature, and the pressures of war and her isolation in Sydney and Melbourne made combustion almost inevitable. A possible ending for 'The Young Know' would have been a break with Frank Clancy. The more likely that break became, the less Elizabeth wanted to publish the letters with the somewhat anodyne ending Mary proposed. Better, she thought, to leave it to 'our bathchair years'. The manuscript, typed and edited by Mary, was set aside while the Clancy marriage faltered.

Unlike Mary and Horrie, Elizabeth and Frank had much in common. There was 'a great easiness between us from the start', Elizabeth said.[16] Frank, who was fourteen years older than Elizabeth, was well read, witty and charming. He took her seriously as an artist and encouraged her to move on from her role as illustrator. Even in the small matter of calling her Elizabeth, rather than the schoolgirlish Betty or the family's Bet, he helped her prepare for the world of artists, dealers and critics she would soon need to meet.

The Clancys had imagined an idyllic, semi-rural life in a small community outside Sydney, where Frank would write and Elizabeth would draw and paint. After a few escapist months, however, reality became a very small upstairs flat at McMahon's Point. Comparing it with the unhemmed Kimberley spaces, Elizabeth felt like a canary in a cage. She had never minded discomfort, especially when it came with excitement and a touch of danger. The hurricane that took off the roof at Auvergne was exhilarating, and she did not complain about living with no shelter except the part of the verandah that hadn't been blown away. But the Sydney flat was like a doll's house. She was luckier than Ibsen's Nora: the last thing Frank Clancy wanted was a wife who played house. One day, early in their marriage, Elizabeth made an elaborate pudding. It was the sort of thing wives did. Frank picked up the plate and put it under the kitchen tap, saying, 'I didn't marry you to make puddings for me.'[17]

Although they were happy together for a time, neither Elizabeth nor Frank was made for a steady life on a small income. Elizabeth could not manage money; Frank, by her account at least, was even less responsible. And he drank as he spent: heavily. His first book *They Built a Nation*—published in 1939 with a foreword by future

Australian Labor Party leader Herbert Vere Evatt, then a High Court judge—had won praise, but its sales remained modest. Clancy's use of primary sources, well before Manning Clark's *Documents in Australian History*, was enterprising but it was a bad time to publish, just on the eve of war. A novel, *Haunted Tenement*, which he sent to an American publisher, failed to rouse interest.

With financial pressure, Frank's failing career, the war and Elizabeth's isolation in Sydney, the marriage was under strain. Elizabeth had no close friends in Sydney, no one to talk to. Their baby, Perpetua, born in March 1941, was strong and beautiful, but Elizabeth herself was tense and tearful after the birth. Frank's anti-war beliefs kept him out of the army until the war with Japan brought a threat of invasion and he was sent to non-combatant wartime duties in Brisbane in August 1942. Elizabeth took Perpetua to the railway station to see him off. 'Her love of Frank is frightening,' she wrote of Perpetua's desolation when she realised that his departure wasn't just their usual game of hide-and-seek.[18]

Rather than openly admit her unhappiness to her parents, Elizabeth turned to Reg and Mary, who had an almost parental role in her life. In turn they exchanged anxious letters about Bet. Mary lent or gave her money, some of it in the form of her own share of the royalties in their joint publications. Although thrifty Horrie did not allow her more than the minimum needed to run the Durack-Miller house, Mary could never refuse Elizabeth. She was just as responsive to Kim, who was drawn into the family business in 1936 and whose letters from Ivanhoe and Argyle kept Mary in touch with the problems of the north. Elizabeth, however, was needier in this wartime period, and Mary was well aware of the effort involved in taking their joint projects from one Sydney publisher to another, carrying the protesting baby Perpetua.

While Mary and Bet's creative lives were hard to reconcile with motherhood, the sisters never let go of the north as their source of inspiration and their emotional centre. What was happening at Ivanhoe and Argyle was more urgent than anything in Perth or Sydney; for Elizabeth, at least, the brothers seemed more important than her husband. The sisters were passionately involved in the fortunes and the disputed future of their father's empire. If it were lost to the family—and MPD seemed determined to shake himself free of it—what would happen to Reg and Kim and their ideas of a better way of life on the stations and in the north generally? In a letter to Mary, Elizabeth was forthright about MPD's inability to change or give up authority:

> Poor old Dad—he stands in the pathetic position of the pioneer who has outlived his time and conditions. To him— poor befuddled old muddler—it must appear that his very flesh and blood are turning against him. I'm not saying he should be dead of course but the reins of Government should be handed over—should have been handed over long ago to his more than able sons.[19]

MPD was more inclined to cut loose than to hand over. In June 1939, while Elizabeth was still in the Kimberley, a chance to sell all the stations had appeared in an astonishing proposal from Dr Isaac Steinberg, who was in Australia as an envoy, looking for a place to establish a Jewish homeland. MPD was ready to listen. The impending outbreak of war with Germany made it more urgent from the Jewish point of view, but less likely to persuade an Australian government wary of 'enemy aliens' and more inclined to intern Russian and German Jews than to welcome them to the north-west.

Elizabeth was not much impressed by 'Dr Steinberg trotting about with his little attaché case',[20] but MPD thought him a charismatic personality. A social revolutionary, a left-winger and an observant Jew, Isaac Steinberg had been expelled from Tsarist Russia for 'subversive activities'. His map of the proposed homeland took in the Durack stations: Ivanhoe and Argyle, Newry and Auvergne. He envisaged close settlement for 75,000 Jews. Farms would be established with livestock and crops. There would be secondary industries such as tanning and canned fruit and vegetables. The settlers would dam rivers, including the Ord, and build hydro-electric stations. They would create an agricultural miracle that would not only populate the north but also create new exports and stimulate economic growth.[21]

Steinberg, MPD and Kim Durack toured the stations together. Steinberg was excited, MPD was thoughtful and Kim was worried. Kim had his own ideas for irrigation and rural development. His future and that of Reg was bound up in the north. All their plans would disappear in a utopian scheme which might easily fail. 'How do you feel about it, boys? Hopeful or sad at heart?' Mary asked Reg and Kim.[22]

Steinberg's campaign continued after the outbreak of war. He won support from a remarkable range of public figures with widely differing political and religious opinions. Prime Minister Menzies was said to favour the scheme but his cabinet was divided. Some saw the populating of the Kimberley as a safeguard against invasion from Asia. 'Better the Jews than the Japs' was a pithy phrase of the time. There was a humanitarian response in which the Christian churches gave unexpectedly united support. The Anglican Primate of Australia, Archbishop Le Fanu of Perth, sent a message to Menzies, saying that Australians should support the scheme 'out of pity's sake and for Christianity's sake'.[23] Melbourne's Catholic Archbishop Daniel Mannix said that giving the land to Jewish refugees could 'wipe out a stain on our common humanity'.[24]

The scheme also won support from left-wing trade unions which had traditionally followed a restrictive immigration policy. As victims of persecution whose cause was promoted by anti-fascist Steinberg, the Jews were welcomed by the same labour leaders who had denounced Jewish 'Money Power' in the past. But xenophobia and racism also appeared. Some predicted that the Jews would not stay in the homeland: 'They would find their way to the cities if they had to burrow under wire netting.'[25] Others were alarmed at the idea of a ghetto. Some in the government were concerned about security risks. Others were sure the scheme would fail because the Jews knew nothing about the land that had defeated so many would-be settlers in the past. There was opposition from members of the Australian Jewish community who believed in assimilation, were proud of the recognition they had won and did not like the idea of a Jewish peasantry. They did not share Steinberg's vision of a Promised Land 'where the settlers would write Jewish poems about the kangaroos and the kookaburras, the hot days and cool evenings, the magic spell of the earth and the first steps of the wanderer pioneers'.[26]

The debate went on through 1940 while the Duracks waited. If the government had supported Steinberg, MPD probably would have accepted an offer that would clear his debts to the bank and allow him to leave the Kimberley with honour. A sale in 1940 would not have been so bad for MPD's sons. Reg, aged twenty-nine, and Kim, twenty-three, both unmarried, could have found new careers. The longer the properties remained in

MPD's control, the more his sons yearned to have their chance at reform, and the more they were blocked from action and lapsed into self-destructive passivity. When the Steinberg scheme failed for want of government backing, Reg and Kim returned to their planning and waiting, becoming, as the years passed, more and more like characters in a Chekhov play. At least their plans included the Aborigines, whom Steinberg and his supporters did not notice. The anthropologist A. P. Elkin was the only public voice reminding the government that the Steinberg plan overlooked 'some three hundred aborigines living in the region…human personalities who have been "refugees", apparently doomed to extinction from the day we took and occupied their country'.[27]

Reg and Kim had different but complementary ideas for the Aborigines. Reg's solutions lay in political action; he did not believe that anything short of socialism would save them. Some 'bourgeois' ideas about marriage would have to go, he said, airily dismissing deeply ingrained racism, along with the widely held belief that children of mixed race inherited the worst qualities of both antecedents. In the meantime, Reg said, a working wage, proper housing on the stations and education for the children must be provided. In 1943 he asked Mary to send some *First Readers* for the station children; he already had a blackboard and chalk.[28] With the years his radical hopefulness faded, but he held firm to the duty to give equality in education. When he married and had children of his own, his wife Enid taught fifteen Aboriginal children with five Duracks in a highly successful school. Kim, too, had radical ideas. When the vice-regal couple visited Argyle in 1939 he told Lady Gowrie that 'it was a pity but as a class she *must go*'.[29] His plans for the future were based on science. Proper use of the land, which was being abused under the present open-grazing system, would bring work for the Aborigines and a better life for everyone.

Kim brought the first plough to the Kimberley. He was blunt with his father about the need for a revolution in the cattle industry. It was no use just buying a few more bulls and thinking things could go on as before; they must bring in pasture management by means of irrigation. At first sceptical, MPD thought well enough of Kim's experiments with lucerne at Argyle to encourage further research. Between 1942 and 1945, Kim succeeded in growing sorghum and millet on the Ord River at Carlton Reach. This was on Connor, Doherty & Durack land but had government financial support.

Vignettes of all four brothers emerge from the letters of Mary and Bet. Reginald Wyndham and Kimberley Michael, both claimed for the north even in their naming, were closest to their sisters. The letters evoke introspective Reg with the gaze of a thinker and the rough hands of a stockman, oblivious of his chaotic surroundings, eating as if he had a train to catch, assuming that everyone had read Marx. Gentle, tactless Kim, with whom a conversation soon became an excited lecture on soil and crops, was intense, dedicated and indifferent to money or advancement. As primary producers, the brothers were spared the worst pressures of war, but the land provided a tough life for them both.

Elizabeth wrote in distress of the predicament of Bill, an architect with anti-war beliefs, who was designing air-raid shelters in Sydney in 1941. She and Frank did their best to support him in 'that dreadful time'. It seemed to Bill that his beloved profession was being extinguished. Pressure to enlist came from the senior members of his firm. It came from casual encounters, as when a 'nice old girl handed me a white feather…I thanked her and put it in my button-hole'.[30] Worst of all, Bet thought, was the family's inability to understand his convinced pacifism. She herself was astonished at Bill's firmness under extreme pressure: 'Too tolerant even to offend an old crank hovering like a spider to pounce on civilian flies. There is more kindness in [Bill's] nature than in all the rest of us put together. Yet whence that cold white flame? Whence the immovable determination?'[31]

Helping Kim at Carlton Reach became Bill's war work. It was no sinecure. Kim's dedication set a high standard:

> I was under no illusions from the start and just as well, as it was the most demanding job of all my life and Kim, 18 months my senior, the toughest boss I have encountered, before or since. It was a long and arduous trip—train from Sydney to Brisbane, Qantas flight by DH 86 from Sydney via Longreach and Cloncurry to Daly Waters in the Territory. There a full stop for a week where I was made an honorary member of the American Forces camped on the airstrip and eventually went with a commando group perched atop a six ton truck taking supplies to Victoria River Depot Observation Unit. Through Jasper's Gorge and somehow eventually to arrive at Carlton Reach: 'Good to see you here Bill—now you have half a day to put up your tent and get settled, and then to work.[32]

Bill and David, close allies in childhood, took different paths in wartime. Mary remembered the young David as 'an assertive elf', tormented at school for his intellectual precociousness and in need of Bill's protection: 'amusing isn't it [that] Bill, whose whole philosophy revolts against force, should be so well equipped to use it, as was shown on the few occasions when he saw fit to strike a blow in David's defence?'[33]

Ebullient David, the only one of the brothers to join the armed forces, was posted to Sydney in 1942. He was cheerful company for homesick Bet and a willing babysitter for Perpetua. The Clancy flat became his base whenever he had leave. Bet, who still saw the twenty-one-year-old as 'the kid brother', had to look at him afresh:

> He is a bright kid but full of a terrible restlessness and exasperation at all this waste of time and energy. The work at the School of Military Engineering is apparently quite easy to him. From what I gather he sleeps through most of the lectures, but when I ask him if he passes the fortnightly exams he says with scorn: 'Have you ever known me to fail?' He is really very goodlooking in his uniform and is getting brown and tough…[he] brings me cigarettes and chocolates each weekend—you know how scarce these things are—and I have been trying to persuade him to smuggle out some potatoes.[34]

Although he disagreed with Frank about nearly everything, David was Frank's favourite brother-in-law ('not counting Reg…or Kim…or Bill'). But it was Mary whom Elizabeth needed most. When Frank was assigned to essential services in Brisbane, the exchange of letters was Elizabeth's lifeline. Mary worried about the effect of isolation on her mercurial sister and did all she could to keep her working.

One joint project, which brought in some welcome payment, was a weekly set of illustrations by Elizabeth with a story by Mary. It ran in the Sydney *Telegraph* for almost a year. Like nearly everything the sisters did together, it was based on their Kimberley experience. The comic-strip adventures of two Aboriginal children were drawn to amuse and charm, and, although they had some purpose to instruct, they did not claim to be realism. Elizabeth conceived the strip as a way of extending the children's quest in *The Way of the Whirlwind*. She wanted the brother and sister to search the world, travelling back through history, popping out at the Armada or in ancient China.[35] She also worked on a children's book about crocodiles. But she fretted to get back to the north, where she could paint. Sydney stifled her.

In March 1943 Elizabeth alarmed the family, and probably angered Frank, by announcing that she was leaving Sydney and taking Perpetua to Auvergne to stay with Reg. Wartime travel for civilians was strictly limited. Elizabeth was not entitled to a permit simply because she wanted to paint at the source of her inspiration or to be with her brother. Reg was uneasy. Although he was lonely and longing for someone to talk to, he knew that Bet's ideas usually meant trouble. Against his better judgment he gave in and sent her a telegram: 'Suggest you take up duties housekeeping, nursing as soon as possible.'[36] Presented to the authorities in Sydney, this ruse worked and Mrs Clancy, experienced cook and nurse, was on her way to do essential work for Mr Durack, well-known primary producer in the Kimberley.

Elizabeth did not tell Reg that she was pregnant. Whether she told Frank before her departure is uncertain, and because he was working in Brisbane she was free to make her own impulsive decision. Writing to Mary about the birth of Perpetua, she had described the 'primeval' experience which made her feel like 'a tool of God'. This time she wanted to give birth in her own heartland. Instead of the little box-like Sydney flat, where she and Perpetua had wept and wailed in unison, she wanted to nurse this baby beside the Ord River.

The first part of the journey, by train from Sydney to Adelaide and on to Alice Springs, was tedious. Pent up for days in a railway carriage, Perpetua, not quite two years old, was fretful and restless. But the train journey was nothing to the ordeal that followed. Elizabeth had planned to fly from Alice Springs to Wyndham with family friend Eddie Connellan of Connellan Airways. She was aghast to find on arrival that Connellan was just leaving Alice Springs for Melbourne and would be away three weeks. Alternative flights—via Katherine and Hall's Creek—proved too complicated. There was trouble with her permit, which was issued in Sydney but not acceptable to the military authorities in charge of travel in the north. She decided to wait for Connellan, putting in time meanwhile at the Hermansburg mission. It was a hundred and thirty kilometres from Alice Springs, but it would be better and cheaper than a sordid, mosquito- and bug-infested pub.

Time at the mission had rewards as well as discomforts. Elizabeth met painters Albert Namatjira and Rex Battarbee. A portly Aborigine in a torn singlet and battered hat, Namatjira impressed her with his paintings of Mount Sonder in different lights. Elizabeth painted his portrait and thought it 'not bad'. Battarbee, Namatjira's mentor, showed her what could be achieved by simplicity in choice of subject.

But the friendly company of fellow painters was counteracted by the pastor's young daughter, Ruth, who disliked Perpetua and set the other children against her. 'Ven does go Perpetua?' was her constant refrain. When Perpetua developed a worrying eye infection which was slow to respond to treatment, Elizabeth took the next bus back to Alice Springs. With no beds to be had in the town, she camped in the Connellan Airways hangar, which was unbearably hot under its tin roof. Perpetua ran around naked 'except for her beloved shoes and socks'. There were more delays and trouble about the travel permit. Elizabeth moved into a hotel: 'hot stuffy room—thick with dust—voices on verandah outside, glasses clinking and breaking', and had meals in a dirty café. The only comfort was a letter and parcel from Mary, and from Bess Durack a birthday card for Perpetua, which she held tightly as she went to sleep.

After waiting nineteen more days in Alice Springs, Elizabeth and Perpetua were permitted to fly to Auvergne, where Reg met them. Elizabeth's pregnancy must have been obvious to her brother; by early June there was a frantic exchange of telegrams between Mary and Reg. Mary wanted her sister to come to Perth, but this sensible solution was refused. On 29 June, MPD, Reg and Kim put a vigorously protesting Elizabeth on a plane to Katherine, having arranged for her to be admitted to the local hospital when the time came. Somehow she escaped, wrote a cheque on an empty bank account, which she asked Mary to honour, and took a flight to Brisbane. Reunited with an apparently forbearing Frank, she gave birth to a son, Michael Francis, on 11 August 1943 in a private hospital in Brisbane. MPD said he could not understand why Bet had to go all the way round the continent to get to Queensland.

Her seemingly futile wartime journey confirmed Elizabeth's sense of herself as a painter, and her belief that the Kimberley region was essential to her creativity. Although her wish to give birth in the Kimberley was frustrated, the idea found expression in one of her best known paintings, the huge oil 'Broome Madonna' (1946) of an Aboriginal woman, heavily pregnant, with a look of calm acceptance on her face. Of all her paintings, this and 'Ord River Venus' had the closest personal meaning for her—'almost identification'.[37]

Staying overnight in Adelaide with her mother's family on her way to Alice Springs, Elizabeth had heard Mary's voice on national radio, in a 'moving and impressive' talk which made their uncle, Ted Johnstone, shift uneasily in his chair. Elizabeth thought Ted the most narrow-minded person she knew: Mary's logic would get nowhere with that sort of person—the sort who says, 'Put the blacks in a house and give them clothes and they'll get pneumonia.' Reg, whose radio had broken down, read the transcript and thought it excellent. This broadcast marked Mary's emergence as a public figure. Firmly and confidently she tackled the controversial issue of Aboriginal rights, almost certainly enraging many friends and relatives. The title, which may have been chosen for her by the Australian Broadcasting Commission, was 'Solving Our Problems'. There was no solution, Mary said, as long as Aborigines were educationally and socially deprived. Royal Commissions were useless; reserves were not an answer.

The arguments in Mary's radio talk had been rehearsed less formally in letters written to Elizabeth a few months earlier. Mary recalled the gossamer veil that Bess Durack had made her wear when she went north, so as to protect her complexion. It was 'a nice kind dim veil' that came between her and reality.[38] Reality was harsh, and the temperate Mary now allowed herself to be angry about blinkered Royal Commissions and enquiries that did not ask the right questions. She grieved for the bright, funny children of her first visit to Ivanhoe who were growing up lacklustre, aimless and diseased:

> Bet, how many white people do you know who despite many generations of civilisation, were they taken as babies, put down in a grass hovel…taught nothing by the white

man beyond what will make him useful to the white man's needs…how many white people do you know who would turn out even half as bright, half as cheerfully intelligent as the average station Aborigine?[39]

Mary had talked to her father about the Aborigines' needs. 'We just did the best we could at the time,' he said, troubled but unable to think what else could have been done. His generation had believed the race would soon be extinct. He wanted to forget the problems, to sell the stations and retire. He did not want to pass on the Kimberley inheritance to his children, but he did not fully understand that they had already taken it on themselves. The effect would be a hard life for Reg, and a tragedy for Kim.

In the first postwar years Mary and Elizabeth thought of Kim as the hope of the Durack family and the region for which he was named. The region, however, was not ready for Kim. When he stood as an independent candidate for the Legislative Assembly in 1947 he won a respectable number of votes but did not take the seat from Labor.[40] His manifesto, 'A New Deal for Kimberley', would have alarmed many voters. Elegantly produced, with a cover design by Elizabeth and a text that showed unmistakable touches of the hand of Mary Durack, the manifesto challenged too many people. Its support for decentralisation would have unsettled administrators in Perth and in Canberra, as would Kim's plain language. ('Kimberley has no towns. It has dumps.') A question about the pearling industry and the White Australia policy was an implicit criticism of racial discrimination. The last page consisted of a four-page questionnaire which voters were asked to fill in, sign, detach and return. The replies, preserved in Kim's papers, came from station owners and managers, storekeepers in townships and pearlers in Broome. Later, Kim's niece, Patsy, summed up the response to this unusual political strategy:

> One can well picture the getting out of ink and pen, clearing of table and laborious thinking and writing under moth-beset carbide and hurricane lamps, the silence broken only by the noises of the tropical night. But whatever questions were crossed out or left unanswered, no one who returned the questionnaire failed to have an opinion on the Aborigines. 'Do you consider the present state of the natives as generally satisfactory? Firstly in terms of native welfare and secondly in terms of service to the community?' met with vigorous pronouncements: 'The sooner they get rid of the lot of them and replace with white labour the better.' 'They are dying out like they have done in other countries.' Otherwise totally contradictory in comment, the preserved forms nonetheless remain as indicative of northern attitudes of the day.[41]

It is no surprise that Kim was not elected to represent Kimberley. The manifesto probably did him permanent damage, characterising him as a stirrer, a radical, even a socialist. As the 1940s came to an end, he was stubbornly continuing the research on soil and crops for which he could not win the financial backing he needed. Reg was an employee in the Connor, Doherty & Durack company, unsure of his future. His marriage in 1944 brought great happiness, but there was strain and anxiety too when his Perth-born wife Enid was first confronted by the harsh conditions of Auvergne. Elizabeth was homeless, her marriage failing, her career a burden as well as a delight. Mary, mother of five young children, struggled on a moderate income to find time and solitude to write.

The public image of the sons and daughters of a 'cattle king' was one of effortless privilege. None of the Duracks matched that expectation.

CHAPTER 5

Homes and Heartlands

When the war ended in 1945, the northern properties were once more under threat. The question of selling Connor, Doherty & Durack had lapsed after Dr Steinberg's overtures in 1939; no serious buyer would come forward during the nation's emergency. As his family knew, MPD was still inclined to sell, but no one quite believed that it would happen. Mary's three months with her father in 1945, travelling to the Queensland places of his boyhood, helped her to understand his impatience to be done with it all, his weariness of shareholders, banks, incompetent or drunken station managers and their unhappy wives, poor seasons, low prices and hopes of better times too long deferred.

Kim had spent the war years growing crops and vegetables under irrigation on his research station at Carlton Reach. He hoped for bigger achievements in peacetime, and he had grand designs for rationalising the management of the stations. Reg's commitment to the north was confirmed when he married Enid

Tulloch, a city girl whose immense courage and adaptability would give life at Auvergne a new sense of hope. As the postwar era began, the neediest of the four was Elizabeth.

After the birth of Michael, Elizabeth moved to Melbourne where she lived uncomfortably in a series of rented rooms, sometimes with the children, sometimes alone, now and then with Frank, depending on his army postings. The wartime housing shortage and their small means made it impossible to get a permanent base. Sometimes they were lucky: a house in Grey Street, East Melbourne, had pleasant rooms and a nearby kindergarten for Perpetua. Although rents were pegged, the practice of extracting 'key money' was widespread. Landladies did not want children, and when Elizabeth was allowed to have Perpetua and Michael with her they were all made to feel unwelcome. A poignant moment in one of her letters shows Perpetua at the beach, incredulous that she can splash about as she pleases, exulting: 'It doesn't matter! It doesn't matter!' Michael, placed in the care of strangers, shouted, 'Don't you go without me!' as his mother departed. Both were in and out of boarding schools before they were five years old. The Loreto nuns, who had educated Elizabeth and Mary in Perth, agreed to take Perpetua at Mandeville Hall in Melbourne and later at Swanbourne in Perth. Elizabeth worried about the fees, which she could pay only in kind. Frank took a number of paintings to Mandeville, and spread them out on the parlour floor. From these the nuns chose 'The Kid'. This picture of a little Aboriginal girl holding a young goat was to become one of Elizabeth's most popular works, but at the time it was a kindness on the nuns' part to take it.

The contrasts of Elizabeth's life were as extreme as her mood swings from exhilaration to despair. They included a short period in which she took a job as a cook on a country property in Victoria, as well as lunches in expensive hotels with some of Melbourne's most influential people. After meeting the future prime minister Robert Menzies and his political ally Richard Casey, she summed them up as 'nice coves' but not really winners, with Menzies the more able of the two.[1] Casey's artist wife Maie became a friend.

Elizabeth lamented her homelessness even more than the precarious state of her marriage. In all her wanderings she kept in touch with Frank; she seems never to have wanted a divorce—nor, under the divorce laws of the time, did she have grounds for one. If he had been able to give her a home, and if he had tolerated her restlessness, kept a job, stopped drinking—all big ifs—they might have stayed together. The desire for a home was strongest of all:

> Oh Mary, a home…somewhere of my own that I could come back to and know there was a bed and a room for the children…I have a terrible feeling all the time of being someone coming down in a long parachute descent, never seeing the ground…if only I could lay my hands on a few hundred quid I would mortgage and re-mortgage and time-payment and every other jiggle-jaggle under the sun to obtain these simple basic requirements.[2]

Elizabeth's collaboration with Mary was a strong sustaining element, emotionally and financially, in a chaotic time. In 1945 she completed the drawings for Mary's first version of the Duracks' family history in Australia, *They Reached a Land*, which was based more on memories than on documents. But her real passion was painting and to paint in Melbourne seemed impossible: she needed to go north again.

Elizabeth found a refuge at Ivanhoe, where in 1947 she persuaded her father to build her a studio on the bank of the Ord River. She really wanted a house, but MPD was horrified at the idea of her actually living there. On Reg's advice she adjusted the demand to a workplace, a grass studio to which she could come and go. She wanted a long narrow rectangle with a high sloping roof. She got a square box with a flat roof, made from boughs and grass, open to the river on one side. It was 'terribly nice of the old boy', but not what she had in mind. Writing to Kim, she mimicked her father's way of taking charge:

> '12 feet! What!, it doesn't want to be 12 feet—here give me a rule Norman—now what's the height of that post— goodness gracious that's high enough—got reaping hooks here Norman? How many hours will it take them to get those post hooks here? Three men could get them here in half a day—yes, two or three hours would be long enough.'[3]

In the comedy of MPD and the studio, Elizabeth could see her father's attitude to the stations. The idea of his daughter making a home there was a sign of slipping standards. Yet on a long table in the 'grass box' Elizabeth created the 'Ord River Venus' and other paintings. She worked with energy and joy. She often had the company of an elderly Aboriginal artist, Jubul, who at first sat and watched her, seemingly more amused than impressed by her efforts. To get rid of his distracting presence Elizabeth gave Jubul some paper and pencils to see what he could do on his own account. These materials did not suit him: as she later discovered, Jubul was from the Northern Territory where he had practised bark painting. Missing the stimulation of his own group he had all but given up the art. Now, challenged to prove himself, he came back fully equipped:

> It was an exciting experience to see him go to work on a piece of prepared bark with his paper-bark brushes and his tins of ochres mixed with urine and blood. He explained carefully to me that what he was doing was simply 'play-about' art and had no connection with the paintings in the sacred caves which we had, on occasions, visited together. That, of course, was the real thing but this was a pleasant way of filling in the hot hours between camps. The subject matter would be some incident of the day, the hunt or the dance. He drew an aeroplane with the same aplomb as a crow...I never saw him rub out a line. The whole was a kind of building up, ordered by some kind of innate sense of form and design that was never geometrical or precise, though always perfectly balanced.[4]

Elizabeth learned from Jubul as painters always learn from one another, but there was no question of copying his methods. She went on with her Windsor and Newton paints, he with his tins of ochres. At the end of the day she would exchange his works for some tobacco and he would have a good laugh over hers. The question of influence, the fine lines between adapting and copying Aboriginal themes and methods would become problematic later in her career. But as she and Jubul worked side by side on the banks of the Ord, it was a happy, companionable experience.

Elizabeth's first exhibition, *Time and Tide*, which opened at the Art Gallery of Western Australia in August 1946, was a gentle introduction into the perilously competitive world of professional art. The same paintings shown at Melbourne's Athenaeum Gallery were well received there also. By contrast Sydney was harsh and she was alone. *Time and Tide*, shown in the David Jones Gallery in January 1947, was a crushing defeat. A scathing review by the *Sydney Morning Herald*'s art critic Paul Haefliger dismissed the paintings with the offensive headline 'Amateurish Art Show by Miss Durack'. 'Miss Durack may have talent,' Haefliger wrote. 'If she has, she does not give much help to its fruition. She should learn to curb her daring spirit for a while at least, and begin where everyone has to begin—at the beginning.'[5] The review, which appeared on the morning of the opening of the show, did not have even one good or reflective word for the paintings.

Haefliger, who was an artist as well as a critic, was powerful. 'A bad review from him and you were really sunk,' said John Olsen.[6] Elizabeth refused to be sunk. Feeling sick and angry ('so angry I could have killed the man if he had been near me'), she found a solicitor's name in the telephone directory and went out from her city hotel to get advice. It seemed she had no redress unless she could prove malice on the reviewer's part, or monetary loss on her own. She paid half a guinea and left. Next she found Haefliger's address and took a taxi to his house in Double Bay, where his wife, looking nervous, made coffee. Elizabeth, who had watched Haefliger enter and leave the gallery, accused him of neglecting his duty to look at the paintings. She wrote to Frank:

He tried to be nice to me—tried to turn the conversation constantly to make a flippancy of it—was I too cruel then… will they [the Duracks] come after me with a popgun… however overall I got what I wanted—he did not look at the pictures, he did not know there were drawings there, he had never seen another line I'd drawn…by this time I was feeling a bit sorry for him—I keep feeling sorry for him, damn it, and I don't want to, I want to keep feeling wild.[7]

Page after page of her furious account of the opening went the next day to 'dearest Frank' in Melbourne. Estranged as they were, she and her husband were still allies; she still looked to him for understanding. She talked to the gallery's curator Will Ashton and critic Bernard Smith. Ashton said Haefliger's review was an insult to himself and the David Jones Gallery, which would not hang paintings they did not believe in. Smith was awed by her courage in confronting the critic. He had expected Haefliger, who was always complaining about soulless competent technicians, to like Elizabeth's work. This review placed all the weight on technical skill. The Sydney *Sun* gave a more balanced commentary but it was the *Herald* that mattered.

At a later exhibition in Sydney, in October 1954, entitled *Love Magic*, Paul Haefliger accused Elizabeth of copying Aboriginal motifs. This was a recurring charge, almost always made by critics who knew nothing about Aboriginal painting. Haefliger, a European to his fingertips, was only guessing at Elizabeth's way of working. She had learned from old Jubul when they painted side by side on the Ord River, but in no sense had she copied his works. Haefliger was well known for his bossy and patronising attitude towards women painters—Sydney portraitist Judy Cassab felt diminished by his words—but with Elizabeth Durack there seems to have been an added malice. The image of the Durack family coming after him with their 'popguns' shows that he had stereotyped her as a child of pastoralists' wealth and privilege.

In the later 1940s, while her marriage was troubled and her

paintings were receiving more than their share of obtuse and patronising reviews, Elizabeth looked north for comfort and inspiration. Ivanhoe, where from 1947 her grass studio waited and her father and brothers came and went, was a place to think. Critical responses to her exhibitions from James Gleeson as well as Paul Haefliger puzzled and disappointed her. In 1948 these responses provoked her to write a long, eloquent open letter to the art world. After her more or less futile face-to-face encounter with Haefliger she did not think it worthwhile to post the letter, so she let the words flow, clarifying her ideas as she wrote.

She had several challenges to meet. The word 'illustrator' was a belittling one, and she had been known as the illustrator of her sister's books. No use to point out that her work with Mary was an equal partnership and quite separate from her work as a painter. Another persistent word was 'documentary', which usually went with the idea that she was primarily engaged in fighting for Aboriginal welfare.

> That the work embraces illustration, document and social conscience I will concede, but [it] merely embraces and is not specifically any one of these things…One is driven along by invisible impulses. At one moment the whole of the universe resides in the eye of a child. The next, the answer is patent in a group of goats on a stony hill…Subject, thought and idea, with hand and eye mutely obeying, are unified into something whole, complete and often unbelievably simple.[8]

When she painted Aboriginal subjects, she was looking beyond them to all human beings, seeing in them 'qualities inherent in the hearts of all people'. In these subjects, too, she found 'the very land incarnate'. The figures in her landscapes were painted in the same colour as the one on her brush as she painted the earth beneath their feet. If her work had documentary value, she insisted, it was incidental. She honoured welfare workers and missionaries, but she was not one of them. Her paintings might reveal sympathy and 'something of what is meant by love in its broadest sense', but this was not a conscious aim:

> If I paint a native camp, far from being horrified as a welfare worker would be and as I am constantly credited with being, nearer the truth is that I am quite enchanted with the dusty harmonies of sub-bleached dresses, tattered trousers and rusty mias.[9]

The charge of copying made Elizabeth angry, especially because the Sydney critics did no more than assert; they never said what her source might be. Had Paul Haefliger or James Gleeson ever seen a bark painting? Could they name one that she had copied? As to the charge of using Aboriginal motifs, she was no more guilty than the French painters who looked to African carvings or Japanese prints.

In 1953, when she illustrated Kate Langloh Parker's *Australian Legendary Tales,* she took bark paintings as the most appropriate source of inspiration. The compositions were her own conception but individual figures were taken from 'carved nuts, bark paintings, caves, rock faces, boomerangs, shields, coolamons, emu eggs and pieces of mother of pearl':

> They are the work of many artists, some long dead and none known beyond the boundaries of their vanishing

tribes. I am indebted to them all—but mostly to Jubul; and although he died some years ago I like to think he survives a little in some of these illustrations.[10]

Less offensive than the charge of copying, but also irritating, was applause for social criticism which reduced her art to propaganda. A Perth columnist described Elizabeth's Broome paintings as 'the story of the gradual degradation of the Aboriginal since his contact with the whites'.[11] Applause of a different kind came for her large-eyed, wistful Aboriginal children: the public could not get enough of these sentimental images.

It was not a good time for a woman painter, and being a West Australian did not help. Most of Elizabeth's male contemporaries— Sidney Nolan and Albert Tucker among the first—took paintings to London, exhibited and worked there in the 1940s. Elizabeth made some attempts to set up an exhibition without accompanying it. There was a further complication. She was still Frank Clancy's wife and according to the regulations of the time she needed his signature to get a passport. She did not press Frank. Perhaps she meant it when she told friend and historian Geoffrey Bolton: 'I have no intention or wish to leave this country. I don't even want to go to Rottnest. I'm going to stay right here and they can come & get it or BOAC [British Overseas Airways Corporation] can wing it over.'[12]

Staying 'right here' in the early postwar years was the north, with forays for exhibitions in the eastern capital cities. When she went into the larger worlds of Sydney and Melbourne, Elizabeth presented an image of confidence, elegance and charm but, lacking membership of any group of fellow painters, she needed her family's support. The postwar art world had its cliques and cabals.

The Sydney critics favoured abstraction and derided Melbourne's figurative painters. When David Boyd was accused of copying his brother Arthur's style ('as near as dammit to being either plagiarism or parodies'[13]), he had the solidarity of the group to back him. Elizabeth retreated into the world in which she felt most herself: beside the Ord River, with old Jubul working nearby, Kim or Reg at one of the homesteads, and a letter from Mary coming by slow delivery from Perth.

Again and again in her letters to Mary, Elizabeth speaks of the Ord as home. Away from there, in Sydney, Melbourne or Perth, she is 'hunted, haunted, flying, fugitive'. She never had a place that could reflect her personality. The grass studio at Ivanhoe was a compromise. She had hoped that an old building could be brought out from Wyndham and set up among paving stones from the river. In a desperate fantasy of a return to childhood, she dreamed of sharing that house with Mary and Kim. Of course they would move around, but it would always be there, 'somewhere to come back to'.[14]

> The Ord is better for us Mary than the [Perth] Hills. The Ord is our own country, from a vantage point we can watch its destiny unfolding and be there as a part of it...This place could be somewhere for the three of us actually and I am sure we could be happy there, also for the children in the holidays.[15]

When the idea of selling the stations was revived Elizabeth was aghast for herself as well as for her brothers. In a long letter to her father she begged him to think again. There was room to compromise. He could satisfy the impatient shareholders of Connor

Doherty & Durack by selling the Northern Territory stations. A new firm, Durack Brothers, could emerge. He must at least keep Argyle. He must think of Reg and Kim, who loved the land and had given it years of their lives. Without Argyle, 'this garden paradise of Australia', Kim would be no more than a market gardener and Reg would live on a piece of sandy rank grass and become a 'character'. MPD must realise too that the Kimberley was part of his own being: 'Dad, you ARE the North, and the contradictions of the country are contradictions that lie within your own heart.'[16]

'Letter from Bet', her father noted in his diary. His only response was to mark with a red pen her point about selling only the Northern Territory stations. Whether they were a viable proposition is doubtful. Auvergne, where Reg had toiled off and on for more than a decade, was an awkward proposition. It included some good pastoral land but there were vast stretches of wild country, where cattle strayed and were lost and which were hard going for horses and dangerous for mustering.[17] To balance Auvergne and its ramshackle homestead, most buyers would want the better pastures of Argyle Downs, where the stone house, creeper-covered, with garden and flagged path, came close to gracious living.[18]

MPD's confident and decisive personality may have led his sons and daughters to underestimate the pressures that were driving him to sell. It had never been easy to hold the Connor, Doherty & Durack company together, and for all the apparent firmness of his control, he was answerable to the shareholders, among whom his brother Dermot in Ireland had been owed dividends for many years. Historian Geoffrey Bolton traced the decline in the Durack fortunes from the end of the First World War:

…beef export prices slumped into a twenty-year trough because of competition from Argentina. Only the state government's meatworks at Wyndham, opened in 1919, saved many from ruin. As it was, Connor, Doherty & Durack, burdened by the need to provide dividends for family members, went into deficit. By the onset of the Great Depression of the 1930s, they owed the Bank of New South Wales at least £100,000 on which annual interest of about £7000 had to be paid—absorbing nearly their whole annual income.[19]

MPD's attitude to his sons' inheritance seems contradictory. He may have thought he was freeing Reg and Kim from the burdens he had carried, imposed on him by old Patsy Durack. Yet he had brought Reg north, straight from school, and had sent Kim to agricultural college. It was late to change direction. His eventual compromise was minimal, but it did concede that it would be hard for Reg to start a new life with his young family. He marked off a block of two thousand square kilometres for Reg, and paid a fair price for it to compensate the shareholders. It was named Kildurk. Part of Auvergne, it was unfenced, with no house and no stock. It was nothing compared with Argyle. Ruefully considering its primitive state, Reg wondered if it was for this that the Duracks had left Ireland. Yet it was enough to keep him in the north. He built a primitive shelter—little more than a partitioned shed—for himself and his family, and began all over again. Eventually, with the help of a government subsidy and the dedication of his wife Enid, a natural teacher, Reg's ambition to teach the Aboriginal children on the station was fulfilled. His sons and daughters shared schoolwork and outdoor activities with the Aboriginal children.

'Our lives were entwined, every day,' Reg's daughter Anne said.[20] She recalled a happy childhood in which the privations of life at Kildurk were more than balanced by 'much fun and family joy, safety in each other, love and real happiness'.[21] And for this fourth generation too, the sons and daughters of Reg Durack, the hold of the north was strong.

There were other concessions in MPD's last days. He did not think that selling the stations should matter to his daughters; their attachment to the land had always seemed to him to be merely sentimental. Bet's homeless state was acknowledged by the gift of a block of land in Perth and money to build on it. Mary was given a car. Bill, an architect, and David, an engineer, had the security of their professions. Unlucky Kim was left to continue his research projects as best he could and to campaign for better land management by lobbying the federal government. His father's concession to Kim was minimal: the alienation of a piece of land near Ivanhoe Station where the Department of Agriculture set up a research station.[22] Why Kim fared so badly is uncertain. Perhaps his plain speaking about the exploitation of the land by the cattlemen had touched his father's pride. Unlike Reg, Kim was never interested in cattle and he made no secret of his boredom and distaste for that central part of his father's work. He was afraid that the Durack family had forfeited its right to be part of the land, 'though we will probably be condemned to go on haunting it for eternity'.[23]

The sale of the stations went through in March 1950, a few months before MPD's eighty-fifth birthday. It brought the relatively small sum of £250,000, which dwindled after probate and payouts to about £30,000—just enough for Bess Durack's old age, but very far from the returns she and MPD had once expected.[24] He had always hoped that discoveries of oil or gas might make the Duracks a fortune. But these and other buried treasures of the west were for others to exploit. Season after season had brought drought; low prices for beef persisted as markets closer to Britain competed with Australian exports. Discovering that the Ivanhoe manager and his wife were drinking heavily, MPD was disgusted and depressed. Small things, which as a younger man he would have dealt with and forgotten, left him profoundly affected. The sale should have been a relief. Instead it felt as if an essential part of the self had been extinguished. He told Mary that he was happy and satisfied, but, she wrote, 'he was crying and holding my hand like a child'.[25]

Feeling out of place, no more than a visitor, MPD completed his last, sad tour of the stations, erected a memorial to the pioneers of his early days, and said his goodbyes. Leaving from Wyndham airport he felt unwell. Back in Perth he became seriously ill and died three weeks later, on 3 September 1950. He had booked a world tour as a long-deferred reward, to himself for years of responsibility and to Bess for taking the greater share in bringing up their children.

Soon after his death, there was a fire at Ivanhoe, and the old homestead, tinder-dry, was burned to the ground. The station had taken its name from an incident long ago, when the young MPD, camping near the Ord and reading Walter Scott's *Ivanhoe* late at night, had fallen asleep, while the red and green buggy lamp, his reading light, burned brightly beside him. The Aborigines were terrified by this unnatural fire which neither burned itself out nor spread its flames. MPD woke and turned out the light of that little 'false fire' at Ivanhoe. This one was real, and there could be no waking.

CHAPTER 6

Broome

Even before the sale of the stations and their father's death Mary and Elizabeth had another base in the north. Towards the end of the Second World War it was becoming evident that Horrie's career was in decline. Aviation was changing; the growth of the Royal Australian Air Force meant that there were many experienced pilots, some of whom would continue flying when the war ended. Small independent airlines like MacRobertson Miller still had a useful role in the late 1940s, but Horrie could see that, like the Duracks' droving days, the heroic age of the air was coming to an end. His own role had been for some time that of administrator in the Perth office. Aged fifty-two when the war ended, and realising that financiers held the real power in the company he had founded, he began to think of other ways to live. A houseful of children in Perth with a family and social circle peopled by Durack aunts and cousins, as well as sociable Mary's countless friends, was no place for a loner like Horrie. He looked north, to Broome, and in

1945 he bought a bungalow close to Roebuck Bay and moved in. He made himself the airline's regional manager in Broome, took responsibility for overseeing the other northern ports, and went back and forth to Perth for board meetings.

Mary encouraged the Broome move, even though it meant that Horrie's time as husband and father—which had never been full time—would dwindle almost to nothing. With five young children it would have been a huge upheaval for her to go with him. A few years of primary school in Broome would be possible, but after that would come the expense of sending the children to board in Perth. Besides, as a writer, Mary needed some like-minded friends and a good public library; she would not find these in Broome.

There was a cluster of reasons for encouraging Horrie's venture, not least Mary's habit of seeing the good in almost any scheme. As well as its giving a discontented Horrie a fresh start in his airline duties, Mary saw another use for the Broome house. By the end of 1945 Elizabeth's marriage was virtually over; she still had no home and her children were suffering from the displacements of lodgings and boarding schools. Sometimes Perpetua and Michael were looked after by Mary while Elizabeth travelled. It was a huge burden on Mary, who had only intermittent and unskilled domestic help.

The house in Broome offered a temporary answer to Elizabeth's predicament: 'I carry in my head a sort of mud map of my belongings, in storerooms and railway lockers and other people's houses, across the length and breadth of the continent.'[1] And so, prompted by Mary, Horrie made his new Broome property available to Elizabeth and her children.

Although Horrie was wary of his sister-in-law, he was anxious to please his wife. He was not sure that Mary had forgiven his infidelity, and for as long as he was feeling a chill in the Perth air, a gesture to Elizabeth might help towards reinstating himself. Having the Clancys to stay was harder than he expected. He had found his own children difficult enough, but he described Perpetua as 'a devil and a half' and Michael 'a spoiled misery bag'. He camped on the beach in an army van and had his meals at the pub. His letters to Mary complaining of a cough underline his sacrifice in leaving the Clancys in possession.

If it was a gain for Elizabeth, it was qualified by the isolation of the hot and uncomfortable house; it was a long walk to the shops, and she had no car. It was lonely too; she did not fit in with the few well-off white people of Broome, nice people who, she said derisively, 'should be taken out of the north and put in a reserve. Not much we can do for them, but we can make the passing easier.'[2]

During her time in his house, Elizabeth pondered the contradictions of Horrie's personality. In a letter which shows how openly the sisters discussed one another's marital problems, she praised Mary's decision not to end her marriage. Having had a few extra-marital affairs of her own, she was in no position to be censorious about Horrie, whose good qualities she acknowledged:

> Say he is mean & he will make a liar of you with his largesse. Say he is selfish & he will show he is prepared to obliterate himself for the sake of others. Say this or that and another facet of his nature will disprove your statement. But one safe generalisation—a paradoxical one—is that the whole of his life is bound up with creation of the most advanced mechanism man has devised—the power of flight—yet he himself seems to have a horse and cart mentality.[3]

Although he admired women of character and ability—as his choice of Mary indicated—in everyday terms he wanted them to stay, as Elizabeth put it, 'at the level of House Frau'.[4]

Post-war Broome, in Elizabeth's view, was in danger of falling into decay after its brief importance as a wartime base for Australian forces. She did not think the pearling industry would recover from the exit of the Japanese; by the time they were readmitted to Australia they would have established themselves in the cultured pearl business and have no need of Broome's resources.[5] Life in Broome was basic. There was no sewerage system. Food supplies came in by ship. Green vegetables were hard to grow because of the quality of the local water, which was full of iron, salty and barely drinkable. Families depended most on potatoes and onions, and on cabbages, which would last for a week. Milk was tinned, and the amount of meat you could buy was limited by the capacity of the kerosene refrigerators. The daily flight from Perth—there was only one—left at 6 am and took about eleven and a half hours to reach Broome.

In spite of its discomforts, the time in Broome was productive for Elizabeth, and her children, who had endured too many displacements, were happy there:

> Our earliest memories are of Broome. We were there as three- and five-year-olds, just after the war so our recollections are fragmentary. Some memories are vivid: days at the convent school with children of mixed ages and races; the kindness of the Sisters; the dusty walk home past Ellies' store; masonite and paint and the smell of turpentine; the tide always being out when we wanted to go for a swim …it was a time of shortages and rationing but we were

bothered more by sandflies and hard, unpleasant bore water. Mainly our memories are happy ones: of picnics at Gantheaume Point, of the excitement of a boat or plane arriving with mail and stores; of our mother receiving packages from our father in Melbourne of precious, tightly rationed art supplies.[6]

Angry and sad at the collapse of his family life but still forbearing, Frank Clancy continued to encourage Elizabeth's career. On her side too there must still have been affection. Financially, she said, he was 'maniacal', but his understanding of her work bolstered her shaky self-esteem. A chance to remarry came when she met the wealthy businessman and philanthropist William Buckland, owner of a chain of service stations, insurance companies and pastoral properties including Victoria River Downs cattle station. Buckland, who was divorced with an adult son and daughter, told Elizabeth that he did not understand people very well, and he proved it in the terms he offered her. His immense wealth came with impossible conditions. He did not want Perpetua and Michael; he would pay their fees at boarding school. Nor did he want Elizabeth to paint professionally; he regarded her work as a hobby. Strangely, perhaps because she wanted to be saved from being tempted by Buckland's riches, Elizabeth referred the choice to Mary. Unless Mary approved she would refuse the proposal, as she appears to have done.[7] She was not, in any case, free to marry. She had no grounds for divorce, according to the laws of the time, except those of separation over a period of five years. The fact that she never initiated an action suggests ambivalence, as does the continuing link with Frank.

For the Millers, the house in Broome gave a chance of

reconciliation at a time when Mary's forgiveness of Horrie's infidelity was still in doubt. Horrie was not at his best in the busy Perth house, and perhaps he never felt truly at home in a suburban setting which had the Durack stamp on it. At Broome, he could offer holidays to his children as well as a base for Elizabeth, who could come and go to Ivanhoe with comparative ease. Horrie's 1946 letters to Mary alternate a slightly huffy recognition of her own career and her involvement in Elizabeth's Perth exhibitions with a display of his determination to prove himself as a domesticated father. 'I can see how much your work and Bet's means and wish you every success in the result of the exhibition,' he wrote in July. His next letter described his daughters Robin and Julie 'playing happily outside having a party. Cooked tea, steak and veg.'[8] Mary made a brief visit to Broome, after which Horrie wrote sadly: 'Your departure left me in a mood of lonely depression.' Sounding the note of responsible householder he added: 'Washed sheets and pillowslips.'[9]

Mary spent the winter of 1948 in the north, starting with a two-week stay with Horrie in the Broome house before travelling to the Durack stations with her father. Horrie joined her for a week with Reg at Auvergne but was absent from a family party at Ivanhoe for MPD's eighty-third birthday in July. After only one day with Horrie in Broome at the end of a three-month stay in the north, Mary returned to Perth where she focused on Elizabeth's next exhibition. While Elizabeth painted at Ivanhoe, Mary made the arrangements with the Claude Hotchins Gallery, and worried about her sister. As she wrote to Horrie:

> Arrangements for the exhibition are going smoothly and think all will be well. Poor old Bet writes in a desperation

of misery and loneliness from Ivanhoe. I can see that she is trying hard to be 'good and sensible' and put in more months on her own up there but feel definite signs and portends [sic] of explosion and would not be surprised if she had decided to come down for her show. It is not good for her for too long up there under these conditions…her pictures continue to come down in little rolls and are very beautiful.[10]

In spite of Mary's concern, Elizabeth did not come to Perth for the 1948 exhibition. She had been given a friendly reception the year before—one review was headed 'Salute to Genius'—and had excellent sales. Under Mary's management the new show was equally successful, but Elizabeth stayed away until it was over.[11] Ahead of her were more exacting occasions in the other state capitals: first in Adelaide in June 1949 and a few weeks later in Melbourne, where Frank Clancy helped her with arrangements at the Velasquez Gallery. After her disastrous encounters with Sydney critics she may have felt she needed as much time as possible to work on her paintings. Whatever her reasons she left the 1948 Perth exhibition to Mary, who supervised the hanging, sent out invitations, charmed the press, and gave a cocktail party after the opening. All this was in addition to Mary's own work and her growing family responsibilities.

Mary's fifth child Marie Rose was born in 1949, five years after the birth of Andy and the crisis in the Miller marriage. Like the others, Marie Rose was welcome but unplanned. Mary was too embarrassed to tell her mother about this pregnancy. Reg gave Horrie a 'little book' on birth control; Horrie opened and closed it again, very quickly, saying nothing.[12] The Miller marriage worked well enough; it was not perfect, but each of them could accept the other's terms. With five children, or seven when Perpetua and Michael came to stay, Mary's household was said to look like a little orphanage. She was never alone.

Loneliness was part of the price of Elizabeth's time in the north, but the rewards were great. Mary thought that Elizabeth's work in and around Perth was good and interesting but 'lacking the verve and joy of her work of the north'.[13] Broome was a place of creative renewal, as was her grass studio at Ivanhoe. Some of her finest paintings belong to this period: 'Broome Madonna' and 'Ord River Venus' among them. She found sitters among the Aboriginal women and the white residents in Broome; and she produced a series of sympathetic studies of the children in the orphanage at Beagle Bay and the patients in the leprosarium near Derby.[14]

Elizabeth travelled the hundred and thirty kilometres between Broome and Beagle Bay on a weekly delivery truck that carried fresh vegetables. She was enchanted by Beagle Bay. The green and silver of its dense scrub, the mauve flowers on sandy tracks and the lush grasses around the springs of fresh water. And white everywhere: the white east-facing church; white tower with cross and globe above it; white crosses in the little cemetery. The painter's eye caught and held it all:

> Toss from the palette all Indian reds, burnt siennas and umbers, and replace them with greens, purples, black and white. White gulls (the mission is only eight miles from the sea). White gowns of priests and brothers, black sashed. White habits of nuns...White donkeys. White limbs of swamp paper-barks. White cumulus against purple skies that threaten still more rain. Crumbling white of the first

adobe buildings. Whitest of all, the church itself...the only perfectly proportioned building in the whole of Kimberley and designed and completed over half a century ago.[15]

Elizabeth's Beagle Bay paintings and drawings of the late 1940s are gentle and, except for the threat in the purple skies, pastoral in feeling. An old nun feeds chickens; a group of nuns kneel in prayer. Even when the sky is stormy, the church seems to offer comfort. The drawings of the men in the leprosarium are gentle too; they express the patience of the sufferers waiting quietly in little groups or on hospital beds. The stillness of the figures contrasts with wild skies, fierce in colour as in movement.

Elizabeth's intermittent need for the Broome house ended in 1950, when her father gave her the money to build a house in Perth, close to Mary and to her mother. Although this had its drawbacks, including the risk of being caught up again in the Durack network, it gave her children security. Even with their mother's comings and goings to paint and exhibit, there would be no more boarding school periods for Perpetua and Michael. Having a place of their own was comforting, so was the warm and loving presence of Bess Durack. Unique in a nomadic family, Bess was always at home. Her way of life, ordered and serene, had been a reproach to Mary and Elizabeth but its certainty was just what her grandchildren needed. Her habitual 'Well, dear, I am sure it will all turn out for the best' was sometimes exasperating for her daughters, but for the new generation it went with a grandmother's cosy house and her unfailing love and welcome. They called her Gran Central.

The house in Broome was only the first stage in Horrie's new career. Strangely, at a time when his Durack brothers-in-law were undergoing extreme hardships on the land—Reg at the primeval

Kildurk, Kim on his drought-afflicted Camballin project—
Horrie decided to lease a pastoral property for himself. He chose
Dampier Downs, a sheep station near Broome, with no stock and
an abundance of wild donkeys and dingoes. It was no place for a
man of his age. It had been for sale since the Depression, and for
good reason. The homestead was primitive and the outhouses and
fences were broken down. Mary might well have been horrified
at the idea of renewing this outback wreck, but her love of the
north won through. She was enchanted by Dampier Downs'
wild beauty, which was the more startling because, in a time of
drought, its site at the foot of the Edgar Ranges gave it a permanent
water supply. She wrote to Elizabeth, describing the spectacular
caves and waterfalls, and kangaroos beyond number: 'beautiful
creatures, the orange red of the rocks, some of them five to six
feet tall—everywhere leaping, in silhouette or standing, stock-still
against the cobalt sky.'[16]

Camping out with Mary in the dilapidated homestead, Horrie
frightened the dingoes away by firing rifle shots at intervals through
a hole in the wire netting over the windows. His shooting skills
came in handy when their food supplies ran low; Mary 'felt like
an Aboriginal woman in the wake of my man who carries, in
grim pursuit of tucker, a loaded rifle'.[17] In June 1951 when she
spent her first days at Dampier Downs, Mary was thirty-eight and
Horrie fifty-eight. It was an absurd, unnecessary way to complicate
the life of a mother of five and a writer with dozens of ideas for
stories and plays. A letter to her cousin Kath McArthur gave a
comic-ironic perspective on the scene:

> Imagine us though Kath at this stage of our lives raising
> fences, reconstructing broken buildings, painting, planning

and running boundaries! With the shared interest, Horrie
and I can now put up with one another for much longer
at a stretch.[18]

How much longer? Mary could not leave her children in Perth
indefinitely, parcelled out in ones and twos, or as unhappy little
boarders with the Loreto nuns, who could be cajoled into taking
them in an emergency but did not really want such young children.
Horrie's plan was to install a manager at Dampier Downs, sell
the Perth house, make the Broome bungalow a permanent home
and send the children to local schools and later to board in Perth.
They tried Broome for six months in 1952.

Did Horrie know what it would mean to share a small house
with five children aged between thirteen and three? Did Mary
know how much she would miss her friends in Perth and the library
she would need to consult if she were to produce a major work in
family history? All her material, in diaries and letters and other
records of the pioneering Duracks, had to be left behind. Departing
by air for Broome, Mary had to limit the children's possessions.
And on the day-long flight, with her large Remington typewriter
under her seat and three-year-old Marie Rose on her knee, she
could see how hard it would be to balance her commitments.
Horrie, who liked to have her to himself, would not be as genial
as he had been at Dampier Downs. Mary's doubts appear in a
letter to her cousin:

> It is with mixed feelings that I go Kath and I think it is with
> mixed feelings that Horrie receives us. The truth is we are
> too many for him and he can never really understand why
> he has to have us all. When I am up there with him he wants

me to be off with him to Dampier Downs and the kids make it impossible without imposing on people. However…I do love the funny little port with its cockeyed houses and cockeyed people and I hate a southern winter—haven't had to endure one for years in fact and should probably die if I stayed.[19]

The Miller children, like the Clancys before them, were happy in Broome. They had seldom lived together as a family. Horrie, in a relatively optimistic mood, was planning a permanent home. So that he would not be overwhelmed by family life, he extended the house with separate quarters of his own. He valued quietness. He was passionate about clean surfaces and spent freely on Flytox, but comfort was not a priority. During her tenancy of the Broome house, Elizabeth had found Horrie a thrifty fusspot. Mary agreed: 'The frugality, the seclusiveness and the possessiveness verge always on neurosis.'[20]

Broome was still remaking itself, clearing away the debris of war-damaged buildings and rusty fragments of aircraft. The wartime establishments of a civil aviation centre and meteorological station would remain, and the coming of civil servants on three-year contracts would change the social structures of the old pearling town. Meanwhile, it was a paradise for the Miller children. They ranged unsupervised around the town; they splashed through rock pools and collected shells and fragments of coral; they learned the names of the bright tropical fish. Released from school for a long lunch break, they swam in the newly rebuilt town baths. For once, the Perth-bred children saw their father in heroic mode, fishing at Cable Beach or, more dangerously, from the rocks at Ganthaume Point. While they played in Anastasia's Pool, a tide-filled hollow in the rocks, Horrie stood 'fearless against the surging sea, caught amid tremendous green and white curtains of spray', hooking barramundi, mackerel, kingeye and once an iridescently gorgeous but inedible parrot fish.[21]

For the Miller girls, the Broome state school was nothing like the Loreto convent in Perth. They had no exams, no homework and a remarkably flexible timetable. No bother about uniforms, no drilling in manners, none of the ceremonious ways of the nuns. Although she had rejected its faith and practice Mary had chosen a Catholic education for her daughters, as had Elizabeth for the two Clancys. Mary would probably have chosen the Broome convent, but anti-clerical Horrie pre-empted her by enrolling all the Millers in the state school. There they shared desks with the sons and daughter of pearlers and town employees as well as Chinese, Malay and Singhalese children, one Japanese and one Aboriginal girl. Aboriginal families were expected to send their children to the nuns of St John of God at St Mary's School.[22] Mary praised Broome for its multi-racial community, but there were barriers, which included segregated seating at the Sun Picture Theatre in Chinatown.[23]

Horrie was mistaken in thinking that by taking Mary from Perth he could have her to himself. She gathered friends effortlessly wherever she was. Horrie complained about her 'retinue of people who are doing or about to do something in a big way for the natives, or the kindergarten, or the school, or are writing a book or a play, a round of visitors who sit and mumble on for hours'.[24]

Broome brought Mary new friends among the German Pallottine missionaries, one of whom, Father Ernest Worms, she had met years before when he visited Ivanhoe. His name and accent were memorable. It was said that he asked one of MPD's pastoralist friends if there were many 'Cat-olics' in the Kimberley. Because Worms was not wearing clerical dress, he was mistaken for one of the dreaded cattle tick inspectors and told emphatically that they had been eradicated years before.

Worms was a trained and dedicated anthropologist who saw no conflict between his religious vocation and his scientific enquiry. Mary expected him to be troubled by the Aboriginal tribal rites he saw on his bush excursions. Worms thought this was absurd: 'Why do you ask? Is it not all in the heart of God?'[25] He believed the Aboriginal dreaming to be a flame of spiritual vitality which missionaries must not extinguish. Mary wrote:

> [Father Worms] sought similes (with what success he could not say) within the environment—the boab tree, stark and grotesque, burgeoning into foliage and blossom before the coming of the life-saving rain; flood waters, like the blessings of divine grace, filling the parched river beds. He also tried to introduce the Christian teaching of union with God through grace and redemption through the natives' own desire to be united with their tribal spirits in the realm of the dead.[26]

'Father Worms' sort of religion suits me alright,' Mary wrote. It was matters of doctrine and church discipline, as taught by the Irish-Australian priests she knew, that left her cold and unbelieving.[27]

Her time in Broome and her friendship with Ernest Worms inspired Mary's attempts to translate Aboriginal song cycles using an approximation of Aboriginal poetic form. Her 'Lament to Galalan—the Law Giver' was published in a university journal in 1952. This work might later have been disapproved of as cultural

ABOVE: Elizabeth and Mary Durack, 1918. BELOW: Reginald Wyndham, Mary, Elizabeth, Kimberley Michael, William and David Durack, with Bess Durack and Nurse Stevens at rear, at 263 Adelaide Terrace, Perth, 1924.

ABOVE: Mary (standing), David, Elizabeth, MPD, Reg, Bill (with Yacht), Kim, 1924.
BELOW: Ivanhoe Station homestead, c. 1936.
OPPOSITE: Mary, MPD, Elizabeth, Ivanhoe Station, 1930s.

Mary, Bill Jones,
Elizabeth and Reg
at Ivanhoe Station,
mid-1930s.

ABOVE: Mary with daughter, Patsy, and women and children of Argyle Station, 1941. OPPOSITE: Mary at Argyle Station, 1937.

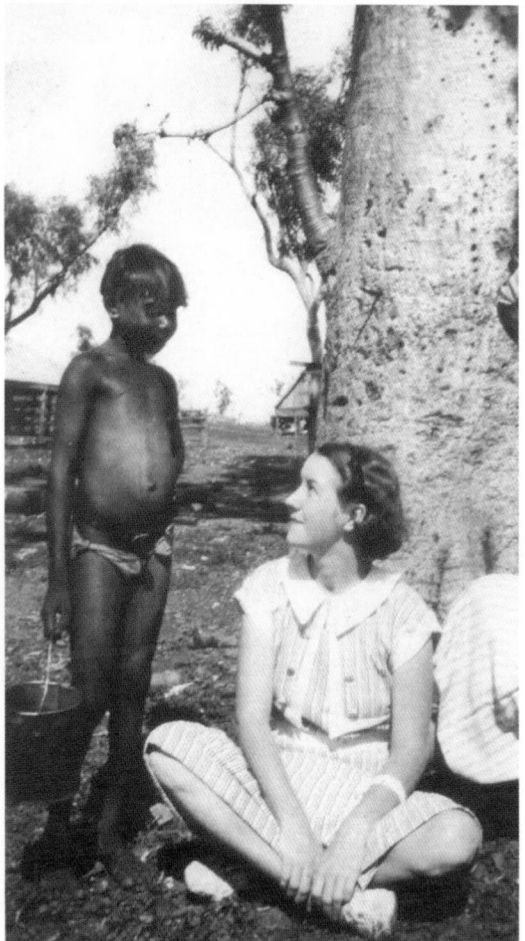

ABOVE: Elizabeth and Mary at Bellevue Ave, Nedlands, 1942.

LEFT: Jeffrey Chunuma Rainyerri and Elizabeth at Ivanhoe Station, 1934.

Mary Durack, 1962.

Elizabeth Durack with 'Broome Madonna', from the series *Time and Tide*, at the Athenaeum Gallery, Melbourne, 1946.

RIGHT: Mary with *The Rock and the Sand*, 1970.

BELOW: Elizabeth at work on *Over in the Limestone* (Eddie Burrup) in courtyard studio, 1997. PHOTO: Robert Garvey.

OPPOSITE: Original cover of *The Way of the Whirlwind*, 1941.

THE WAY
OF THE
WHIRLWIND

MARY & ELIZABETH DURACK

'In the Beginning…
(Genesis 1)', 1997,
from the series *The
Art of Eddie Burrup.*

'Kimberley landscape', 1985,
from the series *Bett Bett's
Wonderful Lonely Palace.*

'The Kid', 1947.

appropriation; at that time it did not seem to trouble anyone, although there were some doubts on scholarly grounds. As well as these poems, Mary produced two children's books, with her own finely detailed illustrations, based on her observations of the sea creatures of Broome.[28]

The Broome experiment lasted barely six months. Mary started a novel with a Broome setting, which she was never to complete. The big project based on the Durack family papers could not be written so far from its sources. The letters and diaries, account books, legal documents, photographs and other records of nearly a century of pioneering endeavours were still packed away in the Perth house, waiting for her. As well as delving into the resources of the State Library, Mary would need to talk to family members in Perth and to start corresponding with others of the Queensland branch and with her father's brother, Dermot Durack, in Dublin. None of this was feasible in the holiday bungalow atmosphere of Broome, nor could it be reconciled with the claims of Horrie's pioneering folly at Dampier Downs. Above all, Mary would need time to think.

Mary's idea of the family story, and her hard-edged view of the Durack achievement, appeared early in 1951 when she wrote to her brother Bill:

> ...we all feel a bit the same re sale of properties—as though the core or actual meaning for doing a lot of things had ceased to exist when they were suddenly snatched away. Bet had felt very much tied up with the places as far as her work was concerned and I, too, also felt strongly that if this generation could do something a bit more enlightened regarding the Aboriginal labour the whole thing would

have been vindicated if you know what I mean.

As it is, there is not much rhyme or reason for any of it—the tremendous pioneering effort, the long years of waiting and hoping, the blind exploitation of land and labour nor even the terrific effort of getting out of debt and on a paying footing again. It was all tied up with what we all hoped to do there some time, or with what we hoped to prove to the powers that could or should be done. However this is an old story now I suppose. I have it all locked up in a couple of tin trunks stored in the garage and hope to reduce it to some form or meaning one of these days.[29]

As this judgment makes clear, Mary saw the family saga in the light of her own generation's frustration. Along with the sale of the stations went their hopes of repairing damage done in 'blind exploitation' of the Aborigines. Her book could not be a triumphalist work, yet it needed to show the pioneers' courage and the hopes that sustained them. Mary came to see that she would need three volumes to do justice to the ups and downs of three generations. Telling the story would be a huge task, and the last volume would have to spell out the failure of vision, and the damage done.

As well as the formidable project of the family saga, Mary had been reconsidering her first novel, which went out to Angus & Robertson under the title *Wandering River* and was refused once more. She offered it as a serial to the *Sydney Morning Herald*; again, there was no interest in a grim story of a remote part of Australia. Not much had changed in the reading public since 1938 when, after a long struggle and many revisions, as well as active promotion by the maverick publisher P. I. (Inky) Stephensen,

Xavier Herbert's *Capricornia* appeared. *Capricornia* had to some degree been softened in revision by Herbert's insistence on the 'loveliness of the land' and his robust comic sense.[30] Mary Durack's novel had these saving qualities; even so, her book was tough, and to promote it as the work of a woman—let alone a cattle king's daughter—would have tested an Australian publisher's nerve.

Mary was still in Broome when her luck changed. Her friend from Ivanhoe years, the anthropologist Phyllis Kaberry, put her in touch with Florence James, a New Zealander who read manuscripts for Constable of London. James was excited about the prospect of the family saga, and she was also willing to recommend Mary's novel to this distinguished London firm.

Wandering River was under consideration by Constable while Mary and Horrie were making their decision to keep separate bases: his in Broome and hers in Perth. It was not a separation: they wrote often, with affection on both sides; each spent time with the other and neither was excluded from the other's future. Mary was indulgent about Horrie's 'new toys', which included a tractor and a bulldozer. She and the children visited Broome and loved it as something more than a holiday place. Horrie wrote plaintively to Mary about his solitary state, but he did not yearn for the Perth household with its human abundance. When Mary sent the children north, usually only two at a time, Horrie made sure she knew what hard work it was to cook and wash for them. He did not cut his ties with Perth, but the idea of a family united in one place collapsed in Broome for its sheer impracticality. Mary's writing and the children's schooling could not be reconciled with the life that suited Horrie.

CHAPTER 7

Kings in Grass Castles

Back in Perth at the end of 1952, after her Broome interlude, Mary was almost ready to begin the family saga. She had the material, or at least the means to find it; she had a publisher; she had a subject that would fully engage her powers. Yet, as a mother of five, with little or no help, an absent husband and a budget that was no more than adequate, she needed heroic energy to accomplish any sustained work. But in some ways her responsibilities were lessening. The three older girls were clever, capable and independent. Patsy and Robin, aged thirteen and twelve, had a sense of order that was beyond their mother. As they grew older they began to protect her, as far as anyone could, from an openness to the world that gave her little time for her writing. Mary's house was usually in a state of cheerful clutter, with people dropping in at will. Night was the only quiet time. Her children went to sleep to the sound of the typewriter:

Days are swamped by the details of life—the sewing, washing, cooking, thinking for them all…There are few hours not interrupted by the telephone, the doorbell and the consciousness of ironing not done, unanswered letters, unpaid bills.[1]

Mary's first major work, *Keep Him My Country*, appeared in August 1955. Under contract for three years, it was delayed by Mary's optimistic habit of mind—just one more revision would put it right—and by her ever-increasing number of tasks undertaken for others. If someone asked her to give a talk, write a book review or read a manuscript, she found refusal impossible. She sighed over some of the manuscripts ('what E [Eleanor Smith] can do to a sentence is nobody's business'[2]), but when asked to arrange a charity function or to entertain a visiting writer, she did it with zest and flair. Her parties were well known; invitations were prized and few would grudge a donation to a mission or an orphanage that went with a cheerful evening in the Durack-Miller garden. All of these came at a cost to her writing.

In October 1953, Michael Sadleir, director of Constable, had told her that *Keep Him My Country* was 'one of the best first novels ever to pass through our hands'.[3] For most writers that would have been the signal to carry out the revisions suggested by the editor and send the book on its way. Not Mary Durack, the compulsive improver. She revised it from start to finish, adding, subtracting, rethinking. Eventually she had to let go. Constable indulged a promising author; they even allowed her to have a book jacket designed by Elizabeth, although the one they used was less striking ('tamer,' Elizabeth said) than Mary's first choice.[4] Mary was not allowed to publish under a pseudonym, as she would have liked. It is 'not a ladylike book', she told Florence James. In writing it, she had chosen a voice that was not her own; she thought it should go out to the world as the work of 'George Hurley', a middle-aged stockman.

From her publisher's viewpoint, a pseudonym would be self-defeating. Better to establish Mary Durack as a Constable author. Her work in progress, the family saga, would benefit from her being 'a name'; outside Perth at that time Mary was scarcely known. Her publications so far had been *All-About* and the children's books, with Elizabeth, a few short stories in the *Bulletin* and many articles scattered in journals with small circulation, like *Walkabout,* or in her ever-ready outlet the *West Australian.* Her work was too varied in genre to build a reading public, and being based in Perth, far from Australia's east-coast literary centres, was a disadvantage. Elizabeth, with her rapid progress from state to state with exhibitions, her single-mindedness and her prodigious energy, had done more at that stage to take the Durack name into the art world. *Keep Him My Country* was Mary's national and international debut, at the age of forty-two.

Reviews and sales were good. The first print run of 6000 copies sold quickly and there was a reprint within weeks. A serial version appeared in the *Sydney Morning Herald* and the *Country-man.* Inevitably, reviewers compared it with Katharine Susannah Prichard's *Coonardoo* (1929) for the treatment of black-white sexual relations. Although the two novels were separated in time by nearly thirty years, there had been little else of their calibre, apart from Xavier Herbert's long-delayed and much revised *Capricornia,* to take up the controversial theme in a little-known region of Australia. Prichard generously ceded the advantage to Mary, for the 'inestimable value of authenticity' that her book possessed.[5]

Prichard was right. *Keep Him My Country* shows how much Mary had absorbed of station life. Ever since her Argyle days Mary had listened and watched as the men went about their work. She caught their idiom, knew their habits of mind. Her novel assembles a cast of white and Aboriginal characters, each one deftly individualised. They all carried their history, often tragic, but with humour and companionship in the daily doings. Some brutal scenes show that Mary was not sheltered by her position as Big Boss's daughter. Her descriptive gift works as well for the scenes of cattle branding as for its evocation of the beauty of the landscape. The scene in which cows judged unfit for breeding are spayed so as to be fattened for meat is clinically precise. The language of the men seems as authentic as the publishers' self-censoring would allow; it is way beyond anything that a convent girl would normally be allowed to hear.

At the centre of the novel, the story of Stan Rolt came close to home. The young manager of Trafalgar Station is perilously like Reg Durack in situation and temperament. The grandson of a legendary pioneer, he is burdened by family tradition; he has been working for years without authority, directed from Perth by the old men whose attitudes are past change. When the novel opens, Stan has lost hope in having any of his ideas carried out. There had been promises that kept him at Trafalgar through the war years:

> There would be big changes when the war ended, they had said. They would concentrate on real development, the improvement of living conditions, the improvement of working conditions and a more modern approach to the welfare of aboriginal employees. And he had hung on believing them until ideas written at fever heat had

faded like the ink, phrases grown brittle and musty like
the paper. That was what this country did to everything
with its sun and dust, its rain and mould. That was why he
must go…He sat down at his desk, took out his letter book
and began briskly: 'My dear Grandfather, It is not without
regret that I today relinquish, finally and irrevocably, the
management of Trafalgar…'[6]

For Reg Durack and all the family members who remembered
his letter of resignation to his father, the echo was unmistakable.
For Grandfather Rolt, the 'Old Immortal', read Patsy Durack
and MPD in part at least. There are differences: Rolt is a Scot,
and there are complications in his family relationships that do not
match the Durack story. But the outlines are there: the overland
trek with cattle, the gold rushes of the 1880s, the tensions between
generations. And as Stan Rolt reads his grandfather's diary, he finds
the same strengths and weaknesses that Mary Durack discerned
in her grandfather and father. Through Stan's perception, she
diagnosed the 'mixture of caution and courage and an imagination
restricted to enterprise'. There was no hint in the diary that 'the
Old Immortal' could see the country's beauty.

Mary's novel was an imaginative preparation for the documentary
work ahead of her. The plot of *Keep Him My Country* is complex,
with many digressions that give a sense of a way of life and the
attitudes that grew from it. The direction, however, is sure. Stan
Rolt learns painfully to understand his relation to the land and
the Aborigines. It is a single lesson, because land and people are
indivisible. His love for an Aboriginal girl, Dalgerie, brings about
his reconciliation to the burdensome life from which he had tried
to escape. The relationship itself is doomed. When Dalgerie is

claimed by her designated husband, Stan offers a way out. 'We'll ask the policeman to marry us,' he says confidently. As his wife, she would be safe; no Aborigine would dare to claim her from a white man. But his proposal comes too late. Dalgerie disappears, and Stan endures some bitter, angry years before he finds her again. By then she is no longer the exquisite young girl of his memory. He sees her disfigured by hardship and disease, a shrunken old woman. Dying, she tells him that she has 'sung' him to the land. 'I cry to my country—Keep him that he may come to my side…' The novel ends on a note of sadness as well as certainty.

> The bonds that he had feared and fought had tightened beyond escape, but the hold of the land was no longer irrational…It was here that he belonged by reason and right for the country knew him and had given him its heart.[7]

The novel expresses Mary Durack's belief that reconciliation is impossible as long as the white people see the Aborigines and the land as possessions to be used for gain. By loving Stan, Dalgerie—more spirit than flesh-and-blood woman—teaches him how to find the right relationship with place. Although central to the meaning of the novel, the love story is only a small part of the narrative. Mary's gift of observation brings the station routine to life. Trafalgar is home to eccentrics, drifters and drinkers. And if at times the novel carries too great a burden of message, the Aboriginal workers and their women and children are drawn as individuals, not as social problems.

Within the Durack family, there were mixed feelings about Mary's novel. Reg must have wished she had not chosen to write a story so close to his own situation. Some readers would wonder

if the Dalgerie story had any basis in fact. Yet in human terms
Dalgerie is the least convincing element in the novel: she is a poetic
theme in a semi-documentary novel.

Reg took several months to respond to Mary's gift of a copy. He
said that it had come as a shock, rousing memories that belonged
to another life. He wished her well and was pleased that the book
had been so well reviewed. Kim was stirred by the novel and wrote
more openly: 'It made me wretchedly sad and depressed. Your
book shocked me back into seeing. To no purpose, I'm afraid, for
me. Having seen, I have no eyes to see again.'[8]

The brothers' reactions to the novel reflect their situations at
the time. Reg had found happiness in marriage and fatherhood,
and by 1955 he had overcome the worst rigours of pioneering
life at Kildurk. He could read with a certain detachment about
some aspects of his younger self in *Keep Him My Country*. Kim's
situation was still precarious. From season to season he lived in
suspense at Camballin—on Uralla Creek, a tributary of the Fitzroy
River—trying out different strains of rice. His quarters, 'living
under a boab tree', sound provisional, even primitive, but they
had a sense of order and were visually splendid. Kim chose a site
with a wide view of the Fitzroy's alluvial plains and had a caravan
built to his own specifications to which he attached a canvas 'fly'
tent. This gave added shade to that of the boab tree, and the whole
establishment made an enchanting holiday place for nieces and
nephews. Although, after six years of outdoor living, Kim was
confident enough to build himself a house, he was still dependent
on committee decisions and political windchanges. Living alone,
he was more vulnerable than Reg to the sombre mood of Mary's
novel in which love for the land, even when allied to human love,
offers no more than a qualified hope. Kim was giving everything

to the land. He had battled flood and drought to save his crop, but his success could be negated by a political decision. What was it all for?

For Mary and Bet, the brothers were never out of mind; for Kim, as younger brother and as a visionary, they felt a blend of protectiveness and reverence. Once, in a mood of deep depression, Kim sent a telegram to Mary in Broome: 'Come soonest.' She responded at once, taking eight-year-old Andy with her, and, after staying for a few days to make sure of Kim's regained equilibrium, left Andy as a shield against loneliness. She knew that Kim's state of mind swung between an intensity of belief that kept him working to exhaustion and an equally intense desolation of spirit. The conditions in which he worked were almost intolerable. Reg's life at Kildurk was tough, but with his wife Enid and his growing family he had hope and companionship. Kim had no sustaining presences. Itinerant workers helped him with fencing, building levees and pumps, levelling the land and sowing crops, but for a good deal of the time he was alone. Mary's account of Kim's state of mind at this time shows his desperate courage on the edge of despair:

> The brief space between sundown and dark was always the worst for him when he was alone. Sometimes, in order to endure it at all he would sit quite still, like a lizard on a stone. 'One must become part of the landscape,' he would tell himself. 'Not thinking or feeling anything. Nothing at all.' It would not matter once it was dark. He could knock up a feed then and go to bed.[9]

In so far as it dramatises the Durack family in fictional form, *Keep Him My Country* explores the viewpoint of the pragmatic Reg

rather than Kim the idealist. It confirmed Mary's sense of herself
as a writer of fiction. She had not yet faced the intellectual and
structural problems of the pioneering story. Her correspondence
with Constable shows how much she wanted to finish her Broome
novel, even at the expense of the family saga. As early as 1953
Florence James was urging her to give the family story the space
it needed, and to think of it as a three-volume work.[10] James
wanted Mary to follow the creative impulse. 'For goodness sake
if you don't feel like going back to the magnum opus and want to
finish the novel don't feel guilty about it. We are very anxious to
have the first volume of the Durack story of course, but one can't
always do these things to order.'[11]

Florence James was awed by Mary's ability to produce anything
at all, given her domestic responsibilities. The birth of a sixth
child, John Christopher, in May 1955, just before the publication
of *Keep Him My Country,* was more difficult than the earlier
ones; it left Mary tired and weak. Elizabeth did some fetching
and carrying for her sister. Within a week, she was reassured to
see that 'the expression of patiently suppressed impatience had
already left [Mary's] face & the ancient compensatory joyousness
taking charge'.[12] A few months after the birth, Mary went north
to spend time in the warmth of Broome. And there, for once, she
wrote plaintively about being a mother. As always, she qualified the
negatives, but the consolations have a touch of dutiful observation
about them:

> Yes, they grow up so quickly and soon stand on their own
> feet, but I seem rather to have overdone this aspect of life,
> though not deliberately I must say. Am feeling tired to
> the bone of the eternal baby on the hip, the weight on the

arm, the broken nights and the unavailing struggle for a moment to work and think. But I should be thankful that the little one is strong and beautiful and that the older kids adore him and are a great help when they have time from school.[13]

Mary's partly written murder mystery, *The Calm Eye*, with its Broome setting, may have been an evasion of the main task she had set herself after her father's death. As Reg and Kim struggled in their different ways with the pioneering heritage, she too was asking 'what was it all for?' She had the documents: letters, diaries, account books, cheque butts that would have taken a professional historian years to puzzle over. She had the inside knowledge, drawn from her own time on the stations, and from all the stories she had been hearing since childhood. Above all, she had the need to know what it amounted to. So much courage, endurance, planning; so much pain and loss. It hadn't brought the fortune her grandfather hoped for. Now that nearly all the land was in other hands, why didn't her generation of Duracks just walk away, forget it, and be thankful that enough had been salvaged from the sale price to make Bess Durack secure? Yet it was clear to Mary that she and Elizabeth, Reg and Kim, were still in thrall to the north of Grandfather Patsy's dream. In telling his story she might understand what it had all been about. Whether she knew it or not, this was the story she was born to tell.

Part of the power and intimacy of the story came from Mary's gift for listening and for finding the writer's voice in letters and diaries. One line from her grandfather Patsy gave her the book's title. '"Cattle Kings" ye call us, then we are Kings in grass castles that may be blown away upon a puff of wind.' So much more

immediate than *They Reached a Land,* her earlier and rather
plodding title for a family saga. *Kings in Grass Castles* delighted the
publishers and revived their hopes of the long-overdue manuscript
being completed.

Revised more than once, the book finally reached Constable in
July 1958. Opening the parcel, Florence James felt like 'a playful seal
long separated from water, opening it here and there, recognising
incidents, reading the new version for a few pages, remembering
another favourite bit, looking for it, remembering, thoroughly
enjoying myself.'[14]

Florence James thought it a good time to publish *Kings.*
Australia was in the news in London. The outback images created
by Patrick White and Sidney Nolan were making a stir, while Ray
Lawler's off-season shearers in *Summer of the Seventeenth Doll* came
on stage in an unexpectedly popular London production. It was
an added advantage for overseas readers that Mary had decided to
begin the story in Ireland. In that way she took her readers with
her, travelling from the known world to the unknown Australia.

By placing the young Patsy back in 1840s Ireland, the decade
of the Great Famine, she showed the fragile link between life and
land. Even without the disastrous failure of the potato crop in
1845, when a million Irish peasants starved to death, it was evident
that Ireland could not sustain her native population. There were
green and fertile fields, but they belonged to the great English
landowners.

The Irish peasants had no rights. When their landlord—or very
often the agent for an absentee landowner—decided to knock down
stone walls to enlarge the grazing areas, he could also demolish
the tenants' cottages, sending whole families, homeless, on the
road to nowhere. Under centuries of rule by the English invaders,

education beyond the most basic level was barred to the native Irish. Their language was being lost, their religion suppressed. Many could not read or write. The only way out was emigration and without cash, or sponsorship from employers in a New World country, they could stay home and starve. John and Amy Durack, grandparents of Patsy, lost four of their ten children in the famine, and four more to emigration. One of these, Darby Durack, sailed for New South Wales with his wife. He had saved £5.10; the balance of £35 would be repaid from his wages as an indentured labourer.

Patsy's father, Michael Durack, lacking the deposit, could not follow his brother. His family survived precariously while the murderous evictions and land clearances went on. Then came the miracle of young Patsy's reward of a gold coin for having done a good turn to Lord Dunraven. Patsy amassed the £8 deposit on the passage money within the year, and the second Durack family unit arrived in Australia in 1853.

Mary Durack used the family documents with empathy and imagination. Writing in the 1950s, when all her father's striving seemed to have accomplished so little, she was not likely to produce a triumphalist work. She was beginning with a strong sense of loss, and working back to see what combination of personalities, desires and opportunities had brought about such an ambivalent result. There had been heroism in the face of hardship, but at a price. Conflict, doubt, despair and death spoke to her from the old letters and diaries. But there was also evidence of high hopes and a remarkable ability to plan. Swap desert plains for snowy steppes and Grandfather Patsy could have been a French general equipping Napoleon's army for the Russian campaign, but with more success.

An early chapter in which Mary assembled her characters shows the novelistic skills that separate *Kings in Grass Castles* from most pioneering chronicles. The clarity of her writing was tested by the need to sort out members of several intermarrying families who shared the same baptismal names. Too many Michaels and Patricks: how would the reader remember which was which? The family habit of descriptive identification helped, but she needed to place Stumpy Michael, Michael Patrick (MPD), Long Michael, Patsy, Black Pat, Big Johnnie and J. B. by giving a sense of character to each one. Each brought different qualities to the new land. You could say that Stumpy Michael was the strategist and Patsy the visionary, but each had some of the other's qualities. They had to be shown in interaction and argument. Patsy is the centre, the hero of the story:

> From the time of his marriage Grandfather's personality clearly emerged as the expansive, impatient, gregarious fellow, who was to take himself and a lot of other people a long way fast…Although he must often have appeared an autocrat time was to prove him sincere in saying that he wanted nothing more than to see his descendants standing firmly on their own feet.[15]

Through Patsy's younger brother, Stumpy Michael, Mary dramatised the difference—not strong enough to be called a conflict—between the uncompromising Patsy and those who wanted to call a halt and attend to family needs. Stumpy Michael was a natural leader, strong in bushcraft, with a reputation for always 'getting through'. Yet in response to his wife's loneliness, he turned for home in Queensland. Grandfather Patsy and MPD are also placed for contrast. Late in their lives Patsy took his wife Mary to Argyle homestead. MPD placed Bess and his children in

Perth, leaving him free to range from station to station, keeping control of the company and its scattered employees.

Mary had letters and diaries to give her the sense of individual voices. Using the insight these provided, she allowed herself to invent dialogue. Her accounts of the epic journey with cattle to the Kimberley had a basis in firsthand accounts written by the men. To make the women's part real and important she chose to create the words they might have spoken. If she had taken herself more seriously as a historian Mary might have hesitated to claim this freedom, but as an independent writer with a novelist's flair she conjured up the imagined voices of her forebears and their companions. Her great-grandmother Bridget and her grandmother Mary, after whom she was named, emerge as strong women who do their best to bring realism into the dreams of ever-increasing expansion. A wife's protest: 'But Patsy…' is a recurring note.[16] Through Kate Durack, wife of Stumpy Michael, Mary put the woman's case for moderation, knowing when to stop, claiming a separate life instead of being submerged in the overlanders' quest.

The high price paid by the women is a constant theme, as is their essential civilising role. When Patsy and Mary Durack return after some months' absence to the home they made at Cooper's Creek in their Queensland days, they find it derelict, the house wrecked, the garden a wilderness. The 'reliable married couple' whom they had left in charge had deserted their post, and storm damage had done the rest. 'Grandfather sank into a broken deck chair and hid his face in his hands. "Oh. Mary, Mary, heaven help the country when the women go."'[17]

It was inevitable that Mary Durack would read the family history through the prism of her own experience. She judged her father, by comparison with Grandfather Patsy and his brother, as lacking in love of the land. A letter from Stumpy Michael to his wife shows his sense of wonder at the beauty and variety of the Kimberley landscape. It matches eloquent passages written in Mary's voice, but none in MPD's. And while Patsy abdicated, giving power to his sons, MPD did not give Reg and Kim their chance in his lifetime.

Mary recognised the burden placed on the young MPD when he was summoned home from school. His diary entries show a bookish young man whose interrupted education in the classics left its mark on his prose style. The Aborigines are 'our sable brethren'; the women are 'the fair sex'; and in an evening of drinking 'Bacchus reigns supreme'. More of a loner than his father, MPD, however, was sociable enough to give total attention to the strangers he met on the track: stockmen and shearers, drifters and derelicts. Mary sympathised with his restlessness. His dreams of wealth beneath the Kimberley soil went beyond materialism; they were a way of escape from the bleak realities of daily life. His diary entries are an odd mixture of the romantic and the practical.

Mary dedicated *Kings in Grass Castles* to Patsy Durack's memory and 'to the success of my brother Kimberley Michael Durack in his work for the development of the Kimberley district of Western Australia'. In choosing Patsy and Kim, invoking the remote past and the future, she omitted her father, even though he almost displaces Patsy as the central character in the later chapters. One reason might be that she was planning a trilogy and that more of her father's story would be told in the second volume. And yet the second volume did not single out MPD; it was dedicated to 'the memory of my Grandfather Patsy's "sons in the saddle" and all who rode with them'. Writing to her cousin Kath McArthur, soon after MPD's death, Mary judged her father severely. Like the others in the company he controlled, he took no responsibility for the future of the land. Mary felt that the land was being used as a commercial speculation, without the love which would make it flourish.[18]

Grandfather Patsy's ambition is seen more kindly, and is placed in the context of his Irish childhood. Mary's reading of his life makes an implicit parallel between the native Irish, exploited in four hundred years of English occupation, and the Kimberley's dispossessed Aborigines. Just as American frontier stories romanticised the east-west pioneering journeys by emphasising their hardships, so *Kings in Grass Castles* enlists the reader's sympathy in its closely documented account of ingenuity, endurance and stoic acceptance of pain and loss along the way. Yet Patsy Durack and his partners were not driven by need; they had done well in Queensland and could have stayed, as others did, to consolidate their first gains. As Geoffrey Bolton comments:

> It is romantic but insufficient simply to say that Patrick Durack and his family were consumed by a hunger for land bred of generations of dispossession in Ireland. Others, not all of them Irish, were also eager to acquire large holdings in the [Kimberley] district.[19]

Bolton believes that Mary Durack made a 'conscientious attempt' to grapple with the overlanding Duracks' encounters with the Aborigines. She recorded minor conflicts, soon resolved, perhaps by the mediation of Pumpkin, the Queensland Aborigine who came with them. In the absence of evidence of more serious clashes, Patsy Durack makes a fitting hero for a romance which has captivated generations of readers, and played a great part in giving Australia its overlanding legend.

Kings in Grass Castles is not as tough-minded on the racial question as Mary's novel *Keep Him My Country*. Moreover, the implicit parallel between the native Irish and the Aborigines soon breaks down. The Durack forebears and others in Ireland were dispossessed by English invaders: they were not allowed to practise their religion; their language was taken from them; they did the menial work for absentee English landlords. This might well have contributed to Patsy Durack's sympathy for the Aborigines. He is unlikely to have seen that he and others were in effect turning into landlords on the English model, benign as some Anglo-Irish were, but also caught in the master-servant relationship. In the 1930s his grandchildren, the third generation of Duracks on the land in Australia, were ahead of their time in empathy, and in understanding of the inequalities of the system.

Mary placed her faith in the third generation. Kim's blend of idealism and scientific planning offered hope. Mary believed in the rightness of Kim's cause. His problem stemmed from impatient developers who demanded bigger and quicker results than he thought practicable. His crops did not fail, but because he refused to risk everything in a grandiose expansion, the investors withdrew support. Did Kim resign or was he sacked? The result was the same. Devastated, he left Camballin in 1958 with nothing to show for his years of toil. Having invested most of his salary in the scheme, he had to look for a job—any job—in Canberra where he could continue to lobby the federal government for a new deal in the Kimberley. A pioneer in his thinking about the Ord River's potentialities for irrigation, he was right to point out the risks of creating a dam without doing the necessary research on the river system. He was proved right too in his advice on Camballin, which became an expensive failure. In dedicating *Kings in Grass Castles* to Kim, Mary was asserting faith in her brother at a low point in his career.

Kings in Grass Castles was published in 1959 and was an immediate and brilliant success. Instead of attracting only the local and limited interest of most family histories, its first edition sold out within a few weeks. By 1985 it had been reprinted eight times and has never been out of print since. Reviewers recognised it as something remarkable: a scholarly work that could be read like a novel. Mary's long delay in completing the work did her no harm; postwar nationalist feeling was bringing a new confidence in Australian writing. While the modernist style of Patrick White's pioneering saga *The Tree of Man* (1955) was sceptically received in some quarters, it was a turning point. It showed Australia's rural landscape in a new way: 'dun-coloured realism' was out.[20] Reviewing it soon after the influential poet and critic A. D. Hope had made his much-quoted attack on White's prose ('pretentious and illiterate verbal sludge'), Mary Durack was responsive and open-minded. With a sharp sideways glance at Hope she remarked that 'the critic who dismisses [White's] often broken and unfinished sentences' would also have to dismiss much of Joyce and Faulkner. She wondered at times if the author could not have expressed himself more briefly but summed up with a confident 'Yes' to White's style and spirit:

I have little doubt that this is a book destined to become an important part of our literary tradition. It probes deep below the surface to the inner lives of men and women, the emotions, sensations and dreams they cannot express, either through diffidence, or because they lack words in

which to embody them…It is full of the beauty and poetry
of nature, the turn of the seasons and the passing of the
years expressed in words that ring as clear and true as the
stockman's Condamine bell.[21]

Mary Durack's words about the inarticulate Stan and Amy in
The Tree of Man apply to her heroes of the outback, Grandfather
Patsy and his companions. They did not have the words to express
their dreams. She tried to show the land as they would have seen
it. The poetry was hers; the vision, as far as she could understand
it, was theirs.

While *Kings in Grass Castles* was close to completion, Manning
Clark published his *Documents in Australian History* (1955). Mary
Durack already knew the importance of primary sources; they were
her inheritance and she learned to use them with the aplomb of a
professionally trained historian. Clark's romance with Australian
history in his six volume sequence (1962–1987) had yet to come. In
his later years he regretted that he had given so little attention to
women and Aborigines; *Kings in Grass Castles* should have alerted
him to their neglect.

The 1950s was a remarkable decade—as remarkable as the
1890s—in its exploration of Australia's past. It produced Clark's
Documents and his *Short History of Australia,* and Russel Ward's *The
Australian Legend.* Judith Wright's *Generations of Men* appeared a
few months before *Kings in Grass Castles.* The two were reviewed
together in the *Times Literary Supplement,* along with Eve Pownall's
Mary of Maranoa. Like Mary Durack, Judith Wright had a family
pioneering history to draw on, and both authors made the women
a strong presence in the narrative. Mary Durack's work has a wider
range of experience, and for all the elegance of Judith Wright's

prose—or because of it—*Generations of Men* seems bloodless, too far removed from all the striving of the messy period it describes. Designer Alison Forbes reinforced the 'prettiness' of *Generations of Men* in choosing a decorous scene of tea in the garden for its cover image. Judith Wright's evocation of her grandmother, May Wright, musing on the Aborigines—did they have souls she wondered?—is abstract compared with Mary Durack's dramatisation of actual encounters, violent and disturbing, between two sets of people whose common humanity was clear to her but not to one another. Not till a much later work, *Cry for the Dead* (1981), would Wright bring passion to her view of the past and write openly about her family's record.

Somehow Mary had to face the fact that her father's generation was even less enlightened than that of her grandfather. Patsy Durack's attitude to the Aborigines, she thought, had a patriarchal recognition of responsibility which was not shared by MPD:

> The younger generation [sons of Patsy and their contemporaries] had none of the patriarchal attitude of their fathers and the things they did as a matter of course would make your hair stand on end. Even Dad who was a sort of symbol of upright dealing in his day, thought nothing of 'picking up' a few likely looking lads from a blacks' camp when going through with cattle. On one occasion he remarks in his journals 'The little fellow I picked up three days [ago] is still crying for his mother and refuses food. Expect he will pick up when we get back to the station.'[22]

Mary's defensive 'even Dad' is revealing; so is the fact that when she came to write about the period in which the 'picking up' took place, she did not include this heartbreaking episode in her narrative. Reading on in her father's journals she found that the child—eleven years old when 'picked up' by MPD—was killed in a fall from a horse three years later. She did, however, quote a more compassionate moment when her father was distressed by the removal of a four-year-old from his mother by police who wanted the child as a witness in some criminal case. 'The wailing of this poor little devil was pitiful.'[23] MPD was disgusted at the way the police treated black prisoners: chained together, neck to neck, and wrist to wrist, looking half starved. The police cruelty was compounded by their exploitation of the Aboriginal women, whom they sent into the bush to catch lizards and snakes for subsistence while they themselves pocketed the food allowance.[24]

Of the three Aborigines whose stories Mary Durack wove most closely into the family saga, Pumpkin and Boxer were acquired in the same casual 'pick up' style, while the third, Ulysses, was a child survivor of a retaliation raid, taken home by a white man as likely to be useful. All three lived long, active and seemingly happy lives in the service of the Duracks. Pumpkin, who belonged to the Cooper's Creek Boontamurra people, went to the Kimberley of his own choosing. It seems likely that Ulysses and Boxer became close to the Duracks because they were in effect tribal orphans. Pumpkin negotiated between black and white, a loner and a middleman. Patsy Durack spoke of him as a friend, and in his despondent old age it was Pumpkin whose company he most wanted. Boxer, whom Pumpkin bought on behalf of MPD in exchange for a horse and a tin of jam, formed an alliance with the Duracks which gave him an unusual degree of independent agency. One of MPD's last acts was to place a memorial plaque for Pumpkin and Ulysses at Argyle in which their 'faithful service' was acknowledged: a recognition which placed MPD as somewhat more aware of indebtedness than most of the pastoralists of his generation. At the same time, it needs to be said that 'faithful service' is a phrase for a servant not a friend. The time and place of Boxer's death were unknown until Mary sought out the records and found that he had died from leprosy in 1949.

Mary Durack thought that, unlike Patsy Durack, MPD did not see the Aborigines as equal in humanity to white men. In her text, Patsy worries about his sons: would they remember that 'these too were "the children of God"'?[25] Her troubled conclusion about her father's generation was that 'we can't sit in judgment' on people of another time. 'It would have taken a brave and extraordinarily independent fellow in the old days to suggest that the blacks had human rights.'[26] Reaching for a comparison she cited the bombing of Germany and Japan, which her own generation had not blinked at.

Long before *Kings in Grass Castles* was completed, Mary recognised that the family history could not be contained in one volume. Constable's preference for a trilogy made sense. Yet she was not ready in 1959 to move on to the period after Grandfather Patsy's death; having made herself at home with the family papers she could see that there would be sensitive issues in the next volume. As long as there were living representatives of her father's generation she would need all her tact to negotiate the story of the Connor, Durack & Doherty partnership. And if she made MPD the central character, as she had made Patsy the hero of *Kings in Grass Castles,* would she have to sit in judgment on him? Although most of the family would agree that, for better or worse, he was the dominant figure in the management of the stations, she needed to be fair to his brothers and cousins who had views of their own. MPD's death in 1950 made an obvious conclusion, but it would involve writing about Reg and Kim, and in 1959 they were still struggling with the consequences of the sale of the stations.

The price of success with *Kings in Grass Castles* came in an avalanche of correspondence: congratulations, queries, requests for advice and public appearances. Mary's family life was as demanding and varied as ever. With Horrie coming and going from Broome, Patsy, Robin and Julie entering on careers, Andy and Marie Rose at school and four-year-old Johnny at home, the household was never tranquil, and Mary did not have a room of her own. She worked hard for the West Australian branch of the Fellowship of Australian Writers and gained pleasure and companionship, fun, gossip and stimulation from its meetings and members. Her unfinished Broome murder mystery still beckoned, and as always the north drew her back, not to rest in the sun but to take on other public tasks.

CHAPTER 8

A Place of Her Own

All through the 1940s Elizabeth Durack longed for a house of her own. Ever since she left Perth as an eighteen-year-old, her place of living had been provisional, her future precarious. Apart from the northern homesteads—Ivanhoe, Argyle and Auvergne—all of them lost to the family in 1950, she had had a bewildering series of stopping places: nurses' quarters and a scruffy hotel in Darwin, a series of Sydney flats and Melbourne boarding houses, a brief stay in Alice Springs, Brisbane for Michael's birth, and Horrie's house in Broome. Financial support from Frank Clancy virtually came to an end in 1945, when his wartime job was over. After that, his intermittent earnings in freelance journalism would scarcely keep him afloat, let alone his wife and children. Although Elizabeth worked hard and productively in the first postwar years, she could not hope to buy a house from the sale of her paintings. Help had come when, a few months before his death in 1950, her father faced the fact that her marriage had failed and that she would have to support her children alone. At the cost of three thousand pounds, he gave her a block of land in Browne Avenue, Dalkeith, and the money to build a house. 'It's very small, dear, very small,' MPD said deprecatingly, but it was the best he could do.[1]

In 1950, all new houses were small. Postwar regulations limited them to eleven squares (102 square metres). Rather than have a set of little box-like rooms, Elizabeth did without the usual separate dining and sitting areas so as to have one long open-plan room which combined her work space with family living. High ceilings made it a good place to hang paintings; these she would change from time to time, except for 'War and Peace', a large genre painting which was always in the same place, catching your eye as you entered. As soon as she had some money, Elizabeth had a garage built; this served as her studio. Life at Browne Avenue had to be frugal. The Clancys had no fridge, telephone or car until the mid-1950s. Every second day the iceman came, carrying a block of ice wrapped in hessian. Elizabeth walked to Mary's house to make phone calls and sometimes to borrow Mary's car.

Dalkeith in the early 1950s was not the glossy precinct of wealth it later became. It had a bushland character. The Clancy children and their Miller cousins explored favourite places by the Swan River, where they saw sleepy blue tongue lizards, occasional snakes, frogs, scorpions, soldier ants and redback spiders. They fished for crabs, mussels and prawns. All around in Edenic profusion were native trees and wildflowers: kangaroo paw, pink myrtle, spider orchids, donkey orchids, purple hovea and the ground-running red grevillea. Dalkeith was a safe place for children. Perpetua, who was ten when they moved into this first house, and Michael, who was seven, rode their bicycles to school, and with a new sense of permanence they learned to be self-reliant. Working mothers as sole parents were rare, and an artist mother even more so, but the two Clancys found Browne Avenue a happy, secure haven and family centre:

> For most of the 1950s Michael and I more or less took for granted whatever our mother was doing, probably even thought it was 'normal'. We'd return from school after riding there and back. In winter there'd be a log fire, and Mother would be at work in the 'big room', or in her first studio, built originally as a garage…We remember Mother being there for us and helping with homework and so on. She also made sure we could cook and do household jobs. Mainly she was always working or planning another exhibition and one way or another we were always involved too.[2]

A house of her own was a huge benefit for Elizabeth Durack, but there was still an income to be made. There was no more family money. Reg was struggling at Kildurk in pioneering conditions; Kim had nothing. Gifts from Mary and her practical help with exhibitions made a difference, but with Horrie's watchful eye on Mary's cheque book there were limits in what she could do for her sister. Child endowment, which began in 1941, was welcome, even at the initial payment of five shillings a week for each child. But Elizabeth had to make more from her painting. Her successes in Sydney, negotiating with publishers over *The Way of the Whirlwind* and the *Daily Telegraph* strip were useful experiences as she faced the need to manage her career as an artist.

One of the troubles with Perth from the artist's viewpoint was its small population; exhibiting in the big eastern cities was a necessity, but travel added to the expense. The profits of her 1947 Perth exhibition bought Elizabeth only a new coat and a return fare to Melbourne for the next showing. Sending her finished work across the Nullarbor was an added complication in a precarious career. Most Australian painters had a second string—something to pay the bills while their reputations grew. Teaching art was one way: Guy Grey-Smith, a much-admired landscape painter who was the same age as Elizabeth, taught at Perth Technical College and the Art Gallery of Western Australia. Robert Juniper had a steady income from a series of three schools where he gave art classes from 1954 to 1984.[3]

It was much the same in the other states, even for those who later won fame and high fees. In 1940s Sydney a doleful William Dobell had envied Elizabeth her payments for the short-lived *Daily Telegraph* strip. Arthur Boyd, living with his wife and two children in a makeshift dwelling in the garden of his father's house at Murrumbeena, had a second string in pottery: work produced communally by Boyd family members and friends and sold in a former butcher's shop nearby. Sidney Nolan found powerful patrons in John and Sunday Reed, whose house outside Melbourne, Heide, was a meeting place for artists and writers for many years. In Sydney, recently arrived Jewish-Hungarian painter Judy Cassab depended for most of the 1950s on her husband's uncongenial work as the founder of a small factory that made elastic stockings. Later, she prospered mainly because she was able to leave her children with their father for two months each year and paint portraits of celebrities in London. On her return, Sydney sitters were eager to follow the lead of film stars and princesses.

Elizabeth Durack had none of these advantages. How did she manage? At the end of 1951, having settled in at Browne Avenue, she took stock. A summary of sales and costs, in Elizabeth's elegant handwriting, told a worrying story. The costs of thirteen exhibitions, seven in the eastern states and six in Perth, between 1946 and 1951, outweighed the returns. Materials, framing, transport of paintings, and airfares added up to £1645.[4] Sometimes the gallery paid for the catalogues and invitations, sometimes not. Sales brought in £1335. This left a deficit of £310 for a vast amount of work. At least there was a house to mortgage, but that would only be a temporary stay. Elizabeth had to diversify, seek commissions, find ways to sell prints, reproduce popular works like 'The Kid'.

One important outlet for hand-finished prints, arranged for her by her brother Kim, was Melbourne's Primrose Pottery Shop where Edith and Betty MacMillan were known for their high standards and the energy with which they promoted their artists. The rewards—from two to five guineas for each of Elizabeth's prints—were a small but reliable buttress for the Clancy household.

The biggest bills at Browne Avenue were from art suppliers and framers. Elizabeth was exacting about brushes, pencils and paints but, in a self-defeating effort to keep costs down, she often bought inferior paper. As Perpetua later reflected: 'I know that ED believed in herself but at times it was almost as if she feared she'd muck things up and waste an expensive piece of paper. And so there'd be an exquisite work produced on second-rate paper.'[5]

In the 1950s, West Australian artists had to be self-reliant. One of the main outlets, Newspaper House, was a do-it-yourself space. Another, on the top floor of Boans department store, held an annual group exhibition for the Society of Artists. Elizabeth used both of these. She also exhibited several times in the Claude Hotchin Gallery, whose owner, the noted collector Sir Claude Hotchin, had the much-desired habit of always settling with his artists on the day an exhibition came down. It was a disappointment to Elizabeth when Hotchin closed his gallery in 1951. Rose Skinner, who founded a successful and enterprising gallery in 1958, held several Durack exhibitions, but she did not offer Elizabeth the assured income that some gallery owners gave to favoured artists.

Elizabeth's Browne Avenue studio was an alternative space for exhibitions. She sent out hand-written invitations to openings, held in the afternoons, with Perpetua passing round cups of tea. Later, Michael was deft enough to do some framing; this saved money and the results were better than the rough-and-ready productions Elizabeth used at first.

Elizabeth's first venture in a Melbourne gallery in December 1946 had good reviews and a friendly reception. She was invited to dinner by an affable Sir Keith Murdoch, editor of the Melbourne *Herald*, but he did not buy a painting. As cautious in his taste as Robert Menzies, he would not have liked 'the element of distortion' that baffled the *Age* critic J. S. Macdonald.[6] Only half a dozen paintings were sold. Next came the 1947 disaster at Sydney's David Jones Gallery in which the disappointment of low sales was exacerbated by Paul Haefliger's contemptuous review in the *Sydney Morning Herald*.

An Adelaide exhibition in 1949 was well reviewed, with the added prestige of 'Desert Song' being acquired by the Art Gallery of South Australia. Over all, however, sales were abysmal. Perth welcomed one of its own but local celebrity would not satisfy Elizabeth's sense of her own worth, nor pay the bills. Her contemporaries—Albert Tucker, Russell Drysdale, Sidney Nolan and Arthur Boyd—all travelled and showed their work in London; she could see how much it meant to a cautious Australian art market to have that 'overseas' seal of approval.

In the mid-1950s Elizabeth thought of a London exhibition as a way to cancel out negative reviews, especially those from Sydney, and to show her how to develop her work. In her turbulent years in the eastern states, often with no fixed address, she had not found a place among fellow artists with whom to share ambitions and strategies. It did not help, in that male-centred art world, to be a woman painter, and the Durack name with its connotations of privilege was a handicap. To tackle London, she needed an agent and a plan. In 1954, Elizabeth enlisted a family friend from the Durack inner circle in Perth. Geoffrey Bolton, later a distinguished historian, was then doing postgraduate studies at Balliol College, Oxford. It was asking a lot of the twenty-three-year-old Bolton to set up an exhibition for Elizabeth, but he took on the task readily and generously. Letters between Perth and Oxford show Elizabeth's nervousness competing with her drive to succeed. She wanted to show her work in the wider world, but she was desperately afraid of failure. Might it not be Sydney all over again?

But then, she thought, London reviewers might look with unclouded eyes; they would never have heard of Paul Haefliger and his charge that she was copying Aboriginal paintings. She was probably right. In a similar situation, David Boyd, who had been accused in Sydney of copying the work of his brother Arthur, won high praise in London and Paris. Yet David Boyd had the advantage of being free to spend several years in London, and he had the support of fellow painters, not least his brother Arthur and brother-in-law John Perceval. Elizabeth Durack had no such support, and it would have been nearly impossible for her to leave her children for a long period, or to find the money to take them with her—even if her estranged husband gave permission for them to leave Australia. Without Frank's legal consent, she could not get a passport.

Her doubts surfaced in a series of letters to Geoffrey Bolton. In between his Oxford studies and exams, Bolton found his way around the galleries and reported back to Perth. Elizabeth wrote anxiously about every detail of a possible exhibition; she sent Bolton a range of paintings and drawings, with suggestions as to how they should be hung. But who should open it? She did not know anyone in the London art world. Michael Sadleir, head of Constable publishing house, and well known as a novelist, was a possibility because of his connection with Mary.

Bolton was patient and resourceful, but in the end it was too hard. Elizabeth's letters show her at a crossroads in her career. She was supporting herself and her children, and she was becoming a name in the Perth art community. But her success had its price. As she wrote to Bolton: 'I am already in danger of becoming the tourist's toy, the two-handed koala, and to my shame, I am existing at this moment on such antics.'[7]

> I want to sink a shaft where up to date I've only been picking up a bit of alluvial—the work has to blaze with the horror & excitement and the utter joyment [sic] of the red the black & the sky all *around* not only on top & the sun pouring down enough to melt the wax on [Icarus's] wings.[8]

Some of her paintings sold readily, but these were the potboilers: 'the little child that tugs at the HEART-STRINGS', the Aboriginal children with 'the EYES'. A London exhibition might just be like 'little old Perth'. People would buy 'The Kid' from a neat folder of prints but the critics would pan her as they did in Sydney. 'I couldn't stand the strain and tension of it all.'[9]

Elizabeth's 1950s letters show the complexities of her life. At times she is attending to her children's needs, worrying that Perpetua is more interested in tennis than school work, delighted at Michael's high-achieving academic record, planning their holidays in tandem with Mary and her children. Other letters show her own need to escape alone to the north, to lose track of time and paint in solitude. Coming back to Perth from a stint with Kim at Camballin she missed 'the wind and the dust, the incredible heat, the big cloud-tumbled skies, the red & the blue, the new sharp greens...' She also missed the sense of community, with all the repetitive talk of points of rain, the height of the creeks, the state of the stock and the 'bush bickering and back-biting', which was like any family that 'squabbles indefinitely but unites against attack, criticism or intrusion from outside.'[10]

Elizabeth did not find that sense of community in Perth. There was no equivalent for artists of the Fellowship of Australian Writers, where Mary kept the peace between some fractious authors, enjoyed friendly companionship with others, and fostered the talented and untalented alike. The Society of Artists was less cohesive, and it does not seem that Elizabeth was involved in its affairs. Nor did she have the time to become a public figure; she survived financially only by concentrated, unremitting work. Living in Perth's close-knit community, she was at risk of becoming everyone's friend, as Mary was, at the expense of her time for painting. But, as Mary remarked: 'Bet has a somewhat harder heart and a big cupboard.'

The 'big cupboard' refers to an episode when Bet was besieged by two Perth women who wanted to see the new wardrobe of knitwear given to her as an advertising ploy by the Wool Board after a painting commission. Bet saw them coming, decided to ignore the doorbell and was appalled when, in friendly Perth fashion, the women opened the unlocked door and let themselves in. It would have been hard to explain why she hadn't answered the door, so Bet dived into a big cupboard, where she crouched, waiting for the intruders to depart. Looking around, they eyed that very cupboard. They were sure that Elizabeth would want them to see the Wool Board collection, so they opened the door, to find the cowering artist.

> 'Elizabeth!' screamed the leading intruder. 'What on earth are you doing in there?'
>
> 'Oh', said Bet, feigning an awakening from deep sleep. 'I often come in here for a quiet nap.'
>
> 'Isn't it wonderful, the crazy things that artists do?' said the woman in a reverent tone to her friend.[11]

As a young girl Elizabeth was thought to be shy, and it may be that for all her wit and charm she was not confident among strangers. The few Perth artists who knew her well found her a good and generous friend, as she was to the young Robert Juniper:

> Elizabeth was a great encouragement to me in my formative years as a painter. To me she was the epitome of feminine grace and culture and I loved her. We sat by her fireside and she shed tears for James Joyce when I told her I'd bought *Finnegan's Wake*. The tears were for the Irish music of his poetry and for his excommunication from the church. Several years later I asked her to be godmother to my first daughter.[12]

Elizabeth was not interested in being 'seen' nor did she have the time for it, but she liked to look at new work. A young artist, Philippa O'Brien, was surprised and touched to have a discerning letter from Elizabeth, who had missed the opening of O'Brien's exhibition, and dropped in alone to have a quiet look.[13]

Early in 1956, Elizabeth built an extension to her house, which would replace her garage as a work place and could also house small exhibitions. A simple, elegant design by Perth architect Geoffrey Summerhayes, it harmonised with the off-white bricks and grey roof of the house. Grey concrete blocks contrasted with the dark red-brown of the jarrah walls and terracotta brick porch and steps. The only sign that this might be a public space was the 'Elizabeth Durack' signature in white paint on the door and the separate entrance which protected the privacy of her house.[14] It was ready in time for an exhibition of some new work, created in a mood of sustained excitement. For once, it was a Perth scene. Reporting to Geoffrey Bolton, Elizabeth wrote:

> I worked all the summer like a mad thing finding its way through a tunnel with that extraordinary scene of light, gaiety & colour which is North Cottesloe—eventually after periods of despair & fleeting moments of exultation I distilled a pure & simple essence. It was terribly interesting—I did some thousands of sketches and some hundreds of paintings—at first great conglomerate masses of moving lines & forms where the colour was superimposed in rough blocks. For some time I thought this was it but I wasn't quite satisfied. I went back & back then I saw that the spirit of it lay in the *light*—a lot of sea, a lot of white sand & a lot of white light—I worked on, then one night very late

with all the thrill of someone operating an illicit still—the
first real drop came through...I have never been so excited
about anything as these Cottesloe pictures...

Well the day of showing all this eventually came...about
150 or more kindly turned up, completely overcrowding the
little gallery. But alas they had come to see 'the Aborigin-*ees*
with their wonderful *eyes*'...[15]

Out of this fiasco came the discovery that prints were more readily
sold than paintings. So long as people could see a folio of numbered
prints, all exactly the same, they would pay twenty guineas for
one of them, while the original was left hanging with a fifteen
guinea price on it. The Cottesloe exhibition lost money on catering
expenses but there was a useful lesson in it. Elizabeth was not at
all sure that she would ever be 'an artist's artist'. To paint with
passion, as she had done with the Cottesloe works, would not pay
the household bills. Yet her reputation would suffer from too many
prints of 'The Kid' and others that warmed hearts in Perth. How
to mediate between the two extremes? A needy author could use
a pseudonym. The quickly written railway-novel trash of 'Rann
Daly', the alter ego of the much respected novelist Vance Palmer,
was barely noticed and easily forgiven. But artists, it seemed, had
always to be themselves.

Who was Elizabeth Durack? Elegant, witty, with a sense of
fun, seemingly at home among the wealthy who could afford to
put art on their walls, she felt most herself when she left Perth
to share Kim's camp at Camballin, or the neo-Grecian dwelling
('mad but fun') that succeeded it.

Elizabeth still had admirers, but none seems to have mattered
to her nearly as much as her work. When one of them called at

Browne Avenue with a gift of home-grown vegetables which he 'knew' she would like better than flowers, he was politely thanked. But now she had to cook the damn things.[16] Unlike sociable Mary, Elizabeth guarded her privacy. She read widely, as Mary did, and as her income from painting became steadier, she built a varied collection of books that show intellectual curiosity and eclectic taste. Australian history and anthropology were well represented; authors she admired sat side by side with those she took issue with. She read Darwin and Huxley; she had a reprint of William Dampier's *New Voyage Around the World* (1697). John Mulvaney's *The Pre-History of Australia* (1969) was on her shelves, as was T. G. H. Strehlow's work on religion among the indigenous people of Central Australia. Poetry was a necessity, like breathing. She kept copies of Dante, Blake, Byron, Keats, Matthew Arnold and Francis Thompson. There was not much modern poetry; an exception was Harold Stewart's translation of Japanese haiku, *A Net of Fireflies* (1960) inscribed by Stewart. An expensive item, but close to her heart, was Grahame Walsh's *Bradshaw's Ancient Rock Paintings of North-West Australia* (1994). Elizabeth read all that she could find on Aboriginal culture, and she explored writings on the art of Native Americans which made illuminating comparisons. There were plenty of novels: from Tolstoy and Dostoevsky to James Joyce, Evelyn Waugh and Muriel Spark, Patrick White and Randolph Stow. Her speculative habit of mind appears in the collection of works by and about the contentious French Jesuit priest and palaeontologist Pierre Teilhard de Chardin, a 1950s Galileo, silenced by the Vatican for his speculative writings about man and the universe. Early and late in her life, Elizabeth needed the printed word as well as the challenge of art. Like the other Duracks, she was unable to think of book-buying as a luxury.

As her career began to take shape in the 1950s, Elizabeth acknowledged her dependence on Aborigines as a source of creativity. 'I could paint white people,' she said, 'but I wouldn't feel the same sympathy with my subjects.' When she painted an Aborigine, 'something happens to me…They just come easy.' She was pleased by Albert Namatjira's response when he saw some of her work in 1951: 'That's proper blackfellow alright.'[17]

Perth's art scene had a degree of sophistication unexpected in such a small city. No other Australian university had a set of Sidney Nolans, one of which hung in the University of Western Australia students' coffee shop. The P&O and Orient Line ships from London docked at Perth, long enough for visiting celebrities to be seen or at least heard on Catherine King's radio program. Sybil Thorndike came to Perth, so did H. G. Wells. The ABC sponsored concert performances by Malcolm Sargent, Lotte Lehmann and others. The university's student drama combined high quality with easy access. *Westerly* magazine, published from the department of English from 1956, was never parochial. An arts monthly broadsheet *The Critic*, founded by John O'Brien of the University of Western Australia Press, maintained a high standard.

Elizabeth's first significant Perth sale was 'The Cord to Alcheringa' (1953). Purchased from the Tom Collins Bequest, it hung for nearly forty years on the steps leading to the senate chamber of the University of Western Australia. By the late 1980s, the winds of change had sent it into storage within the university's art collection. The 'Legend of the Black Swan' was commissioned for the Charles Gairdner Hospital in 1956. Work on another 1950s commission, entitled *Look at the State We're In,* took Elizabeth on a tour of some ten northern outback towns, where she did drawings and gouaches of people and places. Of these, only those done in Geraldton have survived to be displayed in the art collection of its place of origin. Elizabeth loved moving about the country and watching people at work: men mining and shearing, Aboriginal women washing clothes in the river. She seldom painted a landscape without figures. The relationship between land and indigenous people was her abiding theme. Looking back three decades later, she said that the crucial time in her development as an artist was at Ivanhoe, painting with Jubul, beside the Ord:

> Here too it was that the major themes of my work began to take shape. I moved from oils to watercolour and developed in this medium the intricate relationship between the Aboriginal people and the landscape—an aesthetic analogy that has been a continuing refrain through the years. I explored the anatomy of movement—figures into landscape, landscape into figures. I poured 'the harvest of the eye' into 'the mill of the imagination' as, walking through the bush with the blacks, harmonies of shape and line and movement fused and flowered before my eyes.[18]

All through the 1950s and afterwards, a period of retreat from Perth was a constant need. 'She disappears from time to time into the desert and walks around with the blacks, and comes back looking as though she has lived on lizards,' Mary wrote.[19] At home, Elizabeth worked hard, even obsessively, far into the night, on the ambitious projects for which she needed space as well as imagination. The long table in her garage became her centre; later, when she could afford a car and needed a garage, she built another studio at the end of the garden.

With Elizabeth's emerging success as a painter, the family focus of concern shifted from her to Kim. By 1957, it looked as if his Kimberley dream might be fulfilled. The irrigation pipes he had installed (each one 'big enough to hold a smoko in') were a huge achievement. In the same year, Mary was close to finishing *Kings in Grass Castles* and Reg's struggles at Kildurk were easing. The new generation of Duracks and Millers was full of promise, and Elizabeth was proud of the two Clancys. Remembering her own irresponsible younger self, Elizabeth felt a fraud when she lectured Perpetua on the need to work hard and make the most of her talents. Michael, a natural scholar, was on track to be dux of St Louis' school in a few years' time.

Going north was strenuous. Elizabeth would join the Aborigines at Ivanhoe and spend three weeks walking with them, absorbing knowledge, making sketches. She carried a light swag and slept on the ground. The Aborigines treated her as a guest, which meant that she was given the best part of cold goanna for breakfast. The group rested in the heat of the day. The main meal was at night, and was always kangaroo. If they had flour they made little johnny cakes in the ashes. To keep up with the group, Elizabeth needed to be fit. She remembered these walks in an interview in 1971:

> You had to be able to walk, the days start very early. They move very early after a very scratchy breakfast, then you'd pad along and then the party would break up. Say, I was with a couple of women and a couple of the older men, but the younger ones—they'd go off and they'd catch a kangaroo or something. We wouldn't see them 'til the evening.

At the end of one three-week trek, they met some old men from the desert with whom they exchanged songs or other 'remnants' of their culture. Elizabeth thought herself privileged to witness some tribal ceremonies, and she was happy to be politely excluded from others. She told an interviewer that the cave paintings she had seen in the 1930s might have been the beginning of her fascination with Aboriginal culture. It was a slow, gradual process, with 'little glimpses of knowledge', small insights into the relationship of the Aborigines to their environment.[20]

Examples of her work eventually reached London, and under the best possible auspices. Bryan Robertson, curator of an important exhibition of Australian paintings at the Whitechapel Gallery in 1961, visited Perth and chose two of Elizabeth's paintings. Only three women were represented among fifty artists, nearly all from the eastern states. Some of the chosen fifty were already living in London. They ranged from the well-established Sidney Nolan, Arthur Boyd and Albert Tucker—all, like Elizabeth, in their forties—to the twenty-one-year-old Brett Whiteley and Perth's Robert Juniper, who was thirty-three. Being included in 'the Whitechapel' was an accolade; it was the first time, so Bernard Smith remarked, that Australian art found a large and receptive audience outside its own country.[21] It was a defining moment in the recognition of Australian painting abroad. Doubtful critics and buyers at home were reassured. Patrick McCaughey described its effect as 'galvanic'. [22]

Aboriginal art, yet to rouse interest in Australia, was not included in the Whitechapel exhibition nor in a subsequent show at the Tate. London viewers saw images of Aboriginal life including Arthur Boyd's 'Shearers Playing for a Bride' (one of a series which Boyd described as 'too pretty'); Lawrence Daws's 'Mining Town

Blacks'; Russell Drysdale's 'Desert Landscape', 'Mullatoonah Tank', 'Boy with Lizard' and 'Snake Bay at Night'. These, with John Olsen's 'Journey into You Beaut Country', showed white perceptions of Aborigines and their relation to the Australian landscape.

Elizabeth never managed to conquer London as her male contemporaries did, although the death of Frank Clancy in 1965 left Elizabeth free of the legal constraints on her travel outside Australia. Frank's last years were melancholy; after a long decline and a stroke he was looked after by his sister Pat in Sydney. With the whole breadth of Australia between him and his family, it was hard for him to keep contact with Perpetua and Michael; his weekly letters to them became the only link. Questioned as to why her marriage failed, Elizabeth thought that it was not in her nature to share her life with anyone. It was 'more my fault than Frank's,' she said of the marriage breakdown.[23] His support for her work had been crucial in the first years of their marriage; he understood her relentless drive and knew he was in part its victim. He also blamed Kim, with whom Elizabeth found intellectual companionship. Her closest relationships were within her family, and among Perth artists she saw herself as a maverick.[24]

Looking back, Elizabeth idealised her early romance with Tom Naughton, while acknowledging his fatal dependency on alcohol and drugs. She had married Frank, she believed, in order to forget Tom. The pleasures of sex became less important with the years. Her work was what mattered. 'Bet is full of creative fire,' Mary said, adding, 'much more than me.' Sometimes Elizabeth envied the women painters whose husbands gave financial and emotional support to their work. Not that there were many women in that situation—only Margaret Preston and Judy Cassab came to mind—while many male painters had essential domestic and secretarial help from their wives.

From the late 1960s, after Perpetua and Michael had graduated from the University of Western Australia and left home, Elizabeth was free to travel as she pleased, following opportunities to paint, taking commissions from big companies like Conzinc Rio Tinto, and town or shire councils like Geraldton. In 1966, for the first time since her early travels with Mary, she left Australia. She went to Africa to visit Perpetua, who was teaching there. She moved on to London where she was persuaded by West Australian writers Henrietta Drake-Brockman and Gerry Glaskin to join the international writers' association, PEN, and go with them to a New York conference. Enthralled with New York, Elizabeth learned worldly wisdom from the Americans. 'Apply for a grant,' they told her, and a quick success with the Ford Foundation took her across the United States, studying Native-American culture. With later travels came a series of illustrated books: *Seeing—Through Papua New Guinea* (1969), *Seeing—Through the Philippines* (1971) and *Seeing—Through Indonesia* (1977).

She found opportunities to earn money while exploring new places, including a stint on Bougainville Island in 1968, where she was commissioned by Sir Maurice Mawby of Conzinc Rio Tinto to paint a series for the boardrooms of this giant mining company. Elizabeth was enchanted by the rich tropical landscape, excited by the force and energy of the mining operation but alert to the ecological destruction. Her work in Bougainville included some large panels. She painted copper on masonite, then tore up a jungle painting and loosely patterned it on top with the copper showing through. Asked how she justified working for Conzinc—and being paid for some paintings in which she implicitly criticised the 'desecration' of the island—she said that Conzinc tried to be fair: mining would bring wealth to an emerging nation. 'It is an ongoing world argument; development or—God's garden. And we haven't solved it. In fact, you know, we are losing out, aren't we, with the destruction of the huge forest areas.'[25]

The ecological lessons of Bougainville surfaced in the next phase of Elizabeth's work. Her theme became 'the rim of our brittle and disintegrating world'. It was 'our world', she insisted, not 'theirs', not that of the Aborigines alone. Images of disintegration dominated her 1970s and 1980s paintings. She traced them to the disturbing emotions aroused when she returned to Australia after travelling in Africa, Europe and the United States.

> I had to find a new medium—a medium for the rising wind—for the hurricane of the '70s that was upon us— sweeping all before it—uprooting trees, people, shapes, forms, everything that had once stood still—as though petrified—now levitated. Way out east of Mundiwindi— between Mundiwindi and Lake Disappointment—was where I saw the dust—felt the wind rising.
>
> As always, the idea preceded visualisation. The Rim: the rim of our brittle and disintegrating world—goes on blowing itself to shreds.[26]

The Rim and Beyond and *Flightless Birds* were ambitious series. Critic Patrick Hutchings found them horrifying paintings, in which familiar subject matter is 'torn to shreds' and the fragments scattered by a high wind on a barren lunar landscape.[27] Novelist Randolph Stow wrote perceptively of Elizabeth's vision, in which a complete integration of man and nature is visualised:

...nature, however, is always dominant. In 'Sea-Reft' and in the camp series *In Land* and *Landlocked* the figures shimmer in mirage as if whelmed by the sea that once covered their arid country. Not all this desolation is natural...The white slag heaps of 'Mulga Queen' and 'Snow Queen' are more barren than the desert itself.[28]

In a backward glance at her own childhood reading Elizabeth produced a big series of pastels called *Bett-Bett's Wonderful Lonely Palace*. These caught the moment when Bett-Bett, the central character of Mrs Aeneas Gunn's *Little Black Princess of the Never-Never* (1905) leaves the white woman and disappears into the bush. 'Somehow I identified with Bett-Bett, and it would be a drift of figures against a Kimberley landscape.' They were serene, gentle paintings in which Elizabeth found relief from the pressures of change and disintegration in the ecology and in the culture of the Aborigines.[29] The echo of her own name, in a title which reflects the enticement of solitude, suggests a personal meaning. The Kimberley was Bet Durack's 'wonderful lonely palace'.[30]

By the end of the 1990s, Elizabeth had held an astonishing total of sixty-five solo and group exhibitions. Balancing the popular, often sentimental, images and the prints which sold readily, she had at least four series of what she called the 'hot' paintings, the ones painted with passion. She had some important breakthroughs. Her *Explorers and Discoverers* series was shown at the New York Trade Center in 1979; *Out of Sight—Out of Mind* at the Perth Cultural Centre in 1991, and *Derivations and Directions* at the Art Gallery of Western Australia in 1995. *The Art of Elizabeth Durack* by Patrick Hutchings (1981), financed by industrialist and art collector Robert Holmes à Court, was the first monograph on a West Australian painter.

Commonwealth and state public honours kept coming: Order of the British Empire in 1966; Companion of St Michael and St George in 1983; honorary Doctorate of Letters from Murdoch University in 1994. An honorary doctorate from the University of Western Australia came in 1996, just before Elizabeth's eighty-first birthday—an age at which a gentle fade-out from public and professional life might have been expected. Not so: Elizabeth had more to say, and at eighty-one she would walk into an Australia-wide controversy about her next phase of painting.

The house in Browne Avenue, often empty while she travelled, remained Elizabeth's centre. Mortgaged more than once, it helped to keep her more or less solvent through years of striving. As Perth grew affluent and Dalkeith land prices soared, Elizabeth could have sold out at a profit and moved on. Yet, despite her early rebellion against Perth and her restless nature, she kept her safe haven. For the rest of her life she would return to Browne Avenue with the same certainty that took her back to the north. The comfort of coming home to a settled place appears in a letter, to Mary, written when Perpetua and Michael were on holidays and Mary was in Broome:

> Took a taxi from the train—the house was still there—the cat purring loudly and the furniture all in the same position. I turned on all the lights, switched on the radio, poured a drink, ran a bath, laid out the 'roo skins, put the everlastings in a jug—wished like hell you were here to talk and talk and talk to—then I went to bed.[31]

CHAPTER 9

Other People's Books

Mary Durack could never close the door on needy writers. She involved herself in dozens of enterprises which were scarcely worth doing. The human element always engaged her. She knew a goose from a swan, but geese too had feelings. So, even in full knowledge that the memoirs of a paraplegic ex-footballer were almost beyond saving, she took that manuscript home to tidy up and send out with at least a chance. Like other works she adopted, it came at the request of one of her friends in the clergy: priests and nuns were always sure of getting her attention. If she had been hungrier for more literary fame of her own, *Kings in Grass Castles* would have been written in half the time. Telephone, mailbox and doorbell brought new demands. Unpaid and seldom adequately thanked, Mary's editorial labours, more often than not, would produce a mediocre, barely publishable work that the world could have done without. But it was always possible that she would miss real talent, and anyway it would have been ungenerous to refuse.

As an editor, she could be tough. Writing to a fellow professional Florence James she described what was involved in one of many tasks: slashing verbiage, deleting clichés, summarising or dropping uninteresting details, 'chucking out encyclopaedic stuff' and removing authorial moralising. Stripped back, the manuscript might 'read up quite lively and easily and next time might not be turfed back obviously echoing with some poor exasperated reader's sighs'.[1] Even with Elizabeth, who wrote fluently and with verve, Mary could be severe. Asked for an opinion of a little allegory set in Broome, 'The House that Took Off', she reported, 'The story seems less of a caricature of the town than of you yourself.' It was a 'glorious idea' but needed tidying up.[2] She then proceeded to prune and simplify with such thoroughness that her sister wrote back, deflated, that she had gone off the idea.[3]

Some of Mary's severity with Elizabeth's ventures into writing might have been territorial. Always generous about her sister's paintings and drawings, Mary never trespassed into that realm. Even though her own artistic talents were considerable, she kept them low key, enjoying herself now and then with a mural, or an illustrated children's story that she did not seek to publish. When Elizabeth strayed into print, she had to expect an honest professional opinion from her sister.

Mary's directness in commenting on other people's work seemed not to be a deterrent: they kept coming, and she responded at the expense of her own writing. She knew that it was usually a thankless task:

> I wonder how many books Beatrice Davis [of Angus & Robertson] practically rewrote? Xavier Herbert's *Capricornia* was a sow's ear made into a silk purse by the hard

work of Inky Stevenson, though Xavier denied that he had any help. Writers nearly always conveniently forget. Ion Idriess and Frank Clune regarded the heavy rewriting and subbing of their stuff as a mere secretarial job.[4]

When Horrie decided to write his memoirs, Mary was called in as editor. Annoyingly, he called her efforts 'retyping'. *Early Birds* was part autobiography, part history. Horrie had a good story to tell in the founding and early years of his airline, and he wrote with vigour and sardonic humour. Mary's task was to give his chapters shape and to get rid of repetitions and side-tracks. His book appeared in 1963 from the Adelaide publisher Rigby, and was well received. It is doubtful that he could have done it without Mary, not only because of her editorial skill but because *Kings in Grass Castles* had given her such prestige among Australian publishers. Nothing that she recommended would go unread.

Mary and Horrie's time together during the early 1960s was spent mainly in Broome. His pastoral folly at Dampier Downs had failed; undaunted, he bought a sheep property, Debesa, near Derby. Ansett's takeover of MacRobertson Miller in 1963 coincided with a new national regime in civil aviation. Pre-flight plans and other safety procedures meant that Horrie could no longer wander in to a hangar at Broome, choose a plane and say he was 'just going for a spin'. Debesa was a distraction, though an expensive one. Mary seemed not to mind the drain on their finances 'so long as the old boy was happy'. She too had found ways to retreat from the world. Using some royalties from *Kings in Grass Castles*, she had a workroom built on top of the garage of the Nedlands house. And to get further away from the overwhelming life of her family, the Fellowship of Australian Writers and countless other claimants

on her time, she took refuge at Adsett, a house on the coast near
Busselton owned by her friend Dr Ida Mann, an opthalmologist.
Ida was often away, and when she was at Adsett she had writing
of her own to do. The two women worked peacefully in this quiet
seaside setting. Mary's delight in solitude appears in a letter to
Florence James, written from Adsett while Ida was away: 'I have
been here for three heavenly days not speaking to a soul except
myself. I cannot remember ever being so happy in my life. And
I can work.'[5]

One of Mary's unpromising ventures on behalf of others ended
in pure gold. Less well known and less immediately appealing
in its subject than *Kings in Grass Castles, The Rock and the Sand*
(1969) is her finest work. It began in Broome, when the Catholic
Bishop, Johannes Jobst of the German Pallottine order, asked
her help in producing an article for the Catholic press and an
accompanying brochure to celebrate half a century of missionary
work in the north. What he wanted was very simple: something
positive, aimed at benefactors, with the emphasis on the dedication
of the missionaries, the hardships they faced and the spiritual and
temporal gifts they brought. A journalist and a photographer could
have done the job and made the bishop happy. But somehow Mary
found herself agreeing to write the story and offering Elizabeth's
services as illustrator. Bishop Jobst did not want Elizabeth. As he
said to Horrie: 'Vy must she give such a sombre impression [of
Aborigines] and vy limbs like sticks?'[6] He did not know what
he was doing in unleashing Mary's energies in a task that caught
her imagination. After writing a series of illustrated articles,
Missions in a Bypassed Land, published in the Catholic press in
1961, Mary persuaded the bishop to open up his files for a more
ambitious study.

Mary's interest in primary sources made the bishop uneasy. He was a relative newcomer from Germany and he had none of the scholarly expertise and imaginative insight which Father Ernest Worms and other priests of the same Pallottine order had brought to Aboriginal affairs. His diocese of more than 650 thousand square kilometres involved constant travel. He was lonely with no one to talk to and he was not learning much about place or people. Mary found him sad and vague. He was doing his best, and that meant missions and conversions on traditional lines, but he was slow to realise that times were changing. Left to himself he would have produced something outmoded and superficial with a few uplifting photos. When Mary asked for the records held at the Beagle Bay mission, Jobst gave way reluctantly; a searching historical account was not the sort of thing he wanted.

In March 1963 Mary and the bishop set off together in a mission truck to drive the hundred and thirty kilometres from Broome to Beagle Bay. Talking along the way was not easy, given the bishop's soft voice, his German accent, Mary's deaf ear on his left side, and a crate of chirruping day-old chicks in the back of the truck. At first the bishop would not allow her to be alone with the diocesan archives. Other writers of Mary's eminence would have been huffy at the lack of trust. But she persisted gently until he gave in and allowed her to see the files he had tucked away. If she were to write the story, she had to know the seamy side. And, as she said, the seamy side was often the most revealing.

Mary's task would have been easier if all the private letters and confidential reports had been in English; instead she had to struggle with the help of Latin, French, Spanish, Italian and German dictionaries to translate and understand. She had schoolgirl French, she took Spanish lessons, and she had some scholarly priests to help with her translations. Soon she was in deep water. Bishop Jobst had not read the archive but he could guess it would contain stories of disillusionment, quarrels, sexual misdemeanors and heavy drinking among some European priests who were ill prepared for their work. Mary's long experience of the land that the missionaries encountered made her well attuned to their difficulties. The mutual incomprehension of European newcomers and Aboriginal people was dramatised for her in the masses of letters and papers that Bishop Jobst eventually allowed her to read. Her frivolous Broome detective novel was once again set aside for this unexpected, fascinating subject. Mary wrote to Florence James:

> It is hard even to try to tell anyone what this book is 'about'. If I say it is the history of eighty years of missionary effort among the Aborigines of North Australia it sounds as if I've gone round the bend. I mean, utterly un-me. However, at some stage in the past few years I've realised that the whole history of the north was wrapped up in these crumbling letters and papers—the incredible story of a polyglot people, the elusive character and subtle psychology of the Aborigines shown up in relation to the problem they were to the missionaries of these various nationalities and the problem these various missionaries were to them.[7]

As with her discovery of the right title for *Kings in Grass Castles* and its beginnings in Ireland, the new book came to life with the title and the defining moment set out in the first sentence. *The Rock and the Sand* began with the gift of a timepiece to the people of a timeless land:

The people of the dream watched the people of the clock come out of the sea and strike their flagstaff firmly into the ground…Both people were mistaken [in their assumptions] for the clock was not a toy but a way of life, as the dreaming was a way of life, the one defining time by an arrow, the other in terms of heavenly bodies and seasonal change.[8]

The missionaries' documents gave Mary a new perspective on the region and the people she had already described in *Kings in Grass Castles*. The challenge to the indigenous people came by sea as well as overland. In the first chapters of *The Rock and the Sand* the focus was on the west coast, where the pearling luggers brought crews of Japanese, Chinese and Filipino divers. From the 1860s on, there were fortunes to be made in the pearling industry. The temptingly high price of pearl shell and the discovery of some big pearls brought schooners, luggers, sloops and junks to this profitable industry. Diving was a high-risk occupation. The divers—first Aboriginal men and women, later Asians—were never adequately warned or protected against the hazard of the bends. Much of the work of the Catholic missionaries was carried out in this new and complex multi-racial society.

The archives of the diocese of Broome included correspondence with religious orders in France, Spain, Germany and Ireland, and with West Australian government officials. These were supplemented by papers from the archdiocese of Perth. Mary's friendships with German Pallottine priests and with Irish and Australian nuns of the Order of St John of God gave anecdotal material. She knew Broome well, and she soon formed a good sense of the history of Beagle Bay, where Bishop Jobst was based.

The Rock and the Sand is full of stories, skilfully interwoven.

Some are tales of folly; some are tragic; many are heroic. The dominant figure of the late nineteenth century is Irishman Matthew Gibney, who came to Western Australia as a young priest in 1863, and was a bishop from 1887 until 1910. He gave strong leadership, especially in his criticism of the brutal methods with which the police took Aborigines into custody. His trenchant comments on the exploitation of Aborigines by the pearlers were highlighted in *The Rock and the Sand*.

The intricate history of the Spanish and French Trappist missionaries held a story of cultural misunderstanding and clashes of temperament. It was almost impossible to follow a centuries-old monastic rule under the conditions these priests encountered. In Europe they had lived austerely, but always with a standard of hard-scrubbed cleanliness that they could not achieve in rough shacks where water was short and clean linen became a thing of distant memory. Schemes to make the mission self-supporting, through pearling, and through the sale of emu skins and other bright ideas, were tried and failed.

Two stories stand out as triumphs of endurance and wisdom. One is that of the Irishwoman who brought the Sisters of St John of God to the Kimberley. Mother Antonio O'Brien, born in Galway, arrived in 1895 with thirty years of nursing experience and a group of young nuns. The nuns had looked after typhoid patients in extreme heat and primitive conditions on the Kalgoorlie goldfields before accepting the even tougher assignment of the impoverished Beagle Bay mission. From the moment of landing, the nuns had to be stalwart. Wading ashore and walking six kilometres in wet clothes was only the beginning. Their 'convent' was a bark-roofed building with canvas flaps serving as doors. Apart from a few boxes, there was no furniture, and there were no mattresses or pillows on the greenhide stretcher beds.[9]

The nuns had to learn by experience, with many mistakes, the subtleties of Aboriginal culture. Rules which forbade the men of one tribal classification to speak to, or even look at, the women of another classification made no sense to Mother Antonio, but she and her sisters learned to respect the elders and to love the women and children who came to the mission. Mother Antonio discouraged her nuns from thinking of themselves as benefactors. The Aborigines, she said, 'did not ask us to come. We are here of our own choice and we can remain only by their goodwill and the grace of God.'[10]

Once the Beagle Bay mission was established, Mother Antonio moved on to Broome, where the nuns made a squalid hut into an adequate dwelling and soon set up a flourishing multi-racial school. They augmented the meagre earnings from school fees by giving English lessons to the Japanese, Chinese, Filipino and Malay workers in the pearling industry. They also volunteered to help in the understaffed Japanese hospital where divers left paralysed by the bends were taken. A young Irish nun who nursed a Japanese smallpox victim to recovery in 1912, but died of the disease herself, is commemorated in the Catholic cemetery in Broome by a stone plinth and Celtic cross erected by the Japanese community 'in grateful memory'.[11] Mother Antonio is buried in the same section of the cemetery beside many of the Irish nuns of St John of God, a long way from her Galway home. Mary Durack represents her as a woman who never turned aside from the needs of others or judged them harshly for their shortcomings. Generous and resourceful, with a love of company and a sense of fun, she had a good deal in common with her author.

Mother Antonio died in 1923, a decade before the nuns of

her order met a new challenge: leprosy, which was thought to have been introduced by the Chinese who came to the Kimberley goldfields in the 1880s. The disease had spread to the Aborigines, but had not been much noted until the 1930s, when there was panic and 'leper hunts' on Kimberley stations. Under Commonwealth legislation, those suffering from the disease were packed off to Darwin where, lonely and terrified, many Aborigines died. The St John of God nuns recognised the trauma of their being taken away from their spirit country and petitioned to be allowed to nurse them on their home land.

It took five years of persistent lobbying before the nuns were allowed to take over a more or less derelict compound near Derby. There, they found 'chaos, desolation and despair' and brought a measure of hope, order, new buildings and nursing skill to three hundred and forty patients, some of them misdiagnosed in the general panic.[12] In this and other episodes recorded in the church archives, Mary Durack found the altruism that she regarded as the unique gift of the missionaries. Most of the white men and women whom the Aborigines encountered came to the region for their own profit; Mother Antonio, and other priests and nuns from Ireland, Spain, France and Germany, were there to give as best they could, taking nothing for themselves and enduring a harsh and alien way of life.

The Rock and the Sand shows unqualified admiration for the work of the German Pallottine priest, father Ernest Worms, who became parish priest of Broome in 1931. His story is the more eloquent because Mary Durack knew him well and had a vivid sense of his personality and ideas. Having served half a lifetime in the West Australian mission, Ernest Worms looked back with a clear vision and undiminished enthusiasm. The missionary, he said, must be patient and sensitive. He must be prepared to learn the languages of the people to whose service he is sent. He must have a fundamental knowledge of anthropology. 'Otherwise he will feel lost in strange surroundings and blind to the exuberance of human life around him.' His religious convictions should intensify his moral qualities; they should also provide a great tolerance towards native customs and a perception of what should remain untouched or even fostered. 'He should not expect easy success; he might go home after twenty or thirty years of labour, finding satisfaction in the *little* he had achieved.'[13]

What Mary Durack most admired in Ernest Worms was his openness to all that was strange and new, and his total lack of condescension. She remembered him returning from his treks into the desert 'sunburnt, almost inarticulate with excitement and in his own words "stripped as far as decency would allow", most of his clothing having been given away in token of thanks to his native guides'.[14] He explored the caves of the great Wondjina spirit in north-west Kimberley, where he found pictorial and linguistic evidence of the remote past.[15]

Through the prism of the missionaries' records, Mary confronted many of the social and cultural issues of her time, not least the widespread belief that mixed-race boys were destined for crime and the girls for prostitution. Her commitment to integration, with interracial marriage approved, even recommended, would have shocked earlier generations of Duracks. Mary was concerned at the risk of a kind of apartheid, a permanent under-class in a white Australia. In a period when the idea of the orphanage was not yet questioned, she saw the nuns as the only practical way of saving abandoned children from starvation. Her sources described the 'little ones, mostly half-caste girls, some naked, others wrapped in a policeman's shirt or coat', brought in for the nuns to care for.[16]

Reviewers of *The Rock and the Sand* showed respect for Mary Durack's grasp of a complex history and her capacity to show the interactions of places and people. Books about the work of religious orders are seldom lively: discretion and reverence are the norm. Mary Durack's curiosity about individuals, wise and foolish, her tolerance, and her respect for dedicated lives made her the ideal author for this book. It would never achieve the popularity of *Kings in Grass Castles* but it went far beyond the expectations—or even the wishes—of Bishop Jobst. Mary suspected that he never read it. When she sent him a copy she placed a cheque between two of the early pages, as a donation towards his buying a plane. She was never thanked. But she knew the book was worth doing, even if its recognition from Jobst lacked grace. Geoffrey Bolton described it as 'her finest piece of historical research but too objective and too firmly grounded in the district's social history to please hagiographers'.[17]

The writing and publication of *The Rock and the Sand* were shadowed by the deaths, tragic and unexpected, of two of the much-loved members of the family. Kim Durack died in Canberra in May 1968 at the early age of fifty-one. He had been reading Mary's draft chapters up to the day of his death. A diagnosis of aplastic anaemia the year before had not been thought terminal. Kim seemed to be doing well enough with blood transfusions, but his depleted immune system left him vulnerable to infections. He admitted himself to hospital with pneumonia on 27 May and died the next day. Ever since the debacle of his dismissal from the Camballin rice-growing project, he had been living austerely, balancing the boredom of a menial, poorly paid job as a government stores clerk with an adventurous life of the mind. He corresponded with Elizabeth about the visionary Jesuit priest, paleontologist, biologist and philosopher Pierre Teilhard de Chardin (1881–1955) whose work *The Phenomenon of Man* was rousing controversy in the late 1950s. Long before ecology was a common preoccupation, Teilhard de Chardin wrote of the sense of the earth as the only way to take humanity to a new state of peace and unity. And at the time of his death, Kim was writing a commentary on Kant's *Critique of Pure Reason*. Shaken and immeasurably sad, Mary and her daughter Julie packed up Kim's few possessions and took his voluminous papers back to Perth. His notes on the most recent version of *The Rock and the Sand* were waiting for her, seeming to reproach her delay. She took to heart his incisive comment that her last pages sounded like an after-dinner speech. Now she had to finish the book, if only for Kim's sake.

The Rock and the Sand was published in July 1969, a few days after another sudden, tragic death. Julie Miller, married only a few months, had just given the family the happy news that she was pregnant when she became seriously ill. A botched operation for appendicitis in her teenage years had left adhesions which combined with the pressure of the pregnancy caused a bowel obstruction. This was mistakenly entrusted to a small under-resourced hospital and Julie died from a blood clot to the heart after the operation. Mary woke to the 'cold hard reality of having lost, for this life at least, our bright and beautiful darling—the sunshine of our lives—and the little one she had looked forward to with such joyous expectation'.[18] Horrie must have grieved too, but it was not in his nature to share his feelings, and he did not attend his daughter's funeral.[19] Julie's sisters were desolate at the loss. Patsy—whose first child, Mary's first grandchild, was born a few months earlier—was living in Canada: she had to bear the

news alone. Robin, working as a flying nurse, was in Carnarvon
and was not called to Perth in time to see her sister.

It might have been a small comfort for Mary if *The Rock and the
Sand* had appeared with the attractive jacket that the talented Julie
had designed for it; instead Constable chose a drab and unenticing
cover. Too dazed to rejoice in this major work, Mary went back
within weeks to her usual activities. In public she seemed calm; no
one saw her weep openly. Her sorrow overflowed into her diary
and troubled her dreams: 'Dreaming of Julie. Just as in life but I
knew soon to disappear—wanting to hold her but knowing this
to be futile.'[20]

Within a few weeks of Julie's death Mary was back at work,
sorting out competing egos within the Fellowship of Australian
Writers, speaking on assimilation to the Country Women's
Association and afterwards choosing the winners in the jam,
pickle and cake competition. And after a brief interval of respect
for her grief, the claims on her time by aspiring authors were back
to their usual level.

One important intervention as editor and promoter was Mary's
work on *Wild Cat Falling*, a novel by a young man she first met in
1958 just as *Kings in Grass Castles* was close to completion. Colin
Johnson, as he was then known, was about to be released from
gaol, where, like many young Aborigines, he was serving a short
sentence for a minor offence. A country boy, he had nowhere to
go except back to the streets of Perth and more trouble. Mary
was critical of a system that imprisoned Aboriginal youths for
transgressions which would have earned no more than a reprimand
for a white youth. Moreover, Colin Johnson was represented to
her as a special case: 'he reads books', she was told. It was hard to
find accommodation that would keep him from reoffending, so

Mary took him into her own overcrowded house. Escorted by a probation officer, and looking sullen, this tall, thin nineteen-year-old, dressed in 'bodgie black', brought a small parcel of clothes and an uncooperative attitude.[21]

Colin Johnson had grown up in the farming town of Narrogin, one hundred and ninety kilometres south-west of Perth. Fatherless, with brothers and sisters scattered through the state, he had spent time in an orphanage, where he acquired some education. Having passed his junior public exams—a rare feat for an Aboriginal or mixed race boy—he had come to Perth in the hope of getting a job and studying for his matriculation. Mary Durack was astonished at the breadth of his reading; she thought him a 'natural intellectual'.[22] While she looked for ways to give him a new start in life, Colin was welcome to stay in her house. Bess Durack was horrified: "'But, my dear girl," she protested. "You can't think of having the boy stay—not with your girls in the house—and he looks such a..." words almost failing her "...desperado."[23]

After an initial stand-off, the newcomer became almost friendly towards the Miller girls; he entered into their arguments, listened to their pop music, explored their bookshelves. His prejudice against a family of pastoralist exploiters abated a little. Meanwhile, Mary's networking yielded a solution. To separate him from his former associates, she suggested a move to Melbourne. A cool, seemingly indifferent, 'Why not?' was as far as Colin would go in assent. With many misgivings Mary saw him off on the train to the big eastern city, thin and vulnerable in his black jeans, black shirt and an oversized flapping overcoat. Colin's wary manner, his veneer of toughness, was against him; so was his intellectual snobbishness. Mary doubted that she would hear from him again. But before long she had letters describing his journey and returning the

money she had lent him for his fare. He had accepted help from
the Aboriginal Advancement League and from the sympathetic
Barrett Reid of the State Library of Victoria, where he worked
as a cataloguer while studying for his leaving and matriculation.
Soon after came the first draft of a novel. Mary was impressed by
his ideas and his capacity for self-criticism. As he explained in a
letter to Mary, his novel was semi-autobiographical:

> The book concerns a part-Aboriginal boy trying to find
> himself and failing…a stupid, self-broken-down mess,
> barely existing. He is *not* myself, though a little perhaps
> of what I might have turned out.[24]

Back and forth across the Nullarbor, Mary's comments and Colin's
responses crossed and recrossed. She was no longer suspect as a
Lady Bountiful; he could respect her as a professional and take
her criticisms to heart. He accepted her ruling that 'Contradictions
are all right so long as the reader does not suspect it is the *writer's*
mind that is in a stew'.[25] After several years of intermittent work
on new drafts, Mary sent the completed work to Florence James,
her friend at Constable in London. 'What a thrill if we could see
this boy rise as a writer—the first articulate expression of the
mixed blood. No success that might ever come to me would give
me as much satisfaction.'[26]

When Florence James visited Australia in 1964, she and Mary
arranged to meet Colin Johnson at the Adelaide Writers' Festival.
Between them they persuaded Beatrice Davis of Angus & Robertson
to publish his novel. It appeared in 1965. A substantial foreword
by Mary Durack told the story of its evolution (playing down her
own part in it) and placed it as a landmark in Australian indigenous

writing. By this time, her endorsement carried the authority of the creator of *Kings in Grass Castles,* which had been published while *Wild Cat Falling* was still going through its many revisions. Her thirteen-page foreword also added bulk to a slender novella-length book, and an edgy semi-abstract jacket design, contributed by Elizabeth Durack, caught the 1960s counter-culture mood to which *Wild Cat Falling* was attuned.

Mary's delight in Colin Johnson's success was tempered by doubts about the book. Was it all a matter of timing and the author's identity? 'One wonders,' she wrote to Florence James, 'how many reviewers would have paid serious attention to a slim volume by C. Johnson if he had not been introduced as a part-Aboriginal and his background made interesting.'[27] Because much of the interest was her own creation, it was a difficult question.

Under its first proposed title *The Dispossessed,* and marketed as a statement of rebellious white youth, it would have had some immediate popular appeal but nothing like the fourteen reprints and 'set text' status in schools and universities that *Wild Cat Falling* enjoyed between 1965 and 1995. Toiling over the drafts of his novel, Mary sighed to Florence James about Colin Johnson's limitations. He had a 'gift of words' but was 'curiously lacking in imagination'. 'Will he ever see beyond the radius of his own rather dismal personality?'[28]

Introducing the 1992 reprint of *Wild Cat Falling*, which carried the author's Aboriginal name of Mudrooroo, the critic Stephen Muecke asked why it had taken so long for Aboriginal Australia to produce a novel. His conjecture: 'the novel was about the furthest one could move away from traditional Aboriginal genres.'[29] Poetry was closer to song, and dance to the corroboree. Oral narrative came close to the short story.

Mudrooroo became a major figure in indigenous writing.[30] In 1992, one of his sisters, who had done genealogical research on their family, announced that he was in fact of African descent. A sharp and sometimes angry debate followed, in which black and white readers argued as to the difference his racial origin made to the value of his work. Mary would probably have agreed with his defenders in the indigenous community, who said that his belief in his Aboriginal origin, even if mistaken, was crucial, and that because the book came from the experience of someone who had been treated as an Aborigine, it was authentic. She shared Muecke's view that, as the first to use the novel genre, Johnson/Mudrooroo had made a breakthrough.

Musing on the obstacles Mudrooroo had to overcome in using the genre of the novel, Stephen Muecke suggested that he was helped by the idea of the artist as an outcast from society, so that his hero, being both black and beatnik, was doubly alienated. The novel's scorn for white liberal university students came from the Aboriginal perspective but, with only a slight change in terms of attack, it would carry the anger of radical white youth against middle-class condescension:

> 'What I always think,' she comes in, 'it's not the natives need educating so much. It's the whites.'
>
> I guess from the way she looks at me that this is the closest she ever got to an Aboriginal. She offers me this chewed old bit of white corn as though expecting me to seize on it with pleased surprise. How broadminded, how perceptive to express a big, brave thought like that![31]

Editing and promoting *Wild Cat Falling* was only one of Mary's efforts to foster Aboriginal creativity. Watching a performance of *The Merchant of Venice* in the Broome convent school in 1967, she thought the play badly chosen for the children. The young Aborigines who played Portia and Antonio seemed to have little sense of the words. Surely a play could be found that would come closer to their experience and be more fun for actors and audience.

That was the impulse for *Ship of Dreams,* a musical play devised by Mary as a gift to Broome. She recruited a producer and a musical director in Perth, lined up accommodation for them in Broome at the hospitable Catholic presbytery, and tackled the complexities of getting the show on stage with a cast of seventy-two multi-racial children and extras which included a live goat and a cockatoo. Rehearsals were chaotic—the acting was uneven, the lines often indistinctly spoken— but its sheer gusto made up for limitations. The cockatoo was the star of the cast. Twelve Aboriginal boys were tutored by their elders in a corroboree sequence; all were correctly painted with white and yellow ochre by one of their grandfathers. Writing to her mother, Mary described the performance:

> Can you just imagine the scene around the Shire Hall with these boys darting about armed with spears and boomerangs among a bevy of girls and boys in Malay, Chinese and Japanese costume—and their proud parents crowding around the doors to get a look in?[32]

The event was magical for Broome and a triumph for Mary Durack. She went on stage with composer June Fitzgerald and the cast for a standing ovation led by Horrie in the front row. A dismal wet blanket in the beginning, Horrie was so proud and delighted with Mary's achievement that he arranged for the cast to form a surprise guard of honour at the airport when she left for Perth.

Mary's involvement in the Aboriginal Theatre Foundation, in the years following *Ship of Dreams*, took immense patience, time and travel. It included an ambitious production of an opera, loosely based on her novel *Keep Him My Country*, with music by well-known composer James Penberthy. Performed at the Sydney Opera House in July 1973 under the title *Dalgerie*, it took the novel's inter-racial love story as its central thread. It gave a cast of Aboriginal dancers the chance to show their art to a large audience of eastern city-dwellers. *Dalgerie* was well reviewed, and in spite of some tensions inside and outside the cast Mary counted it a success. And, forty years after its first staging, *Ship of Dreams* was performed again in Broome, where it was seen as a crucial step in local theatre and a multicultural event that was ahead of its time.

Through her friendship with South Australian Premier Don Dunstan, whom she had met at an Adelaide Writers' Festival, Mary became involved in the Aboriginal land rights issue. Her habit of mind was always that of the moderator, and in the debates of the 1970s she felt that divisions between 'goodies' and 'baddies' were not helping anyone. She had no faith in the interventions of Oodgeroo Noonuccal (Kath Walker), whom she thought 'phony' as an exponent of Aboriginal lore, overrated as a poet, and an unfortunate influence in stirring Judith Wright to oversimplify the matter of mining leases in the Kimberley.[33] But she admired and liked Nugget Coombs, the chairman of the Australian Council of Aboriginal Affairs, and worked well with him. His long-standing relationship with Wright was not then generally known but their alliance in matters of indigenous policy was strong and influential, and both of them adopted Oodgeroo as a protégé.

Mary's energies on behalf of the Aborigines were dedicated

to whatever causes came her way provided they enhanced pride in indigenous culture and understanding between the races. An important stage came in 1967 after a referendum in which white Australia finally acknowledged the rights of the Aborigines to be counted as citizens of the nation.[34] After that came equal pay, land rights, recognition of sacred places: all good and overdue decisions, but none of them without complications. Mary robustly defended the granting of drinking rights to Aborigines, and, even though she lived to see the disasters that followed, she held firmly to the principle of equality. By nature an optimist, Mary was a realist in practice. Throughout the next decades she held to the view she had summarised in the epilogue to *The Rock and the Sand*:

> Postwar Australian policy, in a precipitate effort to prove its social conscience to the world, had so far done little more for the natives of the north than to deprive them of the few important things they had clung to in their subjection. They had acquired a sense of importance without incentive or self-respect, freedom with nowhere to go, a living without a way of life.[35]

CHAPTER 10

'We Lose Everything that We Belong'

Every year from the early 1960s until the end of her life, Mary Durack went north to see the Aborigines whom she had known when they were all young together. The visits became more important to her than ever when she realised how fragile their common memories had become. Dispossessed in the late nineteenth century, the Miriwoong people had been displaced again. After 1950, when the Peel River Land and Mineral Company (a branch of the Australian Agricultural Company) bought out the Connor, Doherty & Durack holdings and the old Ivanhoe homestead burned down, there was still work for station Aborigines. The 1967 legislation for equal pay for pastoral workers looked like a victory for natural justice. Aboriginal stockmen, whose skills and hard work had made life in a harsh land possible for the pastoralists, were getting their due.

But, as so often before, the Aborigines lost out. As unpaid workers on the stations, they had some compensations for what

Mary Durack uncompromisingly called 'their subjection'.[1] Their extended families—women, children and old people—were maintained on the land to which they all belonged. This seemed the one thing of value in an exploitative system. But worse was to come. When equal pay legislation gave station owners the choice of paying the same wages to black as to white men, they chose white workers because they were thought more reliable—they did not go walkabout, and they had no 'hangers on'. In the blink of an eye, it seemed, the station camps at Ivanhoe and Argyle were emptied of their people. More than half a century of experience in the cattle industry was thrown away, and the stockmen, who had been indirectly supporting their families, were judged worthless. The government provided a reserve some distance away, where the new township of Kununurra would emerge. And there they all were, living on welfare with access to the destructive 'grog' and nothing to do. With some honorable exceptions, like the Kilfoyles at Rosewood, station owners in the cattle country made the change with brutal indifference. The viewpoint of the former stockmen, ignored at the time, is seen in such recent memoirs as John Watson's 'We Know This Country':

> Hundreds of people [in the Kimberley] were forced to leave the stations they'd grown up on and live in appalling conditions in town reserves. Those station managers just came out and said, 'We can't afford to pay you the basic wage and we can't afford to keep feeding you. The welfare mob have lots of money for you to live in the town. So pack up your camp and start walking.'[2]

Displacement was not the only unintended consequence of equal pay for equal work, though it was surely the cruellest. Women all over Australia lost their jobs, or had trouble finding new ones, because men were thought more competent and, as heads of households, more deserving. The women's movement of the 1970s produced articulate leaders to argue their case. The Aborigines were too few and were then unready to make their voices heard. Meantime, their skills were being devalued. The droving days were ending. Better roads meant cattle trucks instead of the leisurely moving of the mobs across country. Eventually, mustering by helicopter would make horsemanship almost irrelevant. Aborigines could have driven the trucks and flown helicopters, and some did. But more often than not, they became dispirited town-dwellers.

Mary Durack was saddened by the way the new deal was marginalising those in greatest need. No one could have worked harder than she did to bring about equality. She underestimated the speed with which the station owners moved into a new era of change, but even when confronted with the facts of redundancies and the disastrous effects of access to alcohol she maintained that equal pay was right and had to come. Her efforts went into any activity that could raise the public image of Aborigines and foster their pride. The Aboriginal Theatre Foundation took an immense amount of her time, as did the Sydney Opera House production of *Dalgerie*. Years of unpaid work, which took time from her writing, taught her a great deal about the hopes and frustrations of new generations of Aborigines who were more politically aware than most of the station people she knew. Because she had connections with both the older generation and the articulate young, she gained an unusual insight into problems which politicians and academics were apt to simplify.

Usually a peacemaker in the family, Mary began to argue with

Reg. He was still employing Aborigines on Kildurk and educating their children along with his own, but he was complaining that the workers were unreliable and lazy. Year after year Mary went to the reserve at Kununurra for reunions with the women who called themselves her 'chisters'. She brought parcels for the whole community: secondhand clothing, tobacco and sweets, and tubes of an anti-inflammatory remedy, Denco-Rub (known as Dingo-Rub), for their rheumatic pains. Dot, Marie, Ruby and the others were now grandmothers. They had stories to tell about their recent and remote past. As always, Mary was carrying pencil and paper, and she began to use a tape recorder to put down the memories that would otherwise be lost.

For Mary, a dramatic moment came in 1972 with the damming of the Ord River and the creation of Lake Argyle. The lake, nine times greater in capacity than Sydney Harbour, drowned Argyle homestead. In giving years of her time to *The Rock and the Sand*, Mary had deferred the second volume that was to follow *Kings in Grass Castles*. Now she felt the need to get back to that work:

> I remember almost the precise moment when I knew that I must carry on [with the family story]. It was in 1972, watching the waters of the Ord River dam rising above the site of the Argyle homestead, blotting out the course of the Behn River and its tributary creeks, drowning the yards and the cattle camps and the sacred sites of the Miriwoong tribespeople. People kept asking me how do you feel? I don't really know how I felt but I do know that I heard, like the voice of doom, a clear command from somewhere or other to take up my pen again and put down the rest

of the story before it too had disappeared under the flood waters of time and change.[3]

The opening ceremony of the Ord River dam, which prompted Mary to record all she could from living memory for a sequel to *Kings in Grass Castles*, was a sad experience for many of the Duracks, but sadder for the Aborigines.

The old homestead would later be represented in the somewhat ersatz form of a museum—an idea that Elizabeth thought 'outlandish'. She refused to attend the opening ceremony in 1972. It was too painful a reminder of Kim, whose years of endeavour to bring carefully planned irrigation to the Kimberley had been frustrated by political and commercial interests.

Bess Durack, who had not seen the north for many years, was persuaded to make the journey with Mary. Perfectly skilled, at the age of eighty-nine, in the art of making conversation with important personages whose names she had forgotten, she chatted with Prime Minister William McMahon and his wife Sonia. In all the self-congratulatory speeches, the Duracks were mentioned as pioneers and former pastoralists, but no one gave credit, or even seemed to know, that the first idea of revitalising the Kimberley by using the Ord for irrigation came from Kim's expedition in the Ord Gorge in 1941. Only four years after his death, it was hard for his mother to accept that he was forgotten. But Bess joined in bravely, even taking a boat trip on the vast waters of newly created Lake Argyle. Down there, she conjectured, was the dining room; and there the remnants of the garden she had tried to make. MPD had brought her to this place, travelling from Wyndham in slow stages by horse and buggy. She could not hold back a lament: 'How could I think [the dam] such a wonderful venture when, because of it, so much that I loved and lived for is drowned for ever?'[4] A lament from Bulla, one of the Argyle Aborigines, was more poignant. 'We feel we lose everything that we belong.'[5]

Mary spent four months in Kununurra, recording memories. Two old stockmen moved into the house she was then occupying and talked non-stop 'except for the occasional nap' for several days. All this and more went onto her tape recorder. Her work extended far beyond the needs of Sons in the Saddle. Although much was being lost in the 1970s, her documentation of the mythology and genealogy of the Kimberley and Dampierland Aborigines was a major work of conservation. Many weeks with notebook and tape recorder safeguarded the memories of Aboriginal communities. She did it alone and for no profit.

She found the Aborigines surprisingly objective about the past, 'recalling events with no hint of bitterness', talking about the white people with neither praise nor blame.[6] She sought out rock paintings in remote places, asked for historical records from the new owners of former Durack properties, looked for gravestones overgrown with weeds, and arranged for some of them to be moved to the Argyle Homestead Museum. With her luggage weighed down with tapes and notes, she went back to Perth well aware that far more than Durack memories went under the waters.

On the flight home, a poem began to compose itself in her head. It was stirred by the sight of an old woman, Maggie Wallaby, catching fish and unaccountably throwing them back into the lake. For Mary, the lake was an ending. 'That's that,' she thought, as the waters closed over the land she knew so well. Maggie seemed to see it differently. Her words, imagined by Mary, brought a message of renewal:

I got to tell that fish: 'You go back—go back now—talk
strong my country. You tell him that spirit can't leave 'em.
You tell him—Wait! Hang on! *This not the finish!*...
Might be close up, might be fifty t'ousand year...
Little fish, you tell him....
Some time you gonna see that sun again. You gonna find
all that moon and star. You gonna feel that warm wind
blowing. *You gonna look-out that sky!*'[7]

Mary's 'Lament for the Drowned Country' grew out of these
words. Written as if in the voice of Maggie, it has been judged her
finest poem. At a later time, her creation of a first-person voice
for Maggie Wallaby might have been questioned. In 1972 it was
taken as she intended it, as a work of empathy and imaginative
identification. Its conclusion reflects Mary's capacity for hope.

All through the 1970s that hopeful temperament was tested in
a time of losses. Without consulting Mary, Horrie sold the Broome
house in 1971 and announced his intention of living in Perth. Ansett
had already taken over MacRobertson Miller Airlines, in 1963.
His rural properties, Dampier Downs and its equally ill-chosen
successor Debesa, were sold at a loss. Horrie had no strong reason
to stay in Broome. Losing the Broome house was a sad deprivation
for Mary and the rest of the Miller family, for whom the northern
base meant winter warmth and holiday pleasures. Horrie's return
to Perth was a gloomy prospect; he would have nothing to do and
he would resent Mary's busy life. Their marriage worked best
when they each had a separate sphere.

Tragedy struck the family in May 1974 when Robin, Mary
and Horrie's second daughter, was diagnosed with a secondary
melanoma. Only six years after Julie's death, it could hardly be

believed or endured. Robin was a beautiful, vibrant young woman, a source of strength and pride within the family. Her training as a triple-certificated nurse, followed by qualification as a commercial pilot, had led to a remarkable career. Mary helped her with a book about her experiences, entitled *Flying Nurse*. This was succeeded by *Sugarbird Lady* which took its title from Robin's work of giving the Salk polio vaccine with sugar cubes to outback children. Horrie's pride in a daughter who followed his example in aviation was unbounded. It broke his habit of thrift; he gave her two planes in quick succession. But neither he nor Mary had been happy about Robin's marriage to Harold Dicks, a medical practitioner more than twice her age, with a reputation as a womaniser. As a partner in Robin's career, however, Harold offered some advantages. Mary and Horrie tolerated him and accepted his advice, sometimes mistakenly, in medical matters.

Medical treatment could not save Robin. She struggled to get back to work after major surgery, flew again, dealt calmly with innumerable cases of accident, disease and death in the outback, until her cancer recurred. Robin died in Perth in December 1975. She had asked to be buried in Broome, and, with the ashes of her sister Julie reclaimed from the Perth grave of her grandfather MPD, her depleted family flew north. A line from Antoine de Saint-Exupéry's *Night Flight* was chosen as Robin's epitaph: 'Can these be the same stars? Is this the same sky? How bright, how clear, what safety I have reached.'

Back in Perth after that desolate day in Broome, Mary was stoic in public. Her diaries show the intensity of her grief. It was against nature for a mother to lose an adult child; to have this tragedy repeated was beyond words. In Robin's death she felt the death of Julie all over again. Recalling the buzz and laughter, the arguments, the parties, and the phone calls from boyfriends that had enlivened her household when her four daughters were growing up, Mary took comfort in her first grandchild, Patsy's daughter Naomi, and in knowing that Marie Rose, recently married, was pregnant. Horrie sat in a darkened room, inconsolable. Bess Durack, in failing health, needed constant visits and supervision. Mary felt herself drowning in sorrows and obligations. No one could rescue her; she had to do it herself. On impulse she escaped for a few days to the Adelaide Writers' Festival, where her sociable self revived a little in the company of other writers: Geoffrey Dutton, Les Murray, Morris West, Tom Shapcott, Dorothy Hewett, Kath Walker. Instead of a formal contribution to the program, Mary read her poem 'Lament for the Drowned Country', which was doubly apt in that time of loss. In reflective mood, she recorded an interview for the National Library in which she summed up her writing career almost as if it had come to an end. She was sixty-three; did it have to be past tense?

> I feel that I have never reached my potential as a writer. I could have written a very great deal more and better than I ever have, though in some ways, perhaps, it is surprising that I wrote anything at all. Perhaps I enjoyed life too much, enjoyed being a person with lots of people in my life. I could have been more disciplined, perhaps less outgoing and more ruthless.[8]

There was no sign of ruthlessness to come. While Constable waited for the sequel to *Kings in Grass Castles*, Mary took on the thankless task of collaborating with Bishop Jobst on a film which he insisted must avoid being 'controversial'—as he thought *The Rock and the*

Sand had been—about Catholic missionary work. Mary's only reward was spending time in Broome and seeing some unfamiliar desert country from the air.

Another distraction, though a more satisfying one than the Bishop's naive and sentimental film, was a script for a one-woman stage performance for actress Nita Pannell. *Swan River Saga* was performed in 1972. Based on the story of the pioneer Eliza Shaw, it was published by Constable of London in December 1976. *Swan River Saga* was another example of Mary Durack's capacity to create a major work from seemingly casual beginnings. Pannell won praise as the white woman's voice from the past, but when she rehearsed a public reading of 'Lament for the Drowned Country' she could not manage the Aboriginal speech rhythms. Mary took over, and read it herself with such feeling that many in the Perth audience were in tears before she reached the last line.[9]

The sequel to *Kings in Grass Castles* was sidelined once more in September 1977 when Horrie had a stroke. His left side was paralysed and his speech was blurred, but his determination to remain in control of his life did not falter. If he could leave hospital and have Mary to care for him, he was sure that he would soon be on his feet again. He did not cooperate with physiotherapists and in a total rejection of hospital care he refused to eat unless Mary fed him. A short trial of home care at Christmas failed dismally. Even with nursing help at home and a house redesigned to take a wheelchair, it was clear to everyone except Horrie that his care would be too much for Mary. Angry and unhappy, he suspected her of planning to put him in the Sunset Home at the end of their street. This was in fact the practical course to take, but it was deferred in the face of Horrie's absolute conviction that he could manage at home—'which means he is sure I can,' Mary said. After some delay following a fall in which he broke a hip, Horrie was discharged from hospital in April 1978. Mary's days and nights as a full-time carer made writing almost impossible. Her diary entries told the story:

> All night up and down to change the bed and full time attention needed to get through the day. He is not responsive to callers, consistently gloomy—not wanting to turn on radio, TV, read papers or even talk to anyone…He sleeps all day and is fitful and restless at night.[10]

With Horrie's misery her main concern, it was hard for Mary to enjoy the public honours that came to her in 1978. The new year began with the announcement of her being made a Dame of the British Empire, an honour conferred by the Governor-General Sir Zelman Cowen in a small private ceremony in Perth. In April she was awarded an honorary Doctorate of Letters by the University of Western Australia. Her speech, in which she did her graceful duty in acknowledging the honour, included a passage with a certain asperity. Mary hoped that the degree would be seen as an acknowledgment of the true role of the writer in the community. Writers, she said, should not become 'off the cuff speakers on current affairs, substitutes for general enquiry bureaus or literary plastic surgeons trained to turn a sow's ear manuscript into a silk purse'.[11] It was a neat summary of Mary's own pitfalls.

Being Dame Mary Durack was a pleasure, but it brought an added sense of obligation. So did a three-year grant from the Literature Board of the Australia Council. The money was welcome. It meant that she could pay for secretarial help, which she needed more than ever. Dealing with hundreds of letters of congratulation on her new honours turned the daily flow of correspondence, which had always been heavy, into a tsunami. Her only solution was to get up earlier. An hour or two each day spared for the family history did not take her far with a major task. The complex sources—letters, diaries, account books, photographs—demanded sustained time and thought.

In September 1978, when Horrie had been at home for five months in her care, Mary decided to end *Sons in the Saddle* at 1920, leaving the final section, up to her father's death in 1950, for a third volume. It was still a big project, but the revised plan deferred dealing with some sensitive issues, not least the sale of the stations. The time span of *Sons in the Saddle*, cut back to three decades, was tricky enough. Instead of the single-focus rags-to-riches story of *Kings in Grass Castles* with Patsy Durack at the centre, the second stage had to deal with Patsy's four sons and two daughters, and a new generation of cousins, many of whom were involved in the story. Too much attention to MPD would upset the cousins whose viewpoint had to be respected. Mary tried to be fair to everyone, but it was hard to keep her uncles John and Patrick Durack equally in mind with her father and hold the narrative line. And telling the whole story of the Connor, Doherty & Durack enterprise, what went wrong, and who was to blame, brought up larger questions.

Mary's own perspective on family history was developing too. Beyond the personal story was the changing scene of Australian policy on Aboriginal affairs and the pastoral industry. In the 1950s it had been possible to give a romantic spin to the overland adventure of Patsy Durack and his team. Not so in the late 1970s. The droving days were over. Station life had changed irrevocably. She and Elizabeth had thought that Mrs Aeneas Gunn's *We of the Never-Never* was a fairy tale. Now her own version of 1930s station

life in *All-About* was being scrutinised. Historians were taking a
sharp look at the period she remembered. Mary knew that the days
when she was 'young Missus' had long since ended. The changes
were dramatised for the family in 1973 when the newly elected
government of Gough Whitlam resumed Reg Durack's lease of
Kildurk, and returned it to its traditional owners. Reg was well
compensated; his sons did not want to succeed him; his wife Enid
had always wanted to retire to Perth. It was a step in the right
direction for the Aborigines. All the same, as Mary struggled with
faded ink on the documents of the family story, she had to ask, as
Elizabeth had asked in 1950: 'what had it all been for?'

That question came back in 1979 with the opening of the Argyle
Homestead Museum. This was a reconstruction of the homestead
that had gone under the waters when the Ord River was dammed.
Mary, Elizabeth and Reg went north to the opening. The sisters
were filmed for an ABC documentary in which an interviewer
asked how they felt about the enterprise. Mary dwelt on the losses
the indigenous people had suffered in the drowning of their 'born
country', the suddenness with which station life had ended, the lack
of work opportunities to replace the old order. Elizabeth spoke of
the failure of her father and others of his generation to see more
in the land than commercial gain. Neither of them wanted to say
much about the homestead itself; even as a museum it was flawed.
Very little had been salvaged of the original. The stone house, with
its wide paved verandah and six rooms, followed Mary's directions
accurately enough and the garden was well laid out. And there
were some evocative photographs and other displays. But without
the separate kitchen, and with none of the outbuildings, it lacked
a full sense of Argyle's eighty years as a working station. Below
the waters of the lake, so divers reported, the saddles still rested

on their wooden horses, the mule chains hung from the rafters and the laundry taps could still be turned, though for no purpose.

With images of displacement in mind, Mary returned to *Sons in the Saddle*. Her depleted energies in times of change and loss may be seen in its tone and structure. She had plenty of material; in fact she had too much. At times the narrative supplies little more than connecting passages between extracts from her father's diaries. In taking 1920 as her cut-off point, Mary argued that this was a key period for the second generation of Duracks. Her father had seen 1920 as the start of an era of expansion in pastoral and mineral development with new means of communication, better roads and river crossings. As an eight-year-old in 1921 Mary had witnessed the historic moment of Norman Brearley's take-off on his inaugural flight north, with her father a passenger. Although one of Brearley's three Bristol aircraft crashed near Geraldton, the resilient MPD spoke to journalists of the wonders of this new age of air travel. With this moment as the dominant image of the last pages of *Sons in the Saddle,* Mary gave a muted open ending, rather than one of doubt and defeat. Although she forecast 'more adversity than prosperity', she closed with a reminder of her father's motto: 'Travel hopefully and trust in God.'

The book was still a work in progress, with drafts of each chapter awaiting revision, when Mary had a near-fatal accident. On a wild winter night in 1979, she helped Horrie to bed and set out for a party. She parked her car and walked in drizzling rain to the median strip on Stirling Highway. Did she start to cross, and stumble into the path of an oncoming kombi van? She never knew. Her injuries were serious: a fractured skull, some spinal injuries, two compound fractures of the left leg, a shattered kneecap and fractured pelvis. She regained consciousness, and even began, after

a few days, to pick up her diary and try to make sense of what
had happened to her. Neurosurgeons decided to operate on the
skull, from which, alarmingly, fluid was still leaking days after the
accident. When the leakage stopped suddenly, Mary half-believed
it was a miraculous intervention:

> Doctor says he will operate on my skull tomorrow. A
> call from somewhere. Broome? Derby? They said from
> Aborigines and wheeled me into the corridor where I took
> the phone to hear the voice of Paddy Roe saying he had
> organised a ceremonial singing of me back to health—they
> were all painted up and bearing magical totems. I heard,
> or at least seemed to hear them chanting. Anyway their
> message of love got through.[12]

In Mary's absence, Horrie had been taken to the Sunset Home,
where with gritted teeth he waited for her recovery. It took five
weeks in hospital and a further period in rehabilitation before Mary
was allowed home, her leg still in plaster, in December 1979. A
few weeks later, Horrie began a regimen of days at his house and
nights in the Sunset Home. Some home help was arranged but
Horrie still called on Mary to take him to the bathroom: an almost
impossible feat while she still carried the weight of her plaster
cast. During that last miserable year of Horrie's life, Mary had the
added sorrow of her mother's death, in April 1980, at the age of
ninety-five. Bess Durack's decline was gentle; her memory faded
but her charm remained. Horrie had a second stroke and died in
September 1980, at the age of eighty-seven. Stoically, Mary had
said: 'I married him for better and for worse and this patch just
happens to be the worst.'[13] Horrie's barely articulated last words,

'Thanks Mum, and God bless you,' ended nearly forty-two years of marriage.[14] He was buried in Broome beside his two daughters, Robin and Julie.

Mary never fully recovered from her accident. As well as permanent damage to her knee, she sustained some memory loss, her ability to concentrate weakened, and her handwriting, always quick and confident, became shaky. Her olfactory nerve had been severed, so she could not smell flowers or enjoy the taste of food, unless it was highly spiced, or drink, unless it had some kind of a kick in it.[15] She would not give up her busy public life, her travels north or her writing, but every achievement was hard won.

As well as her Kimberley interludes, Mary's work for the Stockman's Hall of Fame in Longreach, on which she served as a board member, kept her from her writing. Yet the journeys were a pleasure, and they helped to keep her connections with Queensland friends and the many Durack and Tully cousins.

The big challenge was to finish *Sons in the Saddle*. Even in its truncated form, with the cut-off point of 1920, it was still a substantial book. In some ways it was a more scholarly history than *Kings in Grass Castles*. With her father's diaries beside her as she wrote, there was no need, or temptation, to invent. There is nothing in *Sons in the Saddle* to resemble Patsy Durack's inner monologues and reveries which, although they may be based on letters and hearsay, show Mary Durack the novelist at work. The sequel has a large number of endnotes which help to document the story. *Kings in Grass Castles* had no notes, and its index, compiled in London, left out the names of the Aborigines, even those who play a major part in the story. In the 1930s Mary had questioned the use of those 'silly names', but as these men were not known by their indigenous names she had no choice. She had Pumpkin,

Boxer and Ulysses restored to the index in later editions of *Kings in Grass Castles* and made sure they were included in the index of *Sons in the Saddle*.

Mary's faith in Kim Durack's reparation to the damaged land had helped to make *Kings in Grass Castles* a hopeful book. His death, followed by the doubtful venture of the Ord River dam, must have been in her mind as she wrote the last chapters of *Sons in the Saddle*. As a chronicle of the middle years of her father's life, closely following his diaries, it is perhaps more enlightening than the romance of Patsy Durack, but less appealing to the general reader.

A dramatised version of *Kings in Grass Castles* was made for television; Mary did her best to edit the script but she could not save it from clichés of heroic overlanders battling their way to the Promised Land. Rupert Murdoch approached Mary for the film rights. This came to nothing, but the outback northern romance genre persisted in Australian cinema with Chips Rafferty riding westward and Crocodile Dundee not far behind.

As a respected public figure Mary Durack was much in demand to speak on the issues of the time, including Aboriginal land rights. Mediation was her style, not confrontation, and if her accident had not damaged her health she could have played an even stronger part in the 1980s movements. The belief of her friend, Aboriginal leader Albert Barunga, 'We got to go arm in arm or we get nowhere', was her belief too.

In failing health all through the late 1980s, Mary was found to have an inoperable cancer. Her last visit to her 'chisters' of the Ivanhoe years, in 1993, was made easier by the owners of Carlton Hill and Ivanhoe stations, David and Susan Bradley, with whom she had formed a good friendship in recent years. Mary's daughter

Patsy described this final journey of memory:

> Transported from Kununurra to Carlton in an Ultralite helicopter, she found herself as if in a dream…Down she swooped, skimming the Ord, hovering over House Roof Hill (never before had she seen the top of this so familiar landmark) blowing a myriad of birds from the Ivanhoe Billabong, chasing kangaroo and galloping cattle across the land of her first memories. Beyond the agricultural plots fed by the lake and the place where her brother Kim had first set up his long-ago vision of green pastures, she took a turn above the Argyle Museum site where within a blink of time would stand her own grave. Later there had been a boat trip with the old 'chisters' Daisy, Marie, Peggy, Sheba and Dot—a picnic at Black Rock the waterhole of her youthful idyll.
>
> As the moment came for her departure the Aboriginal women, knowing they would never see her again, began to beat their heads and wail inconsolably. But she was aloft and away to Broome…And there it goes, beneath the wing, the red peninsula jutting into turquoise sea, the white stretch of Cable Beach, the waves breaking against the jumbled rocks of Gantheaume Point where Horrie plucked the big fish from the mountainous breakers. It goes and goes and goes forever…[16]

Mary Durack lived her last days in the house in Bellevue Avenue, Perth, where she had come, newly married, in 1940. Messages of love and concern came from all over Perth and from Kununurra, where, as Susan Bradley told her, the 'Aboriginal relations were singing her better'.[17] Dreams of the past, as she drifted towards death, were sometimes happy, sometimes fearful. One came from a story she had heard about the accidental burns that an Aboriginal child had sustained. Between sleeping and waking, Mary called out: 'Oh help me, don't let me roll into the campfire.'[18] Her daughters Patsy and Marie Rose looked after her at home. Taking the final night shift, Patsy held her to the end and sang her to sleep.

Mary Durack died on 16 December 1994, and was buried, as she had wished, in the garden of the Argyle Homestead Museum, in her 'spirit country'.[19]

CHAPTER 11

The Making of Eddie Burrup

'Mary, my mistakes are my life. If it wasn't for them God bless them I would still be at 184 [Goderich Street].'[1] Elizabeth's words to Mary in 1944 resonated late in her life, when Mary was no longer there to counsel her impetuous sister. Ever since childhood, Elizabeth had relied on Mary for support in her ventures. Not that she always accepted Mary's advice, but it was there to make her stop and think. Sometimes she wanted to be stopped, as when she asked Mary's opinion on a marriage proposal from millionaire William Buckland. Without her older sister, she often said, she would be 'rudderless'.[2] If Mary had lived on as a moderating influence, Elizabeth might have paused before embroiling herself in the biggest tangle of a life that was lived without calculation.

At Christmas 1994, less than two weeks after Mary's death, Elizabeth showed some new paintings to Perpetua, who was then visiting Perth from Broome where she was running an art gallery. Perpetua was astonished by what seemed to be a new direction.

These were 'somehow Aboriginal works', she said, different from
Elizabeth's landscapes with Aboriginal figures, or semi-abstracts
with Aboriginal themes. Elizabeth described them as 'morphological'
works, concerned with the underlying connections between animate
and inanimate forms. Perpetua thought the work was brilliant,
'more striking and pure' than anything her mother had ever done.
But what could possibly come of it? In the 1990s, with indigenous
art reaching new heights of interest and acclaim, these paintings
would be ignored as the work of a seventy-nine-year-old white
woman. There would be no point in exhibiting them. If they had
been painted by a man, an Aboriginal man, Perpetua said, they
would be on the walls of the National Gallery. But Elizabeth would
never use a *nom de brush*. Or...would she?

No more was said. A few days later, as mother and daughter
were walking beside the Swan River, Elizabeth came back to the
idea of exhibiting the paintings under a pseudonym. She already
had an idea about their creator, a second self whom she would call
Eddie Burrup. He was an amalgam of some Aboriginal men she
had known: among them old Jubul, with whom she had painted
beside the Ord, Boxer the stockman and mainstay of Argyle Station,
and Jeffrey Chunuma, whom she and Mary had first known as
an enchanting, mischievous little boy at Ivanhoe.

Elizabeth's diary entry for 1 December 1994 describes the
'morphological works' as 'very private—and removed from the
work I might exhibit or be asked for or the work I guess with
which I am associated'.[3] Yet their inspiration could be traced
back to the wild *Flightless Birds,* and *The Rim* paintings, which
were wilder still. A later entry refers to the tumult of feeling at
the time of Mary's death on 16 December. And on 28 December,
Eddie Burrup was born.

During the Christmas and New Year break, Eddie Burrup took on a shape. In a mood of intense excitement—perhaps a *folie à deux* between mother and daughter—Eddie's history was created. If his work were to be shown, he would need a public identity, including a photograph. Elizabeth's account of the search (unpublished in her lifetime) shows the element of heedless mischief in the Burrup creation. In a temporary escape into unreality from the desolation of Mary's death, Elizabeth and Perpetua went looking for the props needed for the masquerade. Elizabeth's diary traced the process:

There was a serious, almost a reverential atmosphere within the walls of Doyle's Fancy Costumes. Oh! and what walls! From floor to high ceiling they were lined with a phantasmagoria of every article of apparel and every object of disguise ever devised by man or woman to camouflage or conceal, to deceive and belie, to falsify and to misrepresent, to inspire laughter and merriment, to evoke tears, fears, horror or dismay.

Doyle's have been in the serious business of make-believe for three generations. Mr Doyle was courteous and helpful. What was it we were after?

'Something for a bushman—the old style of bushman— not the Reg Williams, not the Tamworth Country-and-Western bushman...' and my eyes were combing the shelves.

'Something more on the lines of Waltzing Matilda?'

'Yes. More like that—like *that*,' and I pointed to Eddie Burrup's hat on the second row from the top.

The long retrieving pole required an extension but eventually a soft furry object with a battered brim and a hole in the crown landed on the counter. From a long row of wigs and beards one intuitively found its way beside the hat. We walked out of the shop with Eddie Burrup's materialising shadow in hand.[4]

The life story came easily. Elizabeth gave Eddie her own birthdate of 1915. He came from the Pilbara region; he had been to a convent school for a few years; he had been in jail twice for minor offences; he had worked as a stockman. From an early age he had made drawings of native animals and station life, just as Elizabeth had done. Eddie was 'he', spoken of in the third person, friend and companion of Elizabeth, his chosen vessel. Did she believe in him? It seems that she did. With Eddie beside her, she felt an extraordinary freedom and happiness. Trying to explain him to herself she looked for definitions:

> Alter ego (Latin lit.) a second self (a) trusted friend (b) a confidential representative (c) a guardian spirit…in S. America a carving of an animal on head, back or shoulders… (so much for Webster's, try Roget's Thesaurus)
>
> Self: I, myself/subconscious…friend…close acquaintance, bosom friend, best friend…fellow man…lover…likeness… analogue, counterpart, reciprocal mate, soulmate… companion…twin…second self…*fidus Achates*…confidant, alter ego.[5]

Back in her Broome gallery, Perpetua gave Eddie his first chance. His work was included in a mixed exhibition in January 1995. All through the year, the Burrups were hanging in the gallery, but not for sale. Offers to buy them were refused. At the end of the year, a small crack appeared in Eddie's retaining wall. The Christmas card sent out from the gallery was presented as his work and was much admired. One of many appreciative comments came from the Director of the Tandanya Institute in South Australia who invited Eddie Burrup to send in some works to a forthcoming exhibition, *Native Titled Now*. Eddie/Elizabeth agreed, and three paintings were shown in Adelaide in April 1996. As before, they were 'not for sale'. Another invitation came in June 1996. Two Burrups were entered in Telstra's 13th National Aboriginal and Torres Strait Islander Art Awards and were shown in Darwin between August and October 1996.

Thus far, Eddie/Elizabeth had a measure of success. No one questioned the authenticity of the paintings and they had been admired when hung among other indigenous works. The next stage, more dangerous, came about by chance. One day in Broome, Elizabeth's brother Bill and his wife Noni were 'minding the shop' for Perpetua, when a buyer made an offer for a Burrup. Pleased with their marketing skills, and knowing nothing about the painter's true identity, Bill and Noni accepted the offer. Perpetua let the sale go through, and once on the slippery slope, she sold several more before allowing herself to consider the implications of the sales.

In September 1996, Perpetua was ready to end the whole masquerade. But Eddie/Elizabeth had one more idea. This was to enter a Burrup for the Sulman Prize, an award for the best subject painting, genre painting or mural project by an Australian artist. For Perpetua, signing off for Eddie in this national competition, with judges appointed by the Art Gallery of New South Wales, was a bridge too far. It was time for the phantom identity to be declared. As soon as that was done, Perpetua would offer to buy back the Burrups sold from her gallery. Elizabeth agreed. She invited Robert Smith, an art historian and contributor to *Art Monthly Australia*, to hear and publish the whole story. They met at her Perth studio in September 1996. Rather than giving Eddie a quiet introduction into public life, Smith's article prompted headline news throughout Australia. And the world came to Elizabeth's door.

Reactions varied. Some commentators were indignant; others sympathetic but puzzled. Why would Elizabeth Durack, well known and long established, choose to exhibit under a pseudonym? Any success that came to Eddie would be his, not hers.

There were other words for what she had done—fraud, hoax, imposture—and these were freely used. Yet none seems quite right. Perhaps the way to start is to ask why, at seventy-nine, Elizabeth wanted a new identity. It was not just a question of putting on Eddie Burrup's hat and having a game at the expense of the art establishment, though that may have been part of it. She wanted a new voice, a new way of seeing. Inspiration came when she distanced her Elizabeth Durack self from the work in progress. There was someone beside her, controlling her brush, the companion whom she chose to call Eddie Burrup. She wrote:

> I felt happy and confident and full of optimism about Eddie Burrup. He was on his way. ED could relax now, hand the reins over to him and settle back into the understood and acceptable role of 'wonderful old woman'.[6]

The use of a male pseudonym has been a common strategy for women writers. Charlotte Brontë trembled at the thought of meeting the great world; she also knew that her work was not what a clergyman's daughter should be writing. Her Currer Bell pseudonym gave her freedom to explore passion and violence. Her sisters Emily and Anne Brontë wrote as Ellis and Acton Bell. Mary Ann Evans chose the pen name of George Eliot in realistic awareness that as a man's work her novels had a better chance of being taken seriously. In a further complication of authorial identity, she was living openly with George Henry Lewes, a married man. As Eliot, she gave her virtuous heroines the respectability she herself had discarded.

Contemporary examples of dual writing identities include such highly respected figures as Joyce Carol Oates and John Banville. Oates found it liberating to become Rosamund Smith; Banville's dense poetic style yields to the fast moving narratives of Benjamin Black. While Banville and Oates lighten up for a general readership, the popular crime writer Ruth Rendell looks on the dark side when she writes as Barbara Vine.

The double self of the expatriate Australian writer Ethel Florence Robertson, née Richardson, is more complex and closer to Elizabeth Durack's invention of a persona. Ethel Robertson, the author insisted, did not write *The Fortunes of Richard Mahony,* (1917–1929) or anything else. The work belonged to Henry Handel Richardson. Her identity as the wife of a London academic shrank almost to nothing. Mrs Robertson gave orders to the cook; Henry sat at his desk and wrote. In hundreds of letters to her French translator, some of them quite intimate, there was no hint that the signature 'Henry H. Richardson' was that of her alter ego, her male self.

There are parallels here with Eddie Burrup. Elizabeth Durack wanted her new paintings to be taken seriously. As a white woman, painting in Aboriginal style, she had been accused of copying in

Sydney in 1947 and again in 1954. And because the political and artistic climate had changed in fifty years, the judgment would be sterner and more knowledgeable than Paul Haefliger's. Her choice of a male identity recalls Richardson's but has an added level of difference. If Ethel Richardson wanted to be Henry, and even to obliterate her female self, that was a private matter. Henry was her creation, a middle-aged, middle-class Londoner who was, of course, white. Creating Eddie, an Aborigine, raised quite different issues. Yet there was a parallel. Writing as Henry, Ethel Robertson felt liberated; so did Elizabeth painting as Eddie.

Perpetua summed up her view of her mother's work:

> Transporting herself imaginatively as a contemporary male with a long past, Elizabeth transferred onto paper and canvas a lifetime of association, shared experiences, adventures, memories, songs and anecdotes heard in the twilight years of lost worlds.[7]

Other examples of a need to hide the self could be found within the Durack family. There was Reg Durack's rejection of privilege when he worked as Jimmy Gale. There was Mary Durack's wish to publish the 'unladylike' *Keep Him My Country* under the name of George Hurley. And, closer to Elizabeth's Eddie Burrup persona, was Mary's poem, 'Lament for the Drowned Country' in which she created the voice of Maggie Wallaby, interpreted Maggie's feelings and used her idiom. There was a real Maggie Wallaby, who might even have heard Mary read the poem in Kununurra in 1972.

In the same year, 1972, Thomas Keneally's novel *The Chant of Jimmie Blacksmith* was published. Keneally's construction of an

Aboriginal consciousness was not questioned. In 2003 (after the Burrup controversy) Keneally said he had been guilty of 'an act of presumption and impoliteness [in] writing as if I were an initiated member of the Aboriginal planet'.[8] Looking back, he believed that he ought to have used the onlooker's perspective of a white man to tell the story. On the difference between empathy (as when a male writer creates a female character) and the 'cultural trespass' involved in *Jimmie Blacksmith*, Keneally spoke of the Aborigines as a special case, needing more sensitivity than other ethnic groups whose worlds his novels had entered. Later the film version of *Jimmie Blacksmith* was criticised by historian Henry Reynolds as an act of presumption and for the essentialist stereotyping of the Aborigines.[9] If Keneally had written the novel under an Aboriginal pseudonym? That would have been self-defeating—as a Keneally novel it sold well and was shortlisted for the Booker Prize—and the idea of cultural trespass was not thought of in the 1970s.

Examples of white Australian women painting in indigenous style are hard to find. Margaret Preston (1875–1963) is the most important exception. From her 1920s art deco images based on a slight acquaintance with indigenous art, she moved to a more serious engagement. Summing up Preston's career in 1962, Bernard Smith wrote approvingly of her growing awareness of the 'aesthetic beauty of aboriginal art...She became the first of many practising artists to champion aboriginal art as an independent art form and to be influenced by it herself.'[10]

Preston's late work expresses cultural nationalism in a generalised Aboriginality, an attempt to find the essence of place. Unlike Durack, Preston did not aspire to a close knowledge of Aboriginal culture. 'My attitude to Aboriginal art is that I regard the use of it as a matter quite apart from its totemic meaning, just as I appreciate the works of El Greco...without having any interest in his religious meaning.'[11]

In 2005, forty years after Preston's death, the question of 'appropriation' in her use of indigenous art was examined in detail. Deborah Edwards, curator of a major retrospective exhibition at the Art Gallery of New South Wales, argued that Preston's work should be seen in the context of her time, when such borrowings were part of normal artistic practice: '...while Preston certainly annexed images from Aboriginal art without understanding the meaning behind those symbols she did so with an absolute respect for the culture.'[12] Could you have respect without understanding? Hetti Perkins, curator of Aboriginal Art at AGNSW, said that although Preston's attempts to engage with indigenous art were 'prescient and beautiful...there's still a way to go'. 'It's like speaking in a French accent without speaking French. The accent is there, the intonation is there but the meaning is not.'[13]

Djon Mundine, Curator of Aboriginal Art at the Museum of Contemporary Art in Sydney, was more forthright. For him it was about ownership and due sensitivity. He likened Margaret Preston's use of Aboriginal imagery to 'crucifixes being used as decoration in heavy metal bands'.[14]

When Robert Smith's *Art Monthly Australia* story was picked up by mainstream journalism in 1997, the issue of intrusion, or cultural appropriation, was vigorously debated. Elizabeth's name was held against her. A stereotype emerged: Elizabeth was a marauding pastoralist's arrogant daughter. This accusation ignored her close association over more than sixty years with the Miriwoong people and the fact that the Durack pastoralists' chapter had closed in 1950 with the sale of the stations.

A revealing parallel is the case of Sreten Bozic, a Serbian

migrant said to be from a peasant family, who spent some years among Aboriginal people in northern Australia, during which he took on a new identity as indigenous writer B. Wongar. As the work of Wongar, his novels and short stories of Aboriginal life were well received, especially in Europe, and when his true identity was exposed in 1981 by Robert Drewe, he received a far less censorious treatment than Elizabeth Durack had.[15] It was later argued by distinguished academic Livio Dobrez that, as a victim of persecution and displacement, Wongar 'was in some sense Aboriginal'. This idea rested on the belief that 'Aborigines played a key role in bringing [Wongar] home to himself'. Thus, there was a sense in which 'a black Bozic actually exists'. Dobrez took for contrast the case of Eddie Burrup, creation of Elizabeth Durack, 'member of a celebrated family which aggressively appropriated black land in the Kimberley'. Her Burrup persona was 'a further and especially patronising expropriation of indigenous Australians'. More could be said about Wongar and Burrup, but it appears that, for Dobrez and others, being a Durack was the unforgivable sin.[16] As Wongar, Bozic's career continued to flourish. He won several literary awards between 1982 and 1997, and was accepted in Australian literary and academic circles even when his deception was well known.[17]

An earlier episode held a warning for Elizabeth. Her *Cord to Alcheringa* paintings, which had hung unquestioned in Winthrop Hall at the University of Western Australia from 1953, stemmed from personal experience. This included the ceremonies she was allowed to witness on her long walks with Aborigines, rock art she had seen in the 1930s, and lessons in the 1940s from Jubul, the Arnhem Land bark painter. In 1995, the *Cord* series roused some controversy when included in a Durack retrospective at the Art

Gallery of Western Australia. It was only when an Aborigine from the Kimberley gave an endorsement, declaring that the works were 'free to be seen by everyone', that they remained on show.

The art community was divided on the Burrup question. 'What's all the fuss?' asked critic Susan McCulloch. Judy Cassab, a judge for the Sulman award, said, 'It's the painting that matters, not the painter.' Djon Mundine was outraged. In a bizarre choice of comparisons he said it was 'like Kerry Packer pretending he's Mahatma Gandhi'.[18] Wayne Bergmann, from the Kimberley Aboriginal Law and Cultural Centre, said it was 'the ultimate act of colonisation'.[19]

In the background of the debate was that celebrated case of concealed identity: the phantom poet Ern Malley, created in 1943 by poets James McAuley and Harold Stewart. Elizabeth was well aware of the Ern Malley hoax. She had a copy of the Malley poems in her library and she had used one of Ern's best lines, 'the black swan of trespass' as the title of her 1979 exhibition at the World Trade Center in New York. She took Ern Malley's last poem as a reflection on her second self, altering it slightly. She began:

> In the eighty-first year of my age
> I find myself to be a dromedary
> That has run short of water between
> One waterhole and the next mirage.

She adjusted Malley's phrase 'the scrub typhus of Mubo' to become 'the scrub typhus of Mabo'.

Like Eddie Burrup, Ern Malley had a life story. It was created through the persona of Ern's sister Ethel, a 'gormless philistine', rather like Edna Everage before fame inflated her. Ethel knew nothing about poetry but having found Ern's tattered manuscripts after his death from Graves disease, she consulted a local librarian in case there was something in them.[20] The story was devised to entrap Max Harris, the eager young editor of the journal *Angry Penguins*, into publishing the modernist poems of the phantom Malley which McAuley and Stewart had concocted on an idle afternoon. The wider aim was to reveal critical naiveté and shoddy verse in the modernist literary movement in Australia. Harris fell into the trap, hailed Malley as a major talent, and was then discredited when the hoaxers were unmasked. To some extent the hoax backfired; the poems, which had to be good enough to fool Harris, were too good to dismiss as total nonsense. They are still in print.

Eddie Burrup was created for a quite different purpose. Durack did not want to discredit Aboriginal art; she revered it. Aboriginal culture, which she had been studying for much of her life, had been her inspiration ever since, as a nineteen-year-old, she saw cave paintings for the first time. She had been given a classificatory kinship place in the Ord River Miriwoong language group. Her account of her weeks-long walks with the Miriwoong shows her sensitivity to 'secret men's business' and her acceptance of the guidance of the women in withdrawing from these ceremonial moments. The Burrup paintings may be understood as her attempt to see as an Aborigine might see, a way of reconciliation, a coming together. It was naive to use the Eddie persona, but not a deliberate exploitation.

The Ern Malley poems were a means to a clearly defined end, an ingenious comic-satiric achievement on the part of McAuley and Stewart. The targets, after Max Harris, were writers of modernist verse and the critics who accepted them as art. If Elizabeth Durack merely wanted to show up the judgment of art critics, a dozen paintings would have been enough to make a point. But her Burrups kept on coming, full of life and creative energy. Painting as Eddie, she said, brought her 'tremendous happiness and a feeling of deep fulfilment'.[21] Puzzling over the meaning of Eddie, Melbourne literary critic John Barnes suggested that Elizabeth Durack's assumption of an indigenous identity was 'simultaneously an assertion of white superiority and a confession of the most profound doubt about that superiority'.[22] Robert Smith saw it differently. While talking to Elizabeth, his misgivings had vanished:

> It seems to me that the work of Eddie Burrup can be seen as not just a homage to Aboriginal Australia but a concrete exemplar for reconciliation between two communities and two cultures in Elizabeth's words 'foundering so badly at the present time'.[23]

Smith noted Elizabeth's lack of sentimentality, condescension or idealisation and her 'true freedom from racial discrimination'. Even with this friendly introduction, Eddie/Elizabeth was given a hard time. Among the few art critics who took time to study the paintings, Susan McCulloch commented:

> There is something profoundly moving about these works [in which] images of animals or figures swim to the surface as if from primordial depths, made more so by their dual titles: 'In the beginning…Genesis 1.1' and 'Well you can see all them ol'fella now comin'.[24]

Reading Elizabeth's own account of the Burrup deception, it is impossible to write the Eddie Burrup story off as opportunistic.

She crossed a line when she misled the public about the authorship of the paintings, and compounded the deception by entering them for awards as indigenous work. Yet it seems clear that she painted from inner necessity—artistic and personal. There was nothing to gain in reputation; either the credit would go to Eddie, or there would be trouble for Elizabeth—as there was.

No one quite knew how to classify the Eddie Burrup art. It was not forgery, not plagiarism. It was imaginative work based on almost lifelong learning from the indigenous people. The element of hoax that evoked Ern Malley coexisted with an ongoing creative impulse. At a time when indigenous paintings were fetching high prices, the Burrups were left to hang as 'not for sale' for two years. Elizabeth's career was not in the doldrums; on the contrary, two major exhibitions were on show in 1994–95 and her work was selling well. Her honorary D.Litt from Murdoch University in 1994 and from the University of Western Australia in 1996 added to her public recognition at this time.

True, she wanted to see if anyone would spot a difference between Eddie's paintings and those of other indigenous artists. She was conducting an experiment in public awareness and critical judgment. But there was more to it than that. A powerful motive, hidden except in her private diaries, was the sense that she needed Eddie, and that Eddie was real:

> My great fear now is that Eddie will be lost to me. I have had no chance to get back to him since my return from Broome a week ago, at Easter where we were together so happily. How I loved sitting under the mango tree with him in the dappled shade with the brilliant sunshine splashing over the fresh Buffel grass and on the red ground…

> Where is he now? Is he still there in Broome? Or has he taken off somewhere over the Leopolds meeting up with all his friends? They'll see him coming and sing out to him from the high rocky summits of the range—and then he'll forget all about me. When and how dare I call him up?[25]

The timing, so close to Mary's death, helps to account for her insistence on Eddie as companion. She had felt the earlier deaths of her siblings: Kim, the beloved brother, and David, the ebullient youngest of the six Duracks. Now, Reg in his mid-eighties was absorbed in his large family. Bill's life was serene; happy in his marriage, family and profession, he was living in Queensland and she seldom saw him. There was no one with whom to share the past.

Another strand in the Burrup tangle is Elizabeth's lively inventiveness. She must have enjoyed creating Eddie's life story. Like McAuley and Stewart she went beyond what was needed in biographical detail. Testing its 'authenticity' she showed Eddie's 'autobiography' to her brothers, Reg and Bill. Reg thought he sounded a nice old chap. Bill accepted it completely, as did his wife, the writer Noni Braham. Perpetua's husband, musician Rex Hobcroft, brought a detached urban perspective to the story, but he too was drawn in. 'What a wonderful character he must be...I didn't know Perpetua was trying to help him.'[26]

There was a political dimension which was also personal. The world had changed since MPD was seen as a model pastoralist, respected for his kindness and fair dealing. Now it seemed that there were no good pastoralists and no virtues in paternalism. As Elizabeth saw it, the new historians were denying that any friendship between black and white had ever existed. It seemed to her that their work spoke only of the violence and exploitation. Elizabeth wanted Eddie to exist as an embodiment of the Aborigines she had known from her Ivanhoe days. Like Mary, she wanted a better deal for the Aborigines, but she was suspicious about land rights and the Mabo decision as likely to bring divisiveness rather than the 'side-by-side' partnership she hoped for.

The men Elizabeth remembered from Argyle and Ivanhoe stations, and others like them, were not being given a voice. As a young woman she and Mary had seen the harshness of station life. They should either tell the truth or 'get the hell out', she wrote in 1939.[27] But what happened after the pastoral workers' equal pay decision—displacement, lack of employment, dependency on the grog—made station life seem almost a golden age. Elizabeth would have agreed with the Aborigines represented in the 1989 collection *Raparapa*, who express pride in the skills exercised in station life[28] and with Nicolas Rothwell who wrote in 2011 of 'many old indigenous stockmen [who] regard the passing of the cattle station days as a tragedy'.[29]

All through the 1980s and afterwards in the Eddie Burrup years, Elizabeth was reading the new historians. Her bookshelves held many volumes, including the work of Bain Attwood and Keith Windschuttle—not quite an A to Z of contemporary writing, but enough to show her attention to current debates. She looked at both sides of the 'history wars', and was offended by the 'black armband' view which seemed to her to obliterate much that was well-meaning in white contact with Aboriginal people. A series of reviews she contributed to *Quadrant* magazine shows her mixed feelings about the way the past that she remembered was being judged.

Her testy piece on Henry Reynolds dismisses *Frontier—Aborigines,*

Settlers & Land as a tedious and largely pointless exercise. She gave no credit to Reynolds's groundbreaking use of official documents. His 'fact on fact, skirmish on skirmish, case after case' approach was seen as futile. 'It totally ignores the pragmatic course of history and evolution of human relations generally,' she wrote.[30] She was angry at the academic's document-based work being preferred to oral history and lived experience. Another academic, Diane Bell, fared better, because she set up a 'fruitful rapport' with Aboriginal women at Warrabri in the Northern Territory, whose ceremonial life she examined in 1976. Elizabeth praised Bell's *Daughters of the Dreaming* for revealing the 'irreconcilable, perhaps irremediable difficulties within Aboriginal communities...[with] the steady degrading of women generally as power swings heavily in favour of "the male-dominated European controls and policies which govern Aboriginal affairs".'[31] What counted most with Elizabeth Durack was Bell's capacity to sit in the shade and listen to the women. She would not allow the fact that oral and documentary history are—or should be—interdependent.

The Mabo land rights decision cut across Elizabeth's belief that indigenous people and white people could share the land. She conceded that things had changed, that stations were run in a quite different way, and that 'not everybody has the attitude that [her] father had'.[32] The aftermath of Eddie's emergence was a shock. As she told an interviewer, she had not expected such hostility:

> I'm not kidding myself that, you know, the blacks love me or anything. It was just fondness and affection there and give and take and of course always very mutual respect. And always the sense that I was learning from them. That was the joy of being out with them by myself in the bush.[33]

Hostility came from those who did not know her. Around Kununurra and Broome she was treated in much the same way as before. She was told that Eddie should stop but the tone was friendly. She relished the moment when, to the astonishment of young white welfare workers, she was greeted as 'Mum' and embraced by Jeffery Chunuma Rainyerri in Kununurra. That was more important to Elizabeth than the attacks of indigenous leaders in Sydney or white academics who had never seen the Kimberley. At the end of a long interview, given over three days in 1997 for Film Australia's national biography program, Elizabeth said that Eddie Burrup's work would continue, and 'perhaps the poor ol' boy might receive some recognition, yes, as an artist in his own right'. He gave her 'a lovely freedom' to move between two worlds; he was a 'cover' that she needed.

> I think I got very tired of being Elizabeth Durack that had been stereotyped as a relic of old colonialism, a relic of conservatism, a daughter of a murderer. You know, I'm very tired of that—it might have been why I liked the idea of working under a *nom de brush*.[34]

When this interview was recorded, Elizabeth was still painting every day. As Eddie Burrup, she was offered the London exhibition she had tried to arrange in the 1950s. The paintings were sent to the Rebecca Hossack Gallery in Cork Street for an opening on 24 July 2000. Elizabeth had planned to be there, but Eddie had to go on without her.

Diagnosed with cancer in 1998, Elizabeth suffered a great deal of pain in her last two years, but she refused to talk about her illness or to stop painting. She was admitted to hospital in 1998 and again in 1999 for treatment which she endured stoically. She had hoped to die in the north, but the end came more rapidly than anyone expected and she died in her Perth house on 25 May 2000. At eighty-four she had a full measure of striving and achievement in an often stormy life. It was characteristic of her unquenchable spirit that the London catalogue, prepared under her direction, gave the final public word to Eddie, not Elizabeth. And that these were borrowed from Ern Malley:

> It is something at least to be speaking
> Though in this No-Man's-language appropriate
> Only to No Man's Land

Two more words were borrowed on Eddie Burrup's behalf: 'Begin here'. Not an ending, then, but a new start: a characteristically intransigent note from Elizabeth Durack.

CHAPTER 12

Returning North

Elizabeth Durack had made her last visit to Ivanhoe Station in July 1995, not long after her eightieth birthday. It was not the last time she saw the north, but it was a farewell to that first and best loved place.[1] As Mary had done a few years earlier, she stayed with Susan and David Bradley, who had owned Ivanhoe since 1989. There was nothing left of the old homestead where as a nineteen-year-old she had worked with Mary saving money for their travels in Europe. That period—less than two years—was meant to be merely an interlude before moving into the wider world. Although they worked hard as station cooks and relished their independence, they had no idea that their 1930s experience would permeate their whole lives. Looking around her in old age, Elizabeth saw changes in almost everything that had inspired her early drawings and Mary's writings. And she herself had changed in many ways, though not in her attachment to the north.

The old homestead, destroyed by fire just after her father's

death, was only a memory, though a powerful one. The 1950s buyers
had left the charred remnants to moulder away while they built a
new dwelling on a different site for a series of managers; this too fell
into disrepair. The Bradleys remade the Ivanhoe garden but lived
at Carlton Hill in a charming, welcoming house with a degree of
elegance and modern comfort unimaginable in the Duracks' time.
Susan Bradley entertained with flair and style. When she organised
fundraisers for the Royal Flying Doctor Service and other good
causes, she invited celebrities to stay—Barry Humphries and Slim
Dusty among them—and included Mary Durack more than once
in the festivities. The newspapers reported the presence of 'Dusty
and the Dames': Dame Mary Durack and Dame Edna Everage.[2]
'Lament for the Drowned Country', recited by Mary to a crowd
of over a thousand on the Bradleys' lawns, had everyone in tears.
In later years, when Mary visited her 'chisters' of the old days,
Susan made their reunions easy, taking care of transport for all the
women and arranging picnics for them at their favourite places.

The Bradleys also kept a friendly eye on Reg Durack, then in
his eighties. After some years in Perth, well-off and secure with a
thriving, gifted family all doing well in the professions, Reg had
returned north. First he bought back the leasehold of Bullita, once
part of the old Connor, Doherty & Durack holdings, and later,
when Bullita was returned to its indigenous owners, he bought
a small holding near Kununurra. The Bradleys worried about
his impulsive burning-off, which might have got out of control.
When Elizabeth came to stay, they were ready to take care of an
old lady who looked as fragile as fine china. During her stay, they
were astonished by her resilience and her apparent capacity to fit
in with the new order. With some misgivings, the Bradleys took
Elizabeth to meet the Ivanhoe 'ringers': a group of young men

with whom she would have little in common. She sat with them, responded to their questions, laughed and told stories for hours. 'They were totally charmed.'[3]

Next day she went with David Bradley, mustering by helicopter. Again, she was eager, responsive, excited. Seeing the landscape from above or driving around the property, she seemed to know every turn of the road, every fence-line, every rock and waterhole. One afternoon she went out walking alone. When the light was fading a few hours later, the Bradleys began to worry. She knew her way, of course, but could she have fallen? David Bradley took the helicopter and went looking. Eventually he sighted a small figure, seated on a rock, making the most of the remaining light.

As she gazed on the darkening landscape, Elizabeth must have reflected on her younger self. Ivanhoe had powerful memories: kneading dough for loaves of bread in the morning; swimming with the Aboriginal women and children in the afternoon. Now the camps were gone; there was no one to call the homestead people to watch a corroboree or to give the hint to stay away when there was secret business. Dot, Marie, Ruby and the others were old women, white-haired, holding their memories on land made alien by many changes. Jeff Chunuma, the bright little boy she had sketched, was old too, living in Kununurra where he was now a respected elder.

The Ivanhoe lagoon was empty, dried up when the Ord River was diverted for the new dam. There were no goats on Goat Hill. The little girl whom Elizabeth had painted in 'The Kid'—where was she? Other figures: MPD, tall and commanding in the saddle, wearing a solar topee that made him look like an Indian Army colonel; Reg, keeping the sun from his neck with a piece of buff-coloured calico tucked under his small-brimmed

R.M. Williams–style hat; Mary on horseback, bringing back
a crocodile her father had shot. Horrie Miller's plane circling
above the homestead, doing stunts to captivate Mary; the riders
on splendid horses who made up the guard of honour when Lord
and Lady Gowrie came to stay at Argyle—where were they?

Memories of Tom Naughton in his new car, turning the
headlights on the Ivanhoe verandah, dazzling them all in his
beautiful white suit. Riding to Argyle with Tom and Reg, or riding
alone with Tom. Dismounting to talk, she and Tom, bridles in
hand, leaning on a post-and-rail fence. The other Tom, drunk
and dishevelled. The sound of his plane overhead, leaving her.

Evenings at Ivanhoe with Kim, his voice from the other end
of the verandah, saying as she fell asleep under her mosquito net:
'And Bet, I've just thought—*We'll move the homestead.* I never did
like this spot here much...And Bet...'[4] The grass studio beside the
river, where she had painted happily beside old Jubul. The need
for the north which had driven her on that nightmare journey
with Perpetua, homing from Sydney by way of Alice Springs
before the birth of Michael.

Dreams and memories: which of them sustained Elizabeth
Durack the painter, soon to create out of these fragments the
insubstantial figure of Eddie Burrup? Driving away from Ivanhoe
at the end of her visit, she said to her host, 'Oh Susan, if only I
could wrench this place from my heart and throw it away, my life
would be so much easier!'[5]

Almost nothing remains of the old Ivanhoe homestead, and Argyle
is fathoms deep beneath the lake. Today tourists come by busload
from Kununurra to look at the recreated Argyle Homestead,

puzzle over the artefacts, battered hats, old saddles, pots and pans, a waterbag, an antique telephone. A large photograph of MPD hangs on one wall, dominant as in life. Spread out on a table, images of the next generation are taken from oddly chosen periods. Kim looking young and eager; his brother Bill photographed in old age; Elizabeth with a 1940s hairstyle and a blank Hollywood look. A mature Mary, touched by experience.

Outside, but close to the house, are the family graves. Reg, Mary and Elizabeth all chose to be buried there. Mary's gravestone is large, central, unadorned, just her name and the years of birth and death. Close by is Elizabeth's memorial, with an epitaph chosen by her son and daughter. Galileo's stubborn words '*e pur si muove*' (but it *does* move) stand for her independence of mind and her questing spirit. Reg chose his own epitaph, '*Exegi monumentum…*' Taken from Horace's ode, the first line translates as 'I have built a monument more lasting than bronze'. The north was his heartland, as he proved by constantly returning to it, but the lasting monument must be the family in whom he took great pride. The words for his wife Enid, carved ten years later, would almost have chosen themselves: Ruth's pledge, taken from the Bible verse: 'Whither thou goest…', pays due respect to Enid's years at Kildurk. She never loved the north, but she loved Reg.

A stone tablet erected by MPD in 1950 was retrieved before the old homestead was drowned. It commemorates the five white men who camped on the Argyle site in 1886, and names Argyle as the place where Patsy Durack spent his last years and where his wife Mary died in 1893. MPD's plaque for Pumpkin of the Boontamurra people of Cooper's Creek speaks of 'faithful service' from 1887 until his death in 1908. His grave is under water, near the drowned homestead. A bronze plaque erected in 2001 lists three generations of family members whose graves are elsewhere: Grandfather Patsy and his wife Mary Durack, MPD and Bess, and their sons Kim, Bill and David 'whose spirits are forever in the land'.

A house that is really a museum and a garden that is also a graveyard make up today's tourist experience of the Durack past, sixty years after MPD sold all his company's holdings in the north. The museum visit is followed by a morning boat trip on Lake Argyle and an afternoon on the Ord River, taking the tourists all the way back to Kununurra. With unconscious irony one of the larger boats is named the 'Kimberley Durack'. The only one of MPD's six children to leave neither a family nor a lasting monument in books or paintings, Kim the visionary is buried in Canberra, the city of bureaucrats.

Mary and Elizabeth, contrasts in temperament, alike in dedication, tried all their lives to understand the region of Australia that they loved. They witnessed the end of the droving days and the second dispossession of the indigenous people, but had no power to avert the tragedy which began in 1788 and continues today. Patsy Durack thought that the land he called his own would be passed down to his sons and grandsons, as 'heirs forever'. He was mistaken. His grandchildren would own nothing of the land; it would hold them forever.

NOTES

ABBREVIATIONS

ADB	*Australian Dictionary of Biography*
Battye Library	J.S. Battye Library of West Australian History, State Library of Western Australia
BN	Brenda Niall
ED	Elizabeth Durack
HCM	Horatio Clive Miller (Horrie)
KMD	Kimberley Michael Durack (Kim)
MD	Mary Durack
MPD	Michael Patrick Durack
NLA	National Library of Australia
RWD	Reginald Wyndham Durack
TLS	*Times Literary Supplement*
TYK	'The Young Know'

AN INTRODUCTION

1 'The family company, Connor, Doherty & Durack, was sold for £250,000 from which, after probate, Bess Durack got just £30,000—reduced to £20,000 after commitments to family were paid out and a modest brick and tile home purchased. Further calls were made on her by Reg, who was desperate on Kildurk, and Kim in order to pay his way into Northern Developments. Bess was worried about her finances and had to be very careful. Kim had taken out no C, D & D shares 'on principle'. He therefore had no entitlement after the sale. Nevertheless MPD contrived to pay him

the same amount as the other boys (£2900) for 'services rendered'. Patsy Millett to BN, 7 September 2011.

2 I am indebted to Mary Durack's unpublished account of the visit to the office, 17 October 1950, and to Patsy Millett's description of the office.

3 *Ibid*.

Chapter 1: BEGINNINGS

1 ED to MD, 1 September 1942, TYK, p. 27.

2 Mary Durack interview. Hazel De Berg, 12 March 1976.

3 ED to MD, 1 September 1942, TYK, p. 27.

4 Bess Durack, quoted in Mary Durack, *Sons in the Saddle,* p. 329.

5 MPD diary, 28 January 1911, quoted *Sons*, p. 352.

6 Bim stood for the initials Bess Ida Muriel.

7 ED, 'The Time of Our Lives', p. 45.

8 *Ibid.*, p. 54.

9 *Ibid.*, p. 61.

10 MPD diary, 26 November 1917, quoted *Sons*, p. 459.

11 'So Much I Loved Is Drowned For Ever', *Australian Women's Weekly*, 3 May 1972.

12 'The Time of Our Lives', p. 1.

13 *Ibid.*, p. 26.

14 *Ibid.*, p. 60.

15 *West Australian*, 4 September 1929.

16 MD interviewed by Stuart Reid, 1990–91.

17 'The Time of Our Lives', p. 158.

18 MD, *Kings in Grass Castles*, p. 24.

19 Geoffrey Bolton, 'Throwing Stones at *Kings in Grass Castles*', 2010, p. 2.

20 Patsy Millett, *The Duracks of Argyle,* pp. 11–12.

21 *Ibid.*, p. 12.

22 *Kings*, p. 280.

23 *Ibid.*, p. 383.

24 MD to ED, 28 September 1944, TYK, p. 66.

25 *Western Mail,* 11 January 1934.

26 'An Outline of North Australian History', *Journal and Proceedings of the Western Australian Historical Society*, vol. 2, no. 12, pp. 1–11.

27 Paul Hasluck, *Mucking About,* pp. 122–23.

28 *Kings* p. 98.

29 'Mr Durack's Story', *West Australian,* 8 December 1921.

30 'A Contrite Crocodile', *West Australian*, 22 February 1934.

31 'WATC Races; Smart Frocking: Newest Millinery', *Western Mail,* 1 April 1934.

Chapter 2: IVANHOE AND ARGYLE

1 ED to family in Perth, 4 April 1934.

2 ED to family in Perth, 29 April 1934.

3 MD and ED, *All-About,* pp. 13, 23.

4 MD to family in Perth, 4 August 1934.

5 ED interview with Robin Hughes, 3 September 1997.

6 *Ibid.*, p. 14.

7 Now part of the Northern Territory's Keep River National Park.

8 MPD to MD and ED, 19 September 1935.

9 *Report of the Royal Commission [on]Aborigines*, p. 4.

10 *All-About*, pp. 17–18.

11 Thalia Anthony, 'Criminal Justice and Transgression on Northern Australian Cattle Stations', p. 35, speaks of the remote interior of northern Australia, from the late nineteenth century to the 1966 Equal Pay decision, as 'sites of transgression' which bypassed the assimilationist tendencies of government policy. For better and for worse, pastoralists exercised their own jurisdiction. Aboriginal people kept their connections with their own country, practised their own ceremonies—but only so long as the pastoralists needed them.

12 MD to ED, 8 October 1942, TYK, p. 88.

13 Kaberry's *Aboriginal Woman* (1939) drew on her experiences at Ivanhoe and elsewhere in the Kimberley.

14 Hasluck, *Mucking About,* p. 230.

15 *Ibid.,* p. 228.

16 *Ibid.*, p. 230.

17 *Ibid.*, p. 235–36.

18 MD to ED, 4 October 1942, TYK, pp. 76–77.

19 MD to ED, 20 September 1942, TYK, p. 54.

20 MD to family in Perth, 6 September 1934.

21 *Ibid.*

22 *Kings*, p. 385.

23 *Ibid.*

24 MD to ED, 7 December 1942, TYK, p. 160.

25 Anthony, 'Criminal Justice…', p. 36.

26 MD to ED, 28 September 1942, TYK, p.68.

27 *Ibid.*, p. 69.

28 *Ibid.*

29 ED to MD, 1 October 1942, TYK, pp. 74–75.

30 MD to ED, 4 September 1942, TYK, p. 31.

31 ED to MD, 1 September 1942, TYK, p. 28.

32 ED to MD, 15 September 1942, TYK, p. 52.

33 George Robertson to Louis Esson (on behalf of Prichard), 3 September 1928, rejecting the offer of the Australian rights to *Coonardoo* which had been published in London by Jonathan Cape. In AW Barker (ed.) *Dear Robertson: Letters to an Australian Publisher*, p. 147.

Chapter 3: LOVE AND MARRIAGE

1   RWD to MPD, 15 September 1937.

2   MPD to RWD, 23 July 1938.

3   ED to MD, 14 October 1942, TYK, p. 90.

4   MD to ED, 3 September 1937.

5   MD to ED, 3 April 1938.

6   MD to MPD and Bess Durack, 20 July 1937.

7   'Old Woman', *Bulletin* (Sydney), vol. 60, no. 3088, 19 April 1939, pp. 4–5.

8   ED to MD, 5 February 1939.

9   KMD to MD, [c. February 1939], TYK, p. 161.

10 MD, 'The Abyss', published for the first time in *Pilgrimage,* pp. 17–27.

11 ED to MD, 2 December 1942, TYK, p. 152.

12 ED to MPD, 9 September 1939.

13 ED to MD, 14 January 1938.

14 ED to MD, 18 December 1937.

15 MD to RWD, [n.d.] c. July 1939.

16 ED to MD, 18 October 1942, TYK, p. 103.

17 MD to RWD, 18 January 1938.

18 MPD to RWD, 18 November 1938.

19 ED to MD, 1 September 1942, TYK p. 28.

20 MD to ED, 12 September 1942, TYK pp. 49–50.

21 KMD to MD, 9 September 1949.

22 Geraldine Byrne, 'Horatio Clive Miller (1893–1980)', *ADB.*

23 MD to MPD, 18 November 1938.

24 RWD to MD, c.1938, TYK, p. 136.

25 ED to MD, 19 December 1938.

26 ED to MD, 19 December 1938.

27 ED to MD, 27 October 1942, TYK, p. 112.

28 RWD to MD, 17 June 1939.

29 ED to MD, 25 November 1942, TYK, p. 146.

30 'Family Notices', *SMH*, 21 August 1939.

Chapter 4: WARTIME

1   ED to MD, 28 March 1938.

2   MD to RWD and KMD, 11 December 1939.

3   ED quoted in Millett, 'Two Sides', p. 19.

4   MD to ED, 11 December 1939.

5   MD to ED, 12 September 1942, TYK, p. 46.

6   ED to MD, 30 November 1941.

7   MD, 'Our Native Population', *West Australian*, 21 October 1944.

8   MD to ED, 7 December 1942, TYK, p. 160.

9   *Ibid*.

10 *Ibid*.

11 MD to Kath McArthur, 29 October 1952, TYK, p. 40.

12 'Round-Australia Trip: Material for Durack Book', *West Australian,* 15 June 1945.

13 *Kings*, p. 388.

14 ED to MD, 18 November 1942, TYK, p. 132.

15 MD to ED, 30 November 1942, TYK, p. 147.

16 ED to MD, 27 October 1942, TYK, p. 113.

17 ED to MD, 25 November 1942.

18 ED to MD, 22 August 1942.

19 ED to MD, 23 February 1939.

20 ED to MD, 24 March 1940.

21 Leon Gettler, *An Unpromised Land*, pp. 76–77.

22 MD to RWD, 31 August 1939.

23 Gettler, p. 83.

24 *Ibid*., p. 114.

25 *Bulletin*, 24 January 1940, quoted Gettler, p. 119.

26 Gettler, pp. 75–76.

27 *Ibid.*, p. 117.

28 RWD to MD, 2 March 1943.

29 Quoted by ED, in ED to MD, 8 September 1942.

30 ED to MD (quoting Bill), c. 17 December 1942, TYK, p. 174.

31 *Ibid.,* pp. 174–75.

32 Bill Durack, conference paper 1991, from Kimberley Heritage Site Museum Display, Carlton Reach Research Station, 1941–45.

33 MD to ED, 28 September 1942, TYK, p. 66.

34 ED to MD, 1 September 1942, TYK, p. 25.

35 ED to MD, 4 June 1941.

36 RWD to ED, 2 March 1943.

37 Interview with Perpetua Durack Clancy, 2 January 2011.

38 MD to ED, 20 November 1942, TYK, p. 134.

39 MD to ED, 7 December 1942, TYK, p. 157.

40 Geoffrey Bolton, 'Durack, Kimberley Michael (Kim), (1917–1968)', *ADB*.

41 Patsy Millett to BN, 15 July 2011.

Chapter 5: HOMES AND HEARTLANDS

1   ED to MD, 31 July 1949.

2   ED to MD, 21 May 1946.

3   ED to KMD, 1 June 1947.

4   ED, 'A Response to Critics—never sent', November 1954. From an unpublished typescript written in response to critic James Gleeson, who had accused her of copying from Aboriginal paintings. ED described her working relationship with Jubul in the 1940s, in her grass studio period.

5   *SMH*, 31 January 1947.

6   John Olsen, *Drawn from Life*, p. 87.

7   ED, to Frank Clancy, 1 February 1947.

8   ED, 'Signature', p. 8.

9   *Ibid.*, p. 6.

10 Elizabeth Durack, 'About the Pictures', in H. Drake Brockman (ed.) *Australian Legendary Tales*, collected by K. Langloh Parker, Angus & Robertson, Sydney, 1953, p. xii.

11 'Between Ourselves', *Western Mail,* 22 August 1922.

12 ED to Geoffrey Bolton, 15 October 1954, Geoffrey Bolton Papers, NLA.

13 Laurie Thomas, quoted in Benko, *The Art of David Boyd*, p. 22.

14 ED to MD, 1 April 1947.

15 *Ibid.*

16 ED to MPD, c. 8 March 1949.

17 *Sons in the Saddle*, p. 103.

18 *Ibid.*, p. 277.

19 Bolton, 'Throwing Stones at *Kings in Grass Castles*'.

20 Durack Dreaming, *Dynasties*, ABC TV [2002].

21 Anne Durack to BN, 26 September 2011.

22 Bolton, 'Throwing Stones at *Kings in Grass Castles*'.

23 KMD to MD, 4 May 1948.

24 MPD's estate was sworn for probate at £61,195. Bolton, 'Michael Patrick Durack', *ADB*. Because the gifts to Reg, Mary and Elizabeth were made shortly before his death they had to be included in the estate and probate paid on them.

25 MD to Kathleen McArthur, 19 October 1950, quoted in Millett, *The Duracks of Argyle*, p. 66.

Chapter 6: BROOME

1   ED to MD, n.d. [1946].

2   *Ibid.*

3   ED to MD, 29 May 1946.

4   *Ibid.*

5   Some Japanese who had been interned during the war returned to Broome and were accepted back into the community where they had lived for many years. Kimberley Male (b.1942), interviewed by Colin Davis, 1 January 2006.

6   Michael Clancy and Perpetua Durack Clancy, 'Afterword', in *With Outstretched Arms*.

7   Buckland remarried in 1951, a year after his affair with Elizabeth Durack ended. Carole Harris, 'Buckland, William Lionel (1899–1964)', *ADB*.

8   HCM to MD, July–August 1946.

9   HCM to MD, 16 September 1946.

10 MD to HCM, 2 October 1948.

11 Out of forty-one paintings shown at the Claude Hotchins Gallery, fifteen sold on the first day and a total of twenty-two within the week.

12 MD to RWD and KMD, 31 August 1939.

13 MD to HCM, 28 June 1948.

14 The series, begun in 1947 and continued in 1963, was not shown until the Kimberley Centenary Celebrations of 2007, when the Sisters of St John of

God arranged an exhibition entitled *With Outstretched Arms*.

15 ED, 'What's Wrong with the NW?', *SMH*, 4 May 1963. The subtitle 'Beagle Bay as a Symbol of Futility', displeased ED and she protested against its use. (Perpetua Durack Clancy to BN, 23 March 2011.) The article takes a backward look at the place where she had painted happily in the 1940s and asks why it had lost hope and energy in the intervening years.

16 MD to ED, 21 June 1951.

17 *Ibid*.

18 MD to Kathleen McArthur, 4 July 1951.

19 MD to Kathleen McArthur, 28 April 1952.

20 MD to ED, 12 July 1951.

21 Millett, 'Two Sides of the Coin', p. 77.

22 Kimberley Male was at the Broome primary school in the early 1950s. He described the enrolment as 'predominantly European' with some Asian and Asian-Aboriginal children; he confirms Patsy Millett's memory of the Aboriginal children being sent to St Mary's Catholic school. Male interview, *op cit*.

23 *Ibid*., p. 69.

24 HCM to Kathleen McArthur, 19 December 1952.

25 MD to Kathleen McArthur, 2 December 1952, quoted Millett, 'Two Sides', p. 65.

26 MD, *The Rock and the Sand*, p. 288.

27 MD to Kathleen McArthur, 2 December 1952.

28 *Ali Bin and the Soldier Crab* and *Creepy the Crab* were never published.

29 MD to Willliam Aiden (Bill) Durack, 8 January 1951.

30 *Oxford Companion to Australian Literature*, p. 148.

Chapter 7: *KINGS IN GRASS CASTLES*

1   MD to Kathleen McArthur, 21 June 1953.

2   MD to Florence James, 4 December 1963, 'Two Sides', p. 154.

3   Michael Sadleir to MD, October 1953, quoted Millett, 'Two Sides', p. 95.

4   ED to Geoffrey Bolton, 27 July 1955 (Bolton Papers).

5   Katharine Susannah Prichard to MD, 11 September 1955.

6   MD, *Keep Him My Country*, p. 8.

7   *Ibid*., p. 267.

8   KMD to MD, 18 September 1955. RWD's letter dated 16 November 1955.

9   MD, 'Figures in a Landscape' (1963), a sketch which evokes Kim's situation

in the early 1950s.

10 Florence James to MD, 30 June 1953.

11 Florence James to MD, 24 October 1955.

12 ED to Geoffrey Bolton, 23 May 1955 (Bolton Papers).

13 MD to Kathleen McArthur, 28 September 1955.

14 Florence James to MD, 27 July 1958.

15 *Kings*, p. 61.

16 *Ibid.*, p. 195.

17 *Ibid.*, p. 183.

18 MD to Kathleen McArthur, 19 October 1950.

19 Bolton, 'Throwing Stones…', p. 6.

20 A. D. Hope, 'The Bunyip Stages a Comeback', *SMH*, 16 June 1956, p. 15.

21 MD, 'Only Time Will Tell', *Westerly*, no. 1, 1957, pp. 44–45. Florence James, more conservative than Durack in her judgment, described White's style as turgid and self-conscious. Florence James to MD, 19 September 1956.

22 MD to Kathleen McArthur, 6 April 1957.

23 *Kings*, p. 354.

24 *Ibid.*

25 *Ibid.*, p. 264.

26 MD to Kathleen McArthur, 6 April 1957.

Chapter 8: A PLACE OF HER OWN

1 Perpetua Durack Clancy to BN, 1 August 2011.

2 *Ibid.*

3 Philippa O'Brien, *Robert Juniper*, p. 150, lists Juniper's teaching posts from 1954 to 1984.

4 Six of the thirteen exhibitions were in Perth; the others, in Adelaide, Melbourne and Sydney, had higher costs and airfares and, on average, a lower rate of sales. Summary by Elizabeth Durack, c. November 1951.

5 Durack Clancy, *op cit*.

6 ED to MD, 12 December 1946.

7 ED to Geoffrey Bolton, 29 November 1954, (Bolton Papers).

8 *Ibid.*

9 ED to Geoffrey Bolton, 28 April 1955.

10 ED to Geoffrey Bolton, 23 '(or 4th)' January 1955.

11 Millett, 'Two Sides', p. 146.

12 Philippa O'Brien, *Robert Juniper*, p. 20.

13 ED to Philippa O'Brien, 2 July 1989. Copy courtesy Philippa O'Brien.

14 *Sunday Times*, 1 April 1956.

15 ED to Geoffrey Bolton, 16 April 1956.

16 *Ibid.*

17 'The Art of the Duracks', *Australasian Post*, 9 July 1951.

18 ED, 'A Maverick in the Perth of the 1940s…' *Fremantle Art Review*, vol. 2, no. 6, June 1987, pp. 4–6.

19 MD to Florence James, 14 February 1957.

20 ED, interview with Robin Hughes, 4 September 1997.

21 Bernard Smith, *Australian Painting 1788–1990*, p. 302.

22 Patrick McCaughey, 'Native Grounds and Foreign Fields', *Australian Book Review*, no. 332, June 2011, p. 11.

23 ED, interview with Robin Hughes.

24 ED, 'A Maverick…'.

25 ED, interview with Robin Hughes.

26 ED, *The Art of Elizabeth Durack*, p. 17.

27 *Ibid.*, p. 12.

28 Randolph Stow, quoted in *The Art of Elizabeth Durack*, p. 11.

29 ED, interview with Robin Hughes.

30 c.f. Mary Durack's 1940 poem 'Piccaninnies', which begins 'Come away, little brother from the ol' white world/Little white piccaninny child…'

31 ED to MD, 7 September 1951.

Chapter 9: OTHER PEOPLE'S BOOKS

1 MD to Florence James, 4 December 1963.

2 MD to ED, 8 March 1963.

3 ED to MD, 15 March 1963.

4 MD to ED, 8 March 1963.

5 MD to Florence James, 17 January 1961.

6 HCM to MD, reporting conversation with Bishop Jobst, April 1953.

7 MD to Florence James, 17 January 1963.

8 *The Rock and the Sand*, p. 21

9 *Ibid.*, p. 191.

10 *Ibid.*, p. 203.

11 *Ibid.*, p. 210.

12 *Ibid.*, pp. 272–73, 278.

13 *Ibid.*

14 *Ibid.*, p. 289.

15 *Ibid.*

16 *Ibid.*, p. 199.

17 Bolton, G. 'Dame Mary Durack', *Independent* (London), 24 December 1994.

18 Millett, 'Two Sides', p. 207.

19 *Ibid.*, p. 208.

20 MD diary, quoted Millett, 'Two Sides', p. 240.

21 *Ibid.,* p. 123.

22 MD, Foreword to *Wild Cat Falling,* p. xvi.

23 Millett, 'Two Sides', p. 123.

24 Colin Johnson to Mary Durack, quoted in Foreword to *Wild Cat Falling*, p. xxi.

25 *Ibid.*, p. xxii.

26 MD to Florence James, 22 June 1964.

27 MD to Florence James, 22 June 1965.

28 MD to Florence James, 28 November 1965.

29 Stephen Muecke, Introduction to *Wild Cat Falling*, pp. v–vi.

30 As Mudrooroo, he became a member of the Aboriginal Arts Committee of the Australia Council and a co-founder with Jack Davis of the Aboriginal Writers, Oral Literature and Dramatists' Association.

31 *Wild Cat Falling*, p. 75.

32 MD to Bess Durack, 6 October 1968.

33 MD diaries, quoted Millett, 'Two Sides', p. 116.

34 Voters were asked to approve a change in the Constitution which deleted two clauses relating to Aborigines. After 1967, Aborigines were no longer excluded from 'the power to make special laws...' (an exemption which was to cause unlooked-for trouble) and from being counted in the census. Voting rights had already been granted.

35 *The Rock and the Sand,* p. 328.

Chapter 10: 'WE LOSE EVERYTHING THAT WE BELONG'

1 *The Rock and the Sand*, p. 328.

2 John Watson, 'We Know This Country', in Paul Marshall (ed.), *Raparapa*, p. 208.

3 MD, Talk for the Warana Festival, Millett, 'Two Sides', p. 249.

4 John Nairn, 'So Much I Loved Is Drowned For Ever', *Australian Women's Weekly,* 3 May 1972, p. 51.

5 Millett, 'Two Sides', p. 203.

6 *Ibid*, p. 251.

7 *Ibid*.

8 MD, interview with Hazel de Berg, 12 March 1976.

9 Philippa O'Brien, phone interview with BN, 22 July 2011.

10 Millett, 'Two Sides', p. 321.

11 Address to the University of Western Australia, 13 March 1978, Millett, 'Two Sides', p. 320.

12 MD diary, September 1979, Millett, 'Two Sides', p. 336.

13 MD diary, April 1980, Millett, 'Two Sides' p. 340.

14 Millett, 'Two Sides', p. 341.

15 *Ibid*.

16 Millett, 'Dame Mary Durack: the Last Chapter', in *Lines in the Sand: New Writing from Western Australia*, p. 84.

17 Millett, 'Two Sides', p. 379.

18 *Ibid*.

19 *Ibid*., p. 384.

Chapter 11: THE MAKING OF EDDIE BURRUP

1 MD to RWD and Enid Durack, 3 April 1944, quoting ED.

2 '… a ship without a rudder', ED to MD, 5 February 1939.

3 ED, 1 December 1994, in 'How I Reinvented Myself in My 80th Year'.

4 *Ibid*.

5 24 April 1994 to 10 May 2000, in 'How I Reinvented Myself'.

6 *Ibid*.

7 'Eddie Burrup: a Daughter's View', *Westerly* (Perth), vol. 54, no. 1, July 2009, pp. 73–4.

8 Thomas Keneally, 'The Borrowers', *Age*, 30 August 2003.

9 Henry Reynolds, *The Chant of Jimmie Blacksmith*, Currency Press, Strawberry Hills, NSW, 2008.

10 Bernard Smith, *Australian Painting 1788–1960*, p. 187.

11 Ian North, 'A National Essence', in D. Edwards and R. Peel (eds.), *Margaret Preston*, Art Gallery of New South Wales, Sydney, 2005, p. 192.

12 Edwards, 'Shadow Cast Over a Painter's Legacy', *SMH*, 25 July 2005.

13 *Ibid*.

14 *Ibid*.

15 Robert Drewe, 'Solved: The Great B. Wongar Mystery', *Bulletin* (Literary

Supplement), 21 April 1981, pp. 2–5.

16 Livio Dobrez and Patricia Dobrez, 'Real Hoaxes, False Frauds and Difficult Authenticities', in Dobrez (eds.), *An ABC of Lying*, pp. 245–46.

17 Several years after Robert Drewe's article was published, Bozic/Wongar was awarded a Senior Fellowship by the Australia Council in 1986 and an emeritus award for an outstanding contribution to Australian Literature.

18 Susan McCulloch, 'Blacks Blast Durack for Her Art of Illusion', *Weekend Australian*, 8 March 1997, p. 1.

19 Mundine and Bergmann are cited by Louise Morrison, 'The Art of Eddie Burrup', *Westerly* (Perth), vol. 54, 1 July 2009, pp. 77–83.

20 Michael Heyward, *The Ern Malley Affair*, p. 104.

21 Robert Smith, *Art Monthly Australia*, p. 5.

22 John Barnes, 'Questions of Identity in Contemporary Australia', in Adi Wimmer (ed.) *Australian Nationalism Reconsidered*, pp. 69–70.

23 'The Incarnations of Eddie Burrup', *Art Monthly Australia*, March 1997, p. 5.

24 Susan McCulloch, *Weekend Australian*, op.cit.

25 ED diary, 24 April 1995, in 'How I Reinvented Myself'.

26 ED interview with Robin Hughes, 5 September 1997.

27 ED to MD, 2 February 1939.

28 Marshall (ed.), *Raparapa*, passim.

29 Nicolas Rothwell, 'Sun Sets on the Pastoralists' Wide Domain', *Weekend Australian*, 20–21 August 2011.

30 ED, 'Counter History', *Quadrant*, vol. 31, no. 7, July 1987.

31 ED, 'Aboriginal Women, Sacred and Profane', *Quadrant*, vol. 28, no. 5, May 1984.

32 ED, interview with Robin Hughes, 5 September 1997.

33 *Ibid.*

34 *Ibid.*

Chapter 12: RETURNING NORTH

1 In the last five years of her life ED was on 'Ivanhoe country' several times, at Kununurra and Ivanhoe Crossing, and she was often in Broome with Perpetua.

2 Susan Bradley to BN, 28 September 2011.

3 Interview with Susan Bradley, Broome, 24 June 2011.

4 ED to MD, 6 November 1942, TYK, p. 123.

5 Bradley, 28 September 2011.

BIBLIOGRAPHY

PRIMARY SOURCES

ARCHIVES & MANUSCRIPTS
Unless otherwise indicated, these are in private collections.
Elizabeth Durack, 'The Art of Eddie Burrup: A Voice of the Artist', 1995–96.
Elizabeth Durack Papers.
Elizabeth Durack, 'Signature: Reflections on Art, Ivanhoe Station, Kimberley WA', 1948.
Elizabeth Durack, 'The Time of Our Lives', 1985 (unpublished memoir).
Florence James Papers, MLMSS 5877 (Mitchell and Dixson Libraries Manuscripts Collection, State Library of New South Wales).
Geoffrey Bolton Papers, NLA.
Geoffrey Bolton, 'Throwing Stones at *Kings in Grass Castles*', Paper presented to the History Society, University of Western Australia, 2010, typescript.
Mary Durack and Elizabeth Durack, 'The Young Know: Letters in a Time of Peace and War', 1942–43.
Papers of the Durack Family, 1886–1991, MN 71 (Battye Library).
Patsy Millett, 'Two Sides of the Coin: Mary Durack, A Daughter's Perspective' [n.d.].

GOVERNMENT REPORTS
'Report of the Royal Commission Appointed to Investigate, Report and Advise upon Matters in relation to the Condition and Treatment of Aborigines' (Moseley Report), Fred Wm Simpson, Government Printer, Perth, 1935.

MARY DURACK & ELIZABETH DURACK WORKS

ARTICLES
'Son of Djaro', *Bulletin*, vol. 58, no. 3016, 1 December 1937, pp. 22–23, 59; vol. 58, no. 3017, 8 December 1937, pp. 6–7.

BOOKS
All-About: The Story of a Black Community on Argyle Station, Kimberley, Bulletin, Sydney, 1935.

A Book of Picture Stories, Imperial Print Company, Perth, 1944 (previously published as a comic strip, *Sunday Telegraph*, Sydney, 1942).

Chunuma, Bulletin, Sydney, 1936.

Kookanoo and Kangaroo, Rigby, Adelaide, 1963.

The Magic Trumpet, Cassell, Melbourne, 1946.

Piccaninnies, Offset Printing, Perth, 1940.

Son of Djaro, R. S. Sampson, Perth, 1940.

The Way of the Whirlwind, Australian Consolidated Press, Sydney, 1941.

MARY DURACK WORKS

ARTICLES & SHORT STORIES
Mary Durack wrote under the name Virgilia for the West Australian *newspaper during 1937–38.*

'The Chase under the Gum Trees', *Western Mail* (Perth), 25 December 1930.

'A Collector in Broome', *Walkabout* (Melbourne), vol. 15, no. 6, 1949, pp. 35–37.

'Dear Tom', *Westerly* (Perth), no. 2, 1956, pp. 49–51 (review of Tom Ronan, *Moleskin Midas*).

'The Double Track', *Coast to Coast: Australian Stories 1961–62*, selected by Hal Porter, Angus & Robertson, Sydney, 1962, pp. 157–64.

'Durack, Patrick (1834–1898)', *ADB*, vol. 4, Melbourne University Press, Carlton, 1974.

'Ernestine Hill', *Walkabout* (Melbourne), vol. 18, no. 3, 1952, pp. 8–9.

'Figures in a Landscape', *Westerly* (Perth), no. 3, September 1963, pp. 19–25.

'Friendly Highway', *Walkabout* (Melbourne), vol. 30, no. 4, 1964, pp. 10–13.

'Genial Ghosts', in *Tom Collins & His House*, ed. Justina Williams, Tom Collins Press for the Fellowship of Australian Writers, WA Section, Perth, 1973, pp. 7–13, photo, p. 48.

'Golden Days of Kimberley', *Walkabout* (Melbourne), vol. 12, no. 6, 1946, pp. 34–36.

'Henrietta as I Knew Her', *Overland* (Melbourne), no. 39, Spring 1968, pp. 46–47.

'In Search of an Australian Frontier', *Texas Quarterly* (Austin, Texas), vol. 5, no. 2, Summer 1962, pp. 10–15.

'Kimberley Epic', *Walkabout* (Melbourne), vol. 14, no. 4, 1948, pp. 29–34.

'Kimberley Saga', *Winthrop Review*, vol. 1, no. 3, Christmas 1953, pp. 17–22 (review of Geoffrey Bolton, *A Survey of the Kimberley Pastoral Industry from 1885 to the Present*).

'A Literature of Loneliness', *Westerly* (Perth), no. 4, December 1968, pp. 64–66 (review of *On Native Grounds: Australian Writing from Meanjin Quarterly*).

'Master Plan', *Summer's Tales 1*, ed. KylieTennant, Macmillan, Melbourne, 1964, pp. 22–31.

'My Week', *Australian Women's Weekly* (Sydney), 12 August 1981, p. 61.

'Ned Kelly—Fearless, Bold and Free?', *Westerly* (Perth), no. 2, 1957, pp. 36–40 (review of Douglas Stewart, *Ned Kelly: A Play*).

'Old Woman', *Bulletin* (Sydney), vol. 60, no. 3088, 19 April 1939, pp. 4–5.

'Only Time Will Tell', *Westerly* (Perth), no. 1, 1957, pp. 44–45 (review of Patrick White, *The Tree of Man*).

'Our Native Population—Asset or Liability: An Evaded Responsibility', *West Australian*, 21 October 1944.

'The Outlaws of Windginna Gorge', *Walkabout* (Melbourne), vol. 7, 1 June 1941, pp. 14–16.

'An Outline of North Australian History from Cambridge Gulf to the Victoria River, 1818–1887', *Journal and Proceedings of the Western Australian Historical Society*, vol. 2, no. 12, pp. 1–11.

'Pumpkin (1850?–1908)', *ADB*, vol. 5, Melbourne University Press, Carlton, 1974, p. 459.

'River of Destiny', *Walkabout* (Melbourne), vol. 12, no. 9, 1946, pp. 33–35.

'The Scroll on Which We Write', *Walkabout* (Melbourne), vol. 31, no. 1, 1965, pp. 26–30.

'Storm Bird', *Summer's Tales 2*, ed. Kylie Tennant, Macmillan, Melbourne, 1965, pp. 1–12.

'Thylungra', *Walkabout* (Melbourne), vol. 12, no. 1, 1945, pp. 9–13.

'The Vanishing Australian', *Walkabout* (Melbourne), vol. 11, no. 10, 1945, pp. 31–33.

'Walter Murdoch: The Man in the Mirror', *Meanjin* (Melbourne), vol. 28, no. 2, Winter 1969, pp. 217–20.

'Xavier Herbert Off Target', *The Critic* (Perth), vol. 5, no. 5, 22 May 1964, p. 40.

'You Can't Take It with You', *Bulletin* (Sydney), vol. 74, no. 3855, 30 December 1953, p. 34.

BOOKS

Child Artists of the Australian Bush, (in association with Florence Rutter), Harrap, London, 1952.

The Courteous Savage: Yagan of Swan River, Illustrated by Elizabeth Durack, Nelson, Melbourne, 1964 (reprinted as *Yagan of the Bibbulmun* illustrated by Revel Cooper, Nelson, West Melbourne, 1976).

Keep Him My Country, Constable, London, 1955.

Kings in Grass Castles, Constable, London, 1959.

Little Poems of Sunshine by an Australian Child, R. S. Sampson, Perth, 1923.

Pilgrimage: A Journey Through the Life and Writings of Mary Durack, ed. Patsy Millett and Naomi Millett, Bantam Books, Milsons Point, NSW, 2000.

The Rock and the Sand, Constable, London, 1969.

Sons in the Saddle, Constable, London, 1983.

To Be Heirs Forever, Constable, London, 1976.

To Ride a Fine Horse, (illustrated by Elizabeth Durack), Macmillan, London, 1963 (children's version of *Kings in Grass Castles*).

The Way of the Whirlwind, Australian Consolidated Press, Sydney, 1941.

INTERVIEWS

Dame Mary Durack Miller, interviewed by Stuart Reid, sound recording, National Library of Australia, 1990–91 (transcript in Battye Library).

Mary Durack, interviewed by Hazel de Berg, videorecording, De Berg tapes, NLA, Tape 933, 12 March 1976 (transcript in Battye Library).

Mary Durack, interviewed in December 1982, videorecording, Film Australia in association with the Archival Film Program of the Australia Council, Lindfield, NSW, 1983.

PLAYS & POEMS

'Lament for the Drowned Country', *Bulletin* (Literary Supplement), vol. 103, no. 5389, 1 November 1983, pp. 70–72.

'Lament to Galalan: In Our Hearts We Know Him', *Winthrop Review*, vol. 2, no. 2, Mid-Year 1954, pp. 18–21.

The Ship of Dreams, 1968.

Swan River Saga, 1972.

ELIZABETH DURACK WORKS

ARTICLES & BOOK REVIEWS

'Aboriginal Life', *Quadrant* (Sydney), vol. 28, no. 1 October 1984, (review of J. G. Steele, *Aboriginal Pathways in Southeast Queensland and the Richmond River*).

'Aboriginal Woman, Sacred and Profane', *Quadrant* (Sydney), vol. 28, no. 5, May 1984, pp. 84–86 (review of Diane Bell, *Daughters of the Dreaming*).

'Albert Namatjira', *Quadrant* (Sydney), vol. 30, no. 11, November 1986 (a memoir and review of *Albert Namatjira—The Life and Work of an Australian Painter*, compiled and edited by Nadine Amadio).

'Art in New York', *Australian*, 18 January 1979.

'Australia's Third World', *Quadrant* (Sydney), vol. 28, no. 4, April 1984 (written under the *nom de plume* Ted Zakrovsky).

'"Chunuma" Strides Out Again', *Quadrant* (Sydney), vol. 31, no. 10, October 1987, pp. 76–77 (review of *Countrymen—Life Histories of Four Aboriginal Men as Told to Bruce Shaw*, Australian Institute of Aboriginal Studies).

'Counter-History', *Quadrant* (Sydney), vol. 31, no. 7, July 1987 (review of Henry Reynolds, *Frontier—Aborigines, Settlers and Land*).

'Instant Books You Don't Even Have To Write!' *Quadrant* (Sydney), vol. 31, no. 12, December 1987 (review of Susan Mitchell, *The Matriarchs—Twelve Australian Women Talk about Their Lives*).

'Land Wrongs', *Quadrant* (Sydney), vol. 29, nos. 1 & 2, January–February 1985, pp. 71–78 (part review, part general comment on Mark Gumbert, *Neither Justice nor Reason*).

'A Maverick in the Perth of the 1940s...' *Fremantle Arts Review,* vol. 2, no. 6, June 1987, pp. 4–6.

'Notes from South Africa', *Quadrant* (Sydney), vol. 19, no. 9, December 1975.

'The Best of Bates', *Quadrant* (Sydney), vol. 30, no. 6, June 1986, pp. 75–77, (review of Daisy Bates, *The Native Tribes of Western Australia*, ed. Isobel White).

'What's Wrong with the North West?', *SMH*, 4 May 1963, p. 12, and 11 May 1963, p. 11.

'White Energy; Black Inertia', *SMH*, 24 February 1962.

BOOKS

The Art of Elizabeth Durack, (introduction by Patrick Hutchings), Western
    Mail, Perth, 1981 (second edition published by Angus & Robertson,
    Sydney, 1982).

Countries of the Indian Ocean, Direct Publications, Perth, 1979.

Face Value: Women of Papua New Guinea, Ure Smith, Sydney, 1969.

Seeing—Through Indonesia, An Artist's Impressions of the Republic, Hawthorn
    Press, Melbourne, 1977.

Seeing—Through Papua New Guinea, An Artist's Impressions of the Territory,
    Hawthorn Press, Melbourne, 1970.

Seeing—Through the Philippines, An Artist's Impressions of the Islands,
    Hawthorn Press, Melbourne, 1971.

CATALOGUES

The Art of Eddie Burrup, presented by the Rebecca Hossack Gallery, at the
    Gallery in Cork Street, London, together with Elizabeth Durack,
    24 July–5 August 2000.

Derivations and Directions—The Work of Elizabeth Durack 1930s to 1950s,
    Janda Gooding, curator, with Silvia Conroy, Art Gallery of Western
    Australia, Perth, March–April 1995.

Elizabeth Durack—Paintings, comment by Randolph Stow, exhibition held at
    artist's studio, Perth, September 1961.

*Elizabeth Durack: Paintings from the series, Battle Cries (1978) and Bett-Bett's
    Wonderful Lonely Palace... (1985)*, presented by Greenhill Galleries, Perth,
    May 2007.

*From Appreciation to Appropriation: Indigenous Influences and Images in
    Australian Visual Art*, Christine Nicholls, curator and commentator,
    Flinders University, Adelaide, March 2000.

Out of Sight—Out of Mind: Exhibition, comment by Lynn Allen, Maureen
    Smith and Elizabeth Durack, Alexander Library Building, Perth Cultural
    Centre, Western Australia, February–March 1991.

Prelude—Early works by Elizabeth Durack, Collin O'Brien and Margaret
    Parker (eds.), Forty7ED, Perth, 2002 (an Art on the Move Touring
    Exhibition).

Recent Australian Painting, Whitechapel Gallery, London, 1961.

Time and Tide: The Story in Pictures of Roebuck Bay, N.W. Australia, by
    Elizabeth Durack, commentary by Mary Durack, Imperial Print
    Company, Perth, 1946.
*With Outstretched Arms: Sisters of St John of God Children, Patients and Friends
    Post-war Broome, Derby, Beagle Bay: Impressions*, by Elizabeth Durack,
    foreword by Pat Jacobs, Forty7ED, Nedlands, WA, 2007 (catalogue
    prepared for exhibition coinciding with the Kimberley Centenary
    Celebrations, 1907–2007).

INTERVIEWS

Elizabeth Durack, interviewed by Robin Hughes, videorecording produced
    and directed by Robin Hughes and Linda Kruger, Film Australia in
    association with SBS TV, Lindfield, NSW, 1997.
Elizabeth Durack, interviewed by Helene Charlesworth for the J. S. Battye
    Library of West Australian History, 1998.
Elizabeth Durack, interviewed for the NLA, 1965 (Hazel de Berg Collection,
    NLA, DeB 103–4) (transcript held by Battye Library).

SECONDARY SOURCES

ARTICLES

'Aboriginal Motifs', *SMH*, 28 October 1954, p. 2.
'Amateurish Art Show by Miss Durack', *SMH*, 31 January 1947, p. 6.
Anthony, Thalia, 'Criminal Justice and Transgression on Northern
    Australian Cattle Stations', in Ingereth Macfarlene, Mark Hannah (eds.),
    Transgressions: Critical Australian Indigenous Histories, ANU E Press,
    Acton, ACT, 2007, pp. 35–61.
'The Art of the Duracks', *Australasian Post* (Melbourne), 9 July 1951.
'Artist's Alter Ego Built Up Over Decades', *West Australian* (Perth), 8 March
    1997.
Barnes, John, 'Questions of Identity in Contemporary Australia', in Adi
    Wimmer (ed.), *Australian Nationalism Reconsidered: Maintaining a
    Monocultural Tradition in a Multicultural Society*, Stauffenberg Verlag,
    Tübingen, 1999, pp. 63–71.
Bechervaise, J. M., 'The Paintings of Elizabeth Durack', *Walkabout*
    (Melbourne), 1 October 1949.

Betts, Mac, 'Elizabeth Durack: The Visual Commitment', *The Gazette* (Perth, Western Australian Institute of Technology Journal), vol. 7, no. 4, July 1974.

Bolton, G, 'Dame Mary Durack', *Independent* (London), 24 December 1994.

Bolton, G, 'Durack, Kimberley Michael (Kim), (1917–1968)', *ADB,* vol. 8, Melbourne University Press, Carlton, 1996.

Bolton, G. C., 'Durack, Michael Patrick (1865–1950)', *ADB*, vol. 8, Melbourne University Press, Carlton, 1981.

Bromfield, David, 'Durack: The Artist We Had to Have', *West Australian* (Perth), 31 May 2000.

Browning, Julie, 'Travel Hopefully: The Duracks', in *Dynasties*, Australian Broadcasting Corporation, Sydney, 2002, pp. 51–83.

Byrne, Geraldine, 'Miller, Horatio Clive (1893–1980)', *ADB,* Melbourne University Press, Carlton, 1986.

Cheater, Christine, 'Kaberry, Phyllis Mary (1910–1977)', *ADB,* vol. 14, Melbourne University Press, Carlton, 1966.

Cranston, M. W., 'The Aborigines and Their Ancestors', *TLS*, 2 April 1970, p. 369 (review of *The Rock and the Sand*).

Daly, Michael, 'Hoax', *Age* (Melbourne), 8 March 1997, p. A23.

Day, Michael, 'Death of an Artist and Her Alter Ego', *SMH*, 26 May 2000.

Devlin-Glass, Frances, 'The Irish in Grass Castles: Re-Reading Victim Tropes in an Iconic Pioneering Text', in *Ireland, Australia and New Zealand: History, Politics and Culture* (eds.) Laurence M. Geary and Andrew J. McCarthy, Irish Academic Press, Dublin, 2008, pp. 104–118.

Dobrez, Livio, '"Late" and "Post" Nationalisms: Reappropriation and Problematisation in Recent Australian Cultural Discourse', in Adi Wimmer (ed.), *Australian Nationalism Reconsidered: Maintaining a Monocultural Tradition in a Multicultural Societ*y, Stauffenberg Verlag, Tübingen, 1999, pp. 47–62.

Drewe, Robert, 'Solved: The Great B. Wongar Mystery', *Bulletin* (Literary Supplement), 21 April 1981, pp. 2–5.

Durack Clancy, Perpetua, 'Eddie Burrup: A Daughter's View', *Westerly* (Perth), vol. 54, no. 1, July 2009, pp. 72–75.

Durack Clancy, Perpetua, 'A Portrait of the Artist as a Young Woman: A Partial View of Elizabeth Durack', *The Journal*, Subiaco, WA, Australian-Irish Heritage Association, vol. 16, no. 3, Spring 2008, pp. 9–32 (Annual Durack Memorial Lecture, 2008).

'Durack Thrived on Bush Life', *West Australian* (Perth), 26 May 2000, p. 11.

Gardello, Muriel, 'Time and Tide', *Western Mail* (Perth), 15 August 1946, p. 8.

Granin, Daniel, 'In an Artist's Studio', *New Times* (Moscow), no. 42, 20 October 1965.

Harris, Carole, 'William Lionel Buckland (1899–1964)', *ADB*, vol. 13, Melbourne University Press, Carlton, 1993.

Hetherington, John, 'Novelist Who Draws on the Outback', *Age* (Melbourne), 26 November 1960.

Hill, Ernestine, 'Co-Authors across a Continent', *ABC Weekly* (Sydney), 26 April 1941.

Hope, A. D. 'The Bunyip Stages a Comeback', *SMH*, 16 June 1956, p. 15.

Hutchings, Patrick, 'The Art of Elizabeth Durack', *Western Mail* (Perth), 1981, p. 9.

Hutchings, Patrick, 'The Durack Show', *The Critic* (Perth), 26 February 1965.

Hutchings, Patrick, 'Elizabeth Durack', *The Critic* (Perth), 2 October 1961.

Hutchings, Patrick, 'Elizabeth Durack, Pictorial Tachiste', *Westerly* (Perth), June 1963.

Kemp, Maud, 'Elizabeth Durack Talks to Australian Artist', *Australian Artist* (Sydney), October 1988.

Keneally, Thomas, 'The Borrowers', *Age* (Melbourne), 30 August 2003.

Kleinert, Sylvia, 'Cooper, Revel Ronald (1934–1983)', *ADB*, vol. 17, Melbourne University Press, Carlton, 2007.

Lancashire, Rebecca, 'Durack Paints a Clear Picture of Her Double Life', *Age* (Melbourne), 8 March 1997.

Laracy, Hugh, 'Durack Mary. *The Rock and the Sand*', *Journal de la Société des Oceanistes*, vol. 28, no. 36, 1972, p. 315.

'Lusty Self-Reliance', *TLS*, 19 February 1960, p. 116.

Marcus, Julie, '...Like an Aborigine—Empathy, Elizabeth Durack and the Colonial Imagination', *The Olive Pink Society Bulletin* (Adelaide), vol. 9 (1 & 2), 1997.

Mayman, Jan, 'Looking at a World in Chaos', *National Times* (Sydney), January 1983.

McCaughey, Patrick, 'Native Grounds and Foreign Fields', *Australian Book Review*, no. 332, June 2011, p. 11.

McCulloch, Susan, 'Blacks Blast Durack for Her Art of Illusion', *Weekend Australian* (Sydney), 8 March 1997, pp. 1, 10.

McCulloch, Susan, 'Painter True to Her Voice', *Australian* (Sydney), 29 May 2000.

McCulloch, Susan, 'What's the Fuss?', *Australian Magazine* (Sydney), 5 July 1997.

McDonald, John, 'Durack: Let's Look at the Big Picture', *SMH*, 12 March 1997.

Mendelssohn, Joanna, 'Durack Needs Art of Sensitivity', *Australian* (Sydney), 10 March 1997, p. 3.

Millett, Patsy, 'Dame Mary Durack: the Last Chapter', in *Lines in the Sand: New Writing from Western Australia*, Fellowship of Australian Writers, Swanbourne, WA, 2008.

Morrison, Louise, 'The Art of Eddie Burrup', *Westerly* (Perth), vol. 54, no. 1, July 2009, pp. 77–83.

Nairn, John, '"So Much I Loved Is Drowned For Ever…"', *Australian Women's Weekly* (Sydney), 3 May 1972, pp. 51–2, 114.

O'Brien, Philippa, 'Prelude: Early Works of Elizabeth Durack', *Art and Australia* (Sydney), vol. 41, no. 1, Spring 2003, pp. 156–57.

'Painting Hoax Has Art World Divided', *SMH*, 8 March 1997, p. 5.

Prerauer, Maria, 'Paradox of Elizabeth Durack', *Australian* (Sydney), 29 December 1982.

'Round-Australia Trip: Material for Durack Book', *West Australian*, 15 June 1945.

Smith, Robert, 'The Art of Elizabeth Durack', *Western Australian Art Gallery Bulletin* (Perth), no. 18, October 1959.

Smith, Robert, 'The Incarnations of Eddie Burrup', *Art Monthly Australia* (Canberra), no. 97, March 1997, pp. 4–5.

Snell, Ted, 'The Fantasist: Elizabeth Durack and Eddie Burrup', *Westerly* (Perth), vol. 54, no. 1, July 2009, pp. 85–87.

Ward, Russel, 'Pastoral Saga', *Meanjin* (Melbourne), June 1960, pp. 211–14.

BOOKS

Adelaide, Debra, *Australian Women Writers: A Bibliographic Guide*, Pandora Press, London, 1988.

Allgemeines Kunstlerlexikon Die Bildenden Kunstler aller Zeiten und Volker, vol. 31, Saur, Munich, 1992, pp. 115–117 (entry on Elizabeth Durack).

Anderson, Roderick, *Western Australian Art: A Selection of Early Works from the Robert Holmes à Court Collection*, Heytesbury Holdings Ltd, Perth, 1986.

Barker, A. W. (ed.), *Dear Robertson: Letters to an Australian Publisher*, Angus &
    Robertson, Sydney, 1982.

Benko, Nancy, *The Art of David Boyd*, Lidums, Adelaide, 1973.

Berndt, R. M. and E. S. Phillips, *The Australian Aboriginal Heritage*, Ure
    Smith, Sydney, 1973.

Bunbury, Bill (ed.), *It's Not the Money, It's the Land: Aboriginal Stories and
    the Equal Wages Case: Talking History with Bill Bunbury*, Fremantle Arts
    Press, North Fremantle, 2002.

Carter, Anne, *Beyond All Telling: A History of Loreto in Western Australia
    1897–1997*, Institute of the Blessed Virgin Mary (Loreto) in Australia,
    Nedlands, WA, 1997.

Clancy, Francis, *They Built a Nation*, with a foreword by the Hon. Mr Justice
    H. V. Evatt, New Century Press, Sydney, 1939.

Dobrez, Livio (ed.), *Identifying Australia in Postmodern Times*, Bibliotech,
    Canberra, 1994.

Dobrez, Livio, Jan Lloyd Jones and Patricia Dobrez, (eds.), *An ABC of Lying*,
    Australian Scholarly Publishing, Melbourne, 2004.

Dutton, Geoffrey (ed.), *Modern Australian Painting*, Collins, London, 1966.

Dutton, Geoffrey, *White on Black: The Australian Aboriginal Portrayed in Art*,
    Macmillan, in conjunction with the South Australian Art Gallery Board,
    Adelaide, 1974.

Edwards, Deborah and Rose Peel with Denise Mimmocchi, *Margaret Preston:
    Catalogue of an Exhibition…Sydney, 29th July–23rd October, 2005*, Art
    Gallery of New South Wales, Sydney, 2005.

Finley, Donald J, *Modern Australian Painting*, Beaverbrook Newspapers,
    London, 1963.

Gettler, Leon, *An Unpromised Land*, Fremantle Arts Centre Press, South
    Fremantle, 1993.

Gilbert, Kevin (ed.), *Black Australia: An Anthology of Aboriginal Poetry*,
    Penguin Books, Ringwood, Vic, 1988.

Gooding, Janda, *Western Australian Art and Artists 1900–1950*, Art Gallery of
    Western Australia, Perth, 1987.

Gray, Stephen, *The Protectors: A Journey Through Whitefella Past*, Allen &
    Unwin, Sydney, 2011.

Greer, Germaine, *Whitefella Jump Up: The Shortest Way to Nationhood*, Profile
    Books, London, 2004 (first published in Australia in 2003 in *Quarterly
    Essay*, with added commentary by Peter Craven and responses by P. A.

Durack Clancy and Patsy Millett, Black Inc, Melbourne).

Hasluck, Paul, *Mucking About: An Autobiography*, Melbourne University Press, Carlton, 1977.

Heyward, Michael, *The Ern Malley Affair*, introduction by Robert Hughes, University of Queensland Press, St Lucia, 1993.

Kaberry, Phyllis, *Aboriginal Woman, Sacred and Profane*, Routledge, London, 1939.

Lofthouse, Andrea (ed.), *Who's Who of Australian Women*, Methuen Australia, North Ryde, NSW, 1982.

Marshall, Paul (ed.), *Raparapa: Stories from the Fitzroy River Drovers*, Magabala Books, Broome, 2011 (first published 1989).

Mason, Murray (ed.), *Contemporary Western Australian Painters and Printmakers*, Fremantle Arts Centre Press, Fremantle, 1979.

Miller, H. C., *Early Birds*, Rigby, Adelaide, 1963.

Millett, Patsy, *The Duracks of Argyle: A Summary of a Pioneering Venture and the Years 1852–1950 in Kimberley, Western Australia*, Access Press, Bassendean, WA, 2008.

Mitchell, Susan, *The Matriarchs: Twelve Australian Women Talk about Their Lives*, Penguin Books, Ringwood, Vic, 1987.

Mudrooroo [Johnson, Colin], *Wild Cat Falling*, introduction by Stephen Muecke, foreword by Mary Durack, Angus & Robertson, Sydney, 1992.

Muir, Marcie, *Australian Children's Book Illustrators*, Sun Books, Sydney, 1977.

New McCulloch's Encyclopedia of Australian Art, by Alan McCulloch, Susan McCulloch and Emily McCulloch Childs, AusArt Editions in association with Miegunyah Press, Carlton, 2006.

Nixon, Marion, *The Rivers of Home: Frank Lacy, Kimberley Pioneer*, 6th ed., The Author, Perth, 2003 (first published 1978).

O'Brien, Philippa, *Robert Juniper*, Craftsman House, Roseville East, NSW, 1992.

Olsen, John, *Drawn from Life*, Duffy & Snellgrove, Sydney, 1997.

Oxford Companion to Australian Literature, W. H. Wilde, Joy Hooton and Barry Andrews (eds.), 2nd ed, Oxford University Press, Melbourne, 1994 (first published 1988).

Parker, K. Langloh, *Australian Legendary Tales*, collected by K. Langloh Parker, selected and edited by H. Drake-Brockman, illustrated by Elizabeth Durack, Angus & Robertson, Sydney, 1953.

Popham, Daphne, K. A. Stokes and Julie Lewis, *Reflections: Profiles of 150*

Women Who Helped Make Western Australia's History: Project of the Women's Committee for the 150th Anniversary Celebrations of Western Australia, Carrolls, Perth, 1979.

Reynolds, Henry, *The Chant of Jimmie Blacksmith*, Currency Press, Strawberry Hills, NSW, 2008.

Reynolds Henry, *Frontier—Aborigines, Settlers and Land*, Allen & Unwin, Sydney, 1987.

Robb, Gwenda and Elaine Smith, *Concise Dictionary of Australian Artists*, Robert Smith (ed.), Melbourne University Press, Carlton, 1993.

Robert Muir Old & Rare Books, *Elizabeth Durack Collection*, introduction by Robert and Helen Muir, foreword by P. A. Durack Clancy and M. F. Clancy, Nedlands, WA, 2006 (Catalogue #142).

Scott, John, *Landscapes of Western Australia*, Aeolian Press. Claremont, WA, 1986.

Skinner, M. L., *The Fifth Sparrow: An Autobiography*, Sydney University Press, Sydney, 1972.

Smith, Bernard with Terry Smith, *Australian Painting 1788–1990*, Oxford University Press, Melbourne, 1991.

Stanner, W. E. H., *The Dreaming & Other Essays*, 2nd ed., introduction by Robert Manne, Black Inc, Collingwood, 2011 (first published in 2009).

Windschuttle, Keith, *The Killing of History: How a Discipline Is Being Murdered by Literary Critics and Social Theorists*, Macleay, Sydney, 1994.

ELECTRONIC SOURCES (VIDEOS)

Durack Dreaming, Dynasties Series 1, Australian Broadcasting Commission, Sydney, 2002.

www.elizabethdurack.com

INTERVIEWS

Kimberley Male, interviewed by Colin Davis, 1 January 2006, NLA.

INDEX